Affinities and Intuitions

The Gerald S. Elliott Collection of Contemporary Art

Affinities and Intuitions

The Gerald S. Elliott Collection of Contemporary Art

Exhibition and Catalogue
Organized by Neal Benezra

Contributions by

Michael Auping	Douglas W. Druick	Mark Rosenthal
Neal Benezra	Judith Russi Kirshner	Norman Rosenthal
Lynne Cooke	Mary Murphy	Charles F. Stuckey
I. Michael Danoff	Roald Nasgaard	

The Art Institute of Chicago

Thames and Hudson

Copublished by Thames and Hudson and
The Art Institute of Chicago

First published in the United States in 1990
by Thames and Hudson Inc., 500 Fifth
Avenue, New York, New York 10110

Library of Congress Catalog Card
Number 89-51745

*Affinities and Intuitions: The Gerald S.
Elliott Collection of Contemporary Art* was
prepared on the occasion of the exhibition
of the same name organized by The Art
Institute of Chicago and on view there
from May 12 through July 29, 1990.

Executive Director of Publications: Susan
F. Rossen; Editors: Margherita Andreotti
and Terry Ann R. Neff; Production
Manager: Katherine A. Houck; Designer:
Michael Glass Design, Inc., Chicago.

Typeset in Walbaum by Typographic
Resource, Chicago. Printed and bound in
Japan by Dai Nippon.

Table of Contents

Foreword

In recent years contemporary art has captured the imagination of a broad public. With this attention has come a great deal of writing and publishing, most of it critical, laudatory, or speculative rather than documentary and historical in intent. In conceiving *Affinities and Intuitions: The Gerald S. Elliott Collection of Contemporary Art*, we have sought to record a single collection of contemporary art in a thorough way, through both analysis and documentation. This publication grew out of our interest in presenting contemporary art as part of a historical continuum and providing it with both the serious consideration and the demanding company that a museum can provide.

We are pleased, as well, to be able to exhibit these works publicly. The depth and focus of the Elliott collection allow us to examine in a concentrated fashion some of the most compelling painting and sculpture made since the advent of Minimalism in the 1960s. Although it was established in the late nineteenth century as a general historical museum, through its acquisition and exhibition policy, The Art Institute of Chicago has built a long and distinguished record of commitment to the art of our time, a commitment that is central to the ambition that has motivated Gerald S. Elliott to assemble this remarkable collection.

James N. Wood
Director
The Art Institute of Chicago

Introduction and Acknowledgments

Soon after my arrival in Chicago in June 1985, I visited Gerald S. Elliott in his apartment high up in the John Hancock Tower. The apartment was filled with works of art and their owner enveloped me in lively conversation and opinion concerning contemporary art. I quickly realized that Elliott was utterly obsessed with art, indeed nothing else really mattered. After three hours of vigorous discussion about art, artists, galleries, dealers, museums, directors, curators, and collectors, I left, a bit dazed, but thoroughly fascinated by this unbelievably intense, enormously opinionated man.

As time passed, it became clear that Elliott was passionately interested, not just in contemporary art, but also in art history and the place the art of our time would occupy in future histories. We spent a great deal of time in the galleries of The Art Institute of Chicago: the curator describing recent acquisitions ranging from Dieric Bouts to Max Beckmann, the collector offering commentaries on the history of collecting in Chicago ("That Manet came from Arthur Jerome Eddy; now he was a great collector!"). Elliott's obsession with the history of art also revealed itself in a desire to document his works. Although he had collected literally stacks of exhibition catalogues and published references to works which he owned, no systematic cataloguing had been done; gradually and informally I began this process. When our conversation turned to this exhibition and catalogue, Elliott continually emphasized the latter; while the exhibition would pass from memory, the book must function as a history both of his activity as a collector and, more importantly, of the art of our time.

Inspired by his ambition for this book, we conceived a publication that should serve simultaneously as a catalogue raisonné of the Elliott collection and as a historical survey with thematic and monographic essays by experts in the field. Thus, the contributions, intended to be useful surveys of selected movements, themes, and individual artists, focus on topics selected both for their general relevance and for their reflection of a particular strength of the Elliott collection. Virtually every object in the collection is illustrated in conjunction with the appropriate text and documented in the catalogue section that follows the essays. The organization of this book into broad aesthetic headings has meant that, in a few instances, artists have been grouped into categories that are not ideal. The catalogue listing serves an important and useful function in locating illustrations.

My efforts in exhibiting and publishing the Elliott collection have been widely and enthusiastically supported at every level of the Art Institute. From the outset, James N. Wood, Director, and James W. Alsdorf, Chairman of the Committee on Exhibitions and the Committee on Twentieth-Century Painting and Sculpture, have lent remarkable support to this project. Since his arrival in 1987, my colleague Charles F. Stuckey has added his strong support to this endeavor. I am indebted to him and to

Douglas W. Druick, Prince Trust Curator of Prints and Drawings, for their essays, as I am to all the authors who have contributed to this book. The process of cataloguing the Elliott collection, which I undertook in 1985, has been completed with single-minded devotion to detail by Research Assistant Mary Murphy. Together she and I have coordinated the extensive efforts required in assembling material for this book. The book itself is the result of the efforts and dedication of many: The text was sensitively edited by Margherita Andreotti and Terry Ann R. Neff and typed by Cris Ligenza of the Publications Department. The fine design is the work of Michael Glass Design, Inc. The book's excellent reproductions are in great part due to many fine photographs taken by Thomas Cinoman, Christopher Gallagher, Robert Hashimoto, and Michelle Klarich under the the direction of Alan B. Newman, and to the production management of Kathy Houck. Susan F. Rossen and Robert V. Sharp were also very helpful. In addition, my sincere thanks go to Dorothy Schroeder, William R. Leisher, Courtney Graham Donnell, Eddi Wolk, Elizabeth Leitgen, Nicholas Barron, Thomas H. Berry, James Pogozelski, Woodman Taylor, and Maureen Lasko for their valuable assistance with various other aspects of this project.

In documenting the Elliott collection, we have made countless inquiries of dealers, collectors, and other individuals in the art world. The demands we have made have been excessive, and we are indebted to Mary Boone and Ron Warren, Mary Boone Gallery, New York; Susan Brundage, Mary Jo Marks, and Rebecca Lincoln, Leo Castelli Gallery, New York; Julie Graham and Gabriella Ranelli, Paula Cooper Gallery, New York; Barbara Gladstone, Richard Flood, and Sophie Hager Hume, Barbara Gladstone Gallery, New York; Marian Goodman, Jill Sussman-Walla, and Lydia Tzagoloff, Marian Goodman Gallery, New York; Richard Gray, Richard Gray Gallery, Chicago; Rhona Hoffman and Susan Reynolds, Rhona Hoffman Gallery, Chicago; Vivian Horan, Vivian Horan Fine Art, New York; David McKee, David McKee Gallery, New York; Helene Weiner and Janelle Reiring, Metro Pictures, New York; Ellie Meyer, Marfa, Texas; Anthony d'Offay, Anthony d'Offay Gallery, London; Julia Ernst and Rebecca Lewellyn-Jones, the Saatchi Collection, London; Susanna Singer, New York; Antonio Homem, Ileana Sonnabend Gallery, New York; Angela Westwater and Joshua Mack, Sperone Westwater Gallery, New York; Donald Young and Barbara Mirecki, Donald Young Gallery, Chicago.

My companion throughout this project, Maria Makela, has been an extraordinary confidant and supporter, both emotionally and substantively. I am especially grateful to her.

Finally, I must express my great admiration and affection for Gerry Elliott. Although this book bears my name as author and general editor, in a very real and essential sense, Gerry has been my collaborator from the outset of this project. His relentless pursuit of quality in art is equaled here by his ambition for this book and its contents. I am very grateful to have had the opportunity to work with such an extraordinary individual.

Neal Benezra

Curator
Department of Twentieth-Century Painting and Sculpture

Robert Ryman (left) and Gerald S. Elliott
in front of *Charter V*, in the artist's studio,
New York, March 1987.

Collecting Contemporary Art: A Profile of Gerald S. Elliott

NEAL BENEZRA

The ascent of the private collector of contemporary art, particularly in the United States, is one of the most thoroughly discussed aspects of today's art world. Historically a discreet and exclusive activity limited to relatively few individuals, the collecting of contemporary art has recently become far more widespread, leading some private collectors to achieve a stature only occasionally reached by artists. This phenomenon can be traced to 1973, with the sale at auction of the Robert and Ethel Scull Collection. That event brought dramatic prices for outstanding works of Pop art by Jasper Johns, Robert Rauschenberg, and Andy Warhol, among many others. The Scull sale established a market for postwar American art and, perhaps more important in this context, it celebrated the Sculls as both preeminent collectors and advocates of contemporary art.[1]

With its bold color and restatement of well-known popular images, Pop art had considerable public appeal. Beginning in the late 1960s, many artists reacted against the growing popularization and commercialization of contemporary art, creating works that were conceptual in nature, their very intangibility placing them virtually outside of commerce. Yet, with the advent of Neo-Expressionism in the late 1970s, the art world again possessed a traditional art form—paintings, by and large—which featured images drawn in large measure from the media. Although more ambivalent and troubling than Pop art, Neo-Expressionism spurred an unparalleled interest in contemporary art and has contributed in the 1980s to the rising power and reputation of a number of private collectors. This phenomenon has been of extraordinary importance, arguably giving new meaning to works of art within a wider cultural context, and altering established relationships and behavior in the art world. Important recent works of art are now considered trophies in the highly competitive scramble among collectors. This overheated atmosphere even caused the great Italian collector Count Giuseppe Panza di Biumo to abandon the endeavor during the late 1970s and early 1980s because, as he noted, "I always bought artists whom nobody was willing to buy. It would be impossible for me to buy artists' work that many other collectors were buying."[2] For Panza, as for many established collectors, the interest in contemporary art reflects a desire for personal discovery, a desire that is frustrated by the current vogue for collecting recent art.

The renewed power of collectors has brought about other structural changes in the art world as well. Given the demand for works of art, it is difficult for dealers to be discriminating. The competition among dealers for the work of the finest artists is perhaps even more fierce than that confronting collectors; as a result, exacting judgments concerning quality are not always exercised. Contributing to this frenzy is the now secondary role of art critics, whose formerly decisive position in discerning quality has been displaced by the lightning pace of the art world. Within the period required to publish a review, new works have often already been validated or discounted by collectors. Accentuating this change has been a shift in interest among critics, away from connoisseurship and toward more interpretative, socio-culturally directed forms of exposition.

Perhaps the most compelling change spawned by the vogue for collecting contemporary art has been the recent direction pursued by many young artists. The current buzzword among them is "commodification," indicating an uneasy fascination with the work of art as an object of commerce, indistinguishable from any other item that can be bought or sold. Although the term is new, the idea is not, even in contemporary art. Indeed, this trend was precisely the concern of those Conceptual artists who attempted to reject the marketplace, relying instead for their support on a small coterie of patrons and intellectually minded critics. By contrast, a current generation of artists is making the commodification of works of art the predominant subject of their work, as they engage in a dialogue concerning private taste in which the participants seem limited to artists and collectors.

The issue of the commodification of art has direct bearing on collecting. If the status of contemporary collectors is newly enhanced, the related challenges that result from operating in advance of the traditional art world are equally new and formidable. Beyond matters of quality lie responsibilities—for storage, conservation, display, loans, and public accessibility.

As a collector for over twenty years, Gerald S. Elliott is keenly aware of the complexity of collecting contemporary art. A native Chicagoan, Elliott attended the University of Illinois, studying business as an undergraduate and receiving a law degree in 1955. Although he did not study art history, he was fascinated by art and spent much of his time in the galleries of the Art Institute. Elliott began to collect Steuben glass and contemporary ceramics; by the late 1960s he had turned to prints; and in 1970 he acquired his first painting, a work by the Dutch artist Karel Appel, from the Chicago dealer B.C. Holland. Emboldened by this purchase, Elliott began to frequent Holland's gallery, as well as that of another Chicago dealer, Richard Gray. Both men steered Elliott in the direction of Abstract Expressionism; in their galleries, Elliott received an informal education in the art of the period. Holland helped Elliott acquire *Duck Pond* of 1948 by Willem de Kooning; Gray sold him an important late work by Arshile Gorky, *Charred Beloved I* of 1946, and Hans Hofmann's *Autumn Sun and Winter Chill* of 1964. Gray recalled that when Elliott was considering the Hofmann, he "was very nervous, very uncertain. We went through a series of long, drawn-out meetings over this picture. He came back any number of times to see it, to talk about it. He was not only getting a measure of the picture, but a measure of me in a way."[3]

Elliott was aware of the living tradition of private collecting that has existed in Chicago since the late nineteenth century. He became conscious of a legacy that includes Mrs. Potter Palmer, Martin A. Ryerson, Arthur Jerome Eddy, and Frederic Clay and Helen Birch Bartlett. He also emulated the example of still active but older collectors, such as Robert B. Mayer, Morton G. Neumann, Joseph Randall Shapiro, and Edwin A. and Lindy Bergman. The last named, distinguished collectors of Surrealist drawings and paintings who developed the world's finest collection of works by Joseph Cornell, had a direct, personal influence on Elliott. Over the course of many years, the Bergmans taught

Plate 1. *Untitled*, 1979
    Mixed media on paper
    11½ x 8½ in. (29 x 22 cm)
    Cat. no. 52

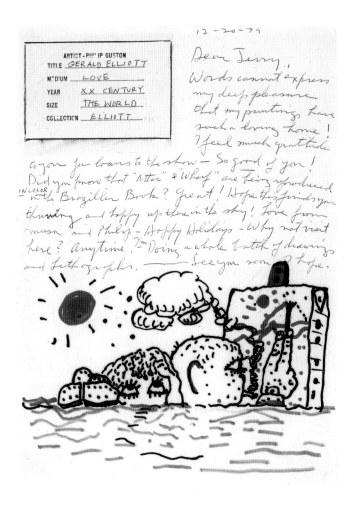

Elliott that obsessiveness is the daily companion of a great collector, a passion for art that "crowds other aspects out of one's life."[4] Elliott was encouraged, as well, by several Chicago collectors of his own generation—Stefan Edlis and Gael Neeson, Helyn and Ralph Goldenberg, Camille and Paul Oliver-Hoffmann, Ann and William J. Hokin, Susan and Lewis Manilow, and Irving and Marcia Stenn—who formed a tightly knit, supportive group whose interests lie in contemporary art and whose collections now rival those of preceding generations of Chicagoans in their depth and quality.

As Elliott's interest and ambition grew, he began to look increasingly to New York. In the early 1970s, Elliott met important dealers from New York and Europe who handled Abstract Expressionist works, individuals such as Harold Diamond, from whom he acquired Jackson Pollock's *The Magic Mirror* of 1941 and Barnett Newman's *Joshua* of 1950, among other works. At this time Elliott also purchased Franz Kline's *Initial* of 1959 and Mark Rothko's *Untitled* of 1956. Another particularly important painting to enter the collection was Newman's *Queen of the Night I* of 1950, which he acquired from the Swiss dealer Ernst Beyeler. Following this purchase, Elliott met and became friends with Annalee Newman, the artist's widow, whose passion for art inspired the collector. Mrs. Newman sold him Newman's *Now I* of 1965, and also persuaded him to purchase Pollock's *Square Pouring*, a fine small painting of 1948.

By the mid-1970s, Elliott had immersed himself in the workings of the New York art world, probing for great Abstract Expressionist paintings with the advice of some of New York's finest art dealers. Indeed, just as his education had begun under B. C. Holland and Richard Gray in Chicago, it now evolved and matured under the tutelage of New Yorkers. Elliott developed a keen eye for art and a profound respect for certain art dealers, individuals who were generous with their time and expertise, and who helped him develop his sensibility without pressuring him to buy. Elliott has recalled time spent with individuals such as Diamond, Xavier Fourcade, Allan Stone, Irving Blum and Joseph Helman, and David and Renee McKee, not with the specific intention of acquiring works, but simply to talk at length and leisure about quality in art.

Among the most important paintings Elliott acquired in those early years was *Attar* of 1953, a great Abstract Expressionist work by Philip Guston. He purchased the painting from David McKee, who represented Guston late in his career and from whom Elliott also bought *Composition* of 1950 by Franz Kline and *Untitled* of 1948 by Clyfford Still. McKee was impressed by Elliott's enthusiasm and recalled that the collector was a permanent fixture in his gallery, always seeking information and asking questions.[5] McKee introduced Elliott to Guston, and the two became good friends. Guston enjoyed Elliott's spirited nature; the two men visited one another in New York as well as Chicago. Guston transformed his work mightily in the late 1960s and 1970s, abandoning his Abstract Expressionist style of the 1950s. Guston had tired of abstraction, feeling compelled to load his canvases with energetically painted images of a more explicitly personal nature. His late paintings are among the most riveting and important of the postwar period, and Elliott met the great painter at the height of his artistic, personal, and rhetorical powers.

Elliott has recalled the eloquence of Guston's words concerning the relationship of human and artistic freedom: the notion that contemporary abstract painting—particularly later Abstract Expressionism and color-field painting—had betrayed the example of de Kooning, Kline, Newman, and Pollock. Elliott came to share Guston's belief that the abstraction of the 1960s had become uninteresting and formulaic. Ultimately, Guston's influence helped transform Elliott's approach to contemporary art. He came to consider works of art not solely on the basis of quality—a characteristic that he could now discern without assistance—but also as expressions of contemporary culture. Of special importance for Elliott was an article titled "Liberation from Detachment: Philip Guston," which the critic Harold Rosenberg published in *The New Yorker* in 1970, as a response to Guston's inaugural exhibition of new works at the Marlborough Gallery, New York.[6] Whereas most critics vehemently rejected the new works, Rosenberg welcomed Guston's new paintings as "stirred by social indignation." For Rosenberg, the existing separation of art from social realities threatened "the survival of painting as a serious activity"; he believed that Guston had "liberated painting from the ban on social consciousness."

In the late 1970s, Elliott's approach to art and collecting began to change. Guston's influence was enormous, and the collector immersed himself not just in matters of connoisseurship, but in the history of art as well. His friends Richard and Mary Gray and Annalee Newman were tremendously influential in this regard, strongly suggesting that Elliott study art history in a formal manner. In 1980 he largely abandoned the active practice of law in order to enter the graduate program in art history at the University of Chicago. Elliott typically would leave his office early; arriving on campus, he would change his clothes in his car in order to appear inconspicuous among his much younger student colleagues. At the University of Chicago, Elliott studied the history of art for the first time in a thoroughgoing way, with coursework ranging from medieval illuminations to Baroque painting. His work in modern art was undertaken under the direction of Reinhold Heller, a well-known expert on Edvard Munch and modern German painting, and Thomas Crow, a young historian of eighteenth- and nineteenth-century French painting, who emphasized a more contextual approach to the study of art. Although Elliott did not complete a master's thesis devoted to Guston, his abiding interest in the artist resulted in extensive research on the changing critical response to his work.[7]

Elliott's new, somewhat more scholarly approach to contemporary art corresponded directly with important shifts in the art market. By the late 1970s, Elliott had developed a small but fine collection of approximately twelve Abstract Expressionist paintings. Although he treasured these works, he was flooded on a daily basis with what he considered to be exorbitant offers to buy them. While the attention initially flattered him, Elliott soon became troubled, both by the imposition, and by the manner in which these offers were beginning to cloud his judgment. Against a backdrop of inflated market values, he found qualitative judgments increasingly difficult to exercise; although he continued to love these paintings, much of the joy he had felt in acquiring them was now being dissipated. Beyond this, the ascent of the market in Abstract Expressionism was slowly making it impossible for him to compete for the finest paintings on the market. Psychologically, the turning point came in 1978, when he found himself unable to afford Willem de Kooning's great *Light in August* of 1946, a work that was purchased by the Shah of Iran. Despite his relative wealth and his growing stature as a collector, the realities of an upturned market increasingly excluded him from this passionate pursuit.

In his readings on the history of art, Elliott paid special attention to the history of collecting; his knowledge of Etta and Claribel Cone, John Quinn, Albert C. Barnes, Sergei I. Shchukin, Ivan Morozov, and Walter and Louise Arensberg taught him that virtually all of the major collections of modern art had been amassed during the respective artists' lifetimes. Although it was a highly risky endeavor, Elliott gradually decided to pursue this direction. Partially a response to economic necessity, this shift toward very contemporary art revealed a deep-seated desire to "relate to the spirit of our time — to the human condition: the ups, the downs, the disruption, the chaos, the ambivalence. The figurative art I collect is a metaphor for man's situation in the '80s."[8]

These words reveal the continuing influence that Guston had upon Elliott. The energetic character and overt, highly expressive content of Guston's late work induced Elliott's shift toward more contemporary figurative painting. With great trepidation and doubt, Elliott began to dismantle his Abstract Expressionist collection, a process that lasted for nearly ten years. Significantly, among the first paintings to be sold was Guston's extraordinarily subtle *Attar*, which was replaced for a time by a powerful late work, *Wharf* of 1978, and ultimately by another, *Night Room* of 1976 (pl. 64; cat. no. 51).[9]

Elliott's growing interest in figurative painting coincided with the emergence of the movement now known as Neo-Expressionism. Elliott saw the major exhibitions heralding the new direction: the "Venice Biennale" (1980), "Westkunst" (Cologne, 1981), "A New Spirit in Painting" (London, 1981), and "Documenta VII" (Kassel, 1982). He immediately began to pursue major works by artists such as Georg Baselitz and Anselm Kiefer of Germany; Francesco Clemente, Enzo Cucchi, and Mimmo Paladino of Italy; and Eric Fischl, Robert Longo, David Salle, and Julian Schnabel, among the Americans.

Elliott's interest in overtly expressive art did not come at the expense of abstraction, however. Although he sold Frank Stella's *Getty Tomb* (first version), a seminal black painting of 1959, this allowed him to purchase Minimalist works in considerable depth. Among these, the works of Dan Flavin, Donald Judd, Sol LeWitt, Robert Mangold, Brice Marden, and Robert Ryman are particularly important, many of them acquired from two dealers then new to Chicago, Rhona Hoffman and Donald Young. In the act of reconstituting his collection, Elliott also began to work with a different group of New York dealers, in particular: Mary Boone, Leo Castelli, Paula Cooper, Larry Gagosian, Barbara Gladstone, Marian Goodman, Vivian Horan, Anthony d'Offay, Ileana Sonnabend, and Angela Westwater.

Elliott's humanist leanings, manifested in his holdings of figurative paintings, are not at odds with a strong taste for Minimalism. Just as Elliott has considered Neo-Expressionism to be metaphorical of the human condition in our time, for him geometric abstraction, "the quieter works — the Brice Mardens, the Rymans, some of the LeWitts, a few of the Judds — evoke a kind of spiritual or mystical sense."[10] It was this pursuit of a more spiritual expression that led Elliott to propose that Ryman create a series of "meditative" paintings. This project (see pp. 92–101) was inspired by John and Dominique de Menil's similar belief in abstraction, as evidenced in their Rothko Chapel project of the early 1970s.

Through the course of the 1980s, Elliott has pursued two principal directions: figurative expressionism, in particular, the painting of Clemente, Kiefer, and Schnabel; and Minimalist painting and sculpture, especially the work of Judd, Marden, and Ryman. These are scarcely exclusive categories, however, as Elliott also possesses a number of important works by Tony Cragg, Jeff Koons, Jannis Kounellis, and Bruce Nauman, among several others.

Neal Benezra

In looking ahead to the 1990s, Elliott hopes to continue to distinguish his collection from others devoted to the art of our time. Commissioning artists, as he did with Ryman, is one means; new works have been commissioned from Sol LeWitt, Joel Shapiro, and, most recently, Francesco Clemente and Bruce Nauman. Beyond his continuing interest in the work of Schnabel, Clemente, and Nauman, in particular, Elliott continues to broaden the range of his collection, having added recently works by Marcel Broodthaers, Mario Merz, and Lawrence Weiner, artists not widely known or collected in the United States. Elliott is saddened by the changes in the contemporary art world in the United States, particularly the pace of movement which allows less and less time for considered decisions. The tradition of collecting that nourished him in earlier years now seems largely lost, and Elliott misses the days when he could live with a work at home prior to deciding on a purchase, and when he could view all the works in his collection rather than storing them—circumstances that inevitably lessen one's personal rapport with a work of art.

And yet, despite an undercurrent of pessimism concerning the current state of collecting, Elliott's all-encompassing enthusiasm for contemporary art remains unabashed. Stories abound in the art world of his nearly fanatical search for works of art. For example, in a recent profile of the collector published in *Art & Auction*, Judith Neisser described a visit that Elliott and the dealer Leo Castelli made to the studio of David Salle in 1986:

> The artist brought out his painting entitled *Dusting Powder* [sic], and Elliott remembers shouting "Oh! Oh! I want it." Castelli, however, had the painting in mind for someone else. Elliott recalls saying, "Leo, I don't want any other painting in the studio." He also recalls having chest pains. Four days later Elliott checked into a Chicago hospital for quadruple bypass surgery. "As they wheeled me into the operating room I kept thinking, 'I'll miss that painting! I'll miss that painting!'"[11]

Elliott recovered from the operation and he got the painting.

---

1. For differing perspectives on the Scull sale, see John Tancock, "The Robert C. Scull Auction," in *Art at Auction: The Year at Sotheby Parke Bernet* (New York, 1974), pp. 137–45; and Barbara Rose, "Profit Without Honor," *New York* 6, 45 (Nov. 5, 1973), pp. 80–81.

2. "Giuseppe Panza di Biumo," in The Museum of Contemporary Art, Los Angeles, 1983, *The First Show: Painting and Sculpture from Eight Collections*, p. 86.

3. Judith Neisser, "A Magnificent Obsession," *Art & Auction* 10, 2 (Dec. 1987), p. 111.

4. Gerald S. Elliott in conversation with the author, Mar. 16, 1989.

5. David McKee in conversation with the author, Mar. 17, 1989.

6. Harold Rosenberg, "Liberation from Detachment: Philip Guston," *The De-Definition of Art* (Chicago, 1972), pp. 139–40.

7. Elliott has written on topics ranging from collecting to the current state of art criticism. An unpublished essay on criticism, written under the pseudonym Jonathan Urnaby, is titled, "Call Me Schwartz or Collecting in the Age of Instantaneous Multiple Ratification." His published essay

devoted to collecting was written under a different pseudonym: Sidney M. Bratherly, "Notes from a Collector," *Issues* 5 (Winter 1986), pp. 47–49.

8. Neisser (note 3), p. 110.

9. In her recent memoir of her father, Philip Guston, Musa Meyer described a visit that the Guston family made to Elliott's home in 1981. See Musa Mayer, *Night Studio: A Memoir of Philip Guston by His Daughter* (New York, 1988), p. 231.

10. Neisser (note 3), pp. 110–11.

11. Ibid., p. 108.

16

Minimalism: The Early Years

CHARLES F. STUCKEY

Nearly thirty years have passed since so-called Minimal art first appeared in the 1960s as something of a novelty and, although collectors and museums now compete vigorously as patrons, the general public remains puzzled by, if not skeptical of, its significance. The relatively arrested development of the style's leading practitioners (Donald Judd, Dan Flavin, Carl Andre, and to a lesser extent Sol LeWitt), the fact that their recent works often appear so similar to their pioneering pieces of the 1960s, contributes to the skepticism, yet for advocates of Minimalism such consistency stresses the artists' integrity. The critical debate that accompanied the complicated genesis of Minimal art has further added to this situation, a debate in which the artists themselves have often participated in an effort to bolster the case for this utterly modern art, predicated on an absence not only of explicit content and meaning, but also of composition and of virtuoso manual skills. These circumstances warrant a brief review of Minimal art as it first appeared in a series of influential exhibitions during the early to mid-1960s. It is hoped that such a review will provide a historical and theoretical framework within which the rich holdings of the Elliott collection can be more fully appreciated.

Broadly speaking, Minimal art may be considered a development of theoretical issues raised by artists such as Josef Albers, Barnett Newman, Ellsworth Kelly, Jasper Johns, Ad Reinhardt, and Frank Stella, all of whom took exception to the dramatically charged gestural brushwork and turbulent compositions popularized by such painters as Hans Hofmann, Jackson Pollock, Willem de Kooning, and Franz Kline. Preferring to work more systematically and advocating for art the power of focused thought rather than that of emotional outburst, the younger artists stressed fact in favor of feeling, no matter how sincere or profound.

The flat geometric relationships in works by Johns, Stella, and the others in turn hark back to the battle cry of early modern art: Maurice Denis, writing in 1890, had insisted, "Remember that a painting—before it is a battle horse, a nude woman, or some anecdote—is essentially a flat surface covered with colors assembled in a certain order."[1] The implications of this statement were subsequently developed by Clement Greenberg and others into a concept called "Modernism" to explain the evolution of the arts since the nineteenth century: "It seems to be a law of modernism...that the conventions not essential to the viability of a medium be discarded as soon as they are recognized."[2] For Greenberg, the recognition that illusionistic space was inessential to painting challenged artists to make paintings that totally asserted their flatness. This objective seemed to find its paradigmatic realization in Pollock's "overall" compositions of the late 1940s, with their dense webs of paint applied uniformly across the canvas. Coextensive with the entire canvas, the painted surface became in Pollock's work a flat field, its shape defined by the canvas's perimeter or "framing edge."

Following Pollock's "breakthrough," most Modernist-minded artists of the 1950s and 1960s felt a need to stress the abstract concepts of both shape and flatness as ultimate essentials. Johns set an influential example in the mid-1950s with paintings of flat objects, such as targets or flags, their readymade, evenly striped compositions dictating the dimensions of his canvases, seemingly objects themselves and hardly different from the flat objects painted all over them. Yet for all his Modernism, John's use of recognizable images of any sort and his commitment to refined brushwork remained inessentials to be purged for other artists, such as Stella. As Stella's friend Andre tersely put it in commenting on Stella's "Black Paintings,"

> Art excludes the unnecessary.... Frank Stella has found it necessary to paint stripes. There is nothing else in his painting. Frank Stella is not interested in expression or sensitivity. He is interested in the necessities of painting.[3]

Judd's art reviews advocating topical Modernist issues provide a more immediate context for a consideration of the early development of Minimalism and, in particular, for Judd's own works of the early 1960s. Around 1962 Judd decided to dispense with canvas for more objectlike flat surfaces, including Masonite and wood, which he covered with a single color, usually a bright shade of cadmium red, to assert his lack of concern for old-fashioned composition. For example, Judd's untitled wall piece of 1962 (pl. 10; cat. no. 61), with its central ring of yellow Plexiglas, resembles works by Jules Olitski and Lee Bontecou that Judd singled out in reviews published in *Arts* in 1960. He particularly admired Olitski's painting *A Hole to Put My Head Through* of c. 1960 because, as he put it, the oval form near the center "establishes a diagonal between the corners."[4] Admiration was also expressed for Bontecou, who likewise placed round voids at the center of her compositions and used canvas over shaped armatures that project outward from the wall. In an article published a few years later, Judd pointed out her historical significance as "one of the first to use a three-dimensional form that was neither painting nor sculpture."[5] Shortly afterwards, in another review, Judd singled out Stella's innovative deep stretchers, constructed with indentations along the sides or at the center, thus extending the convention of the flat rectangular canvas into a Modernist convention of the shaped object.[6] The yellow Plexiglas insert in the piece mentioned above asserts Judd's concern for strictly factual as opposed to illusionary depth; the otherwise uniformly red, roughly textured surface likewise defines the piece as a physical object, albeit one fashioned for presentation on the wall like a conventional painting.[7]

In a group of four other wall pieces made at this time, Judd literally extended the tops and bottoms with curved metal-covered elements that wittily suggest fragments of picture frames. The central plane in three of these (DDS 25, 40, 42) is wood painted red. This intensely assertive color, especially favored by Judd during 1962 and 1963, can be read as a barometer of his admiration for Newman's proto-Minimalist paintings with broad, roughly rectangular cadmium red bands. On the other hand, the sheet of unpainted, galvanized iron tacked onto the central plane of the fourth of these related pieces, an untitled work of 1963 in the Elliott collection (pl. 11; cat. no. 62), appears to be a direct response to Stella's works of 1960 and 1961 painted with metallic aluminum and copper pigments. Judd explained later that he had hand drilled some 900 holes in the metal plane in the Elliott piece to make the surface more "definite": "Without the holes the metallic finish would be too illusionistic, too soft. It's to make a firmer surface."[8] This piece and two of its counterparts with red central planes were among the works that Judd selected in late 1963 for his important one-person exhibition at the Green Gallery (December 1963–January 1964).

In addition to wall pieces, the 1963–64 exhibition also contained some of Judd's earliest floor structures, for the most part simple wood constructions made of planes and ribs painted red. Evidently one of the wall pieces that Judd was making in 1962 became too heavy and cumbersome to hang, leading him to develop a group of freestanding works that initiated the boxlike objects that have since become one of his hallmarks.[9] Although lacking one of these early floor pieces, the Elliott collection does contain a 1978 object (pl. 14; cat. no. 65), the dimensions and red painted surface of which make it a sort of nostalgic reprise of the breakthrough 1962–63 structures. Like its predecessors, the 1978 object is partially open to expose its inner surfaces as spatial compartments, thus intimating, despite its placement on the floor, that the outer shell is analogous to a frame separating art space within it from literal space surrounding it.

Judd's early floor pieces highlight a widespread tendency among artists around 1960 to dispense with the base and to install works directly on the floor like elements in absurd theater sets.[10] In dismissing the base, these artists were building on the precedent of early twentieth-century figures such as Marcel Duchamp, whose *Trap* of 1917 (a coatrack nailed to the floor and apparently never exhibited outside his studio) was probably the very first floor piece, and Constantin Brancusi. The latter was widely revered by Minimal artists, such as Andre, Flavin, and Serra, as the most important innovator in the history of twentieth-century three-dimensional art. Devoting himself to the simplification and refinement of shape and surface, Brancusi created variations of elementary forms that embody as well as symbolize such abstract absolutes as becoming, coupling, and transcending; he also addressed the pedestal issue, fashioning his own bases to integrate his abstract sculptures with their environment.

Shortly after he met Stella in 1958, Andre started cutting simple wood sculptures in the spirit of Brancusi's *Endless Column.* When Stella pointed out to him that the unworked surfaces on the sides of these were no less sculptural than the worked surfaces, Andre decided that carving was inessential to transform material into art.[11] Later he explained, "Up to a certain time I was cutting into things. Then I realized that the thing I was cutting was the art. Rather than cut into the material, I now use the material as the cut in space."[12] Andre did not exhibit until much later most of his early 1960s pieces, like the Elliott collection's *Blue Wood Chain* of 1964 (pl. 2; cat. no. 4), a miniature Brancusi-like totem made from glued-together interlocking blocks of milled lumber. Coated with blue paint, this piece exemplifies a transitional phase, perhaps influenced by Judd's earliest painted wood objects, before Andre resolved to dismiss color and adhesives from his art as unnecessary.

Just as Judd's Green Gallery show was closing in New York, the first museum exhibition of Minimal art, "Black, White and Gray," opened at the Wadsworth Atheneum in Hartford in January 1964. Neither Judd nor Andre were included, possibly because of their use of color. Judd's account of this exhibition, published in the March 1964 issue of *Arts Magazine,* is nevertheless revealing of Judd's thinking at the time and points to Dan Flavin's influential role for subsequent Minimal art. It indicates that Judd was already familiar with the wide variety of Minimal work made by this early date, even though a good deal of it was not to his taste. While he accepted the 1949 painting by Newman in this exhibition as a precedent, Judd surprisingly dismissed the 1953 all-white paintings by Robert Rauschenberg and the wood "boxes" on the floor by Robert Morris and Tony Smith (with whose black works Judd was unfamiliar) as "next to nothing," wondering why anyone would build something barely present. "There isn't anything to look at," he quipped.[13] What he most admired was the aluminum painting by Stella and a fluorescent light tube by Dan Flavin, *the diagonal of May 25, 1963 (to Constantin Brancusi)*, extending on a diagonal across a wall. "It makes an intelligible area of the whole wall," Judd pointed out, adding, "The light is an industrial object, and familiar, it is a means new to art. Art could be made of any number of new objects, materials and techniques."[14] In apparent response to Flavin's works with commercially manufactured components, by March 1964 Judd began to have metal fabricators make his art objects (DDS 47); later that same year, Judd began to order Plexiglas planes from fabricators,[15] evidently to bring ambient light into his structures in recognition of Flavin's use of this "material." Flooding light not only across the wall in a painterly way, but also projecting its "contents" outward sculpturally into a room, Flavin's fluorescent tube cannot be categorized as either painting or sculpture, a quality that would have further appealed to Judd's neither/nor aesthetic.

Judd's review of the Wadsworth Atheneum exhibition, however, neglected to mention that Flavin had also exhibited five diagram drawings along with the bulb piece, thus setting a precedent for Judd and other Minimal artists who would soon likewise exhibit drawings with objects (or just the drawings), as if to stress that the idea for a given work was of equal or greater importance than its physical fulfillment. Each of Flavin's drawings was inscribed exactly with the day, month, and year of execution of the "idea," and Judd would himself soon date his own works with equal precision. One of the Flavin drawings exhibited in Hartford plotted *the diagonal of May 25*, also referred to as *the diagonal of personal ecstasy* (S 73; FR 4); the other four (S 75–76, 78–79; FR 9–12) charted a not yet executed fluorescent bulb piece dedicated to the fourteenth-century Franciscan scholar William of Ockham, famous for his "Razor" axiom: "Principles (entities) should not be multiplied unnecessarily."[16] Realized from these drawings, Flavin's first serial bulb structure, illustrating Ockham's concept with the set 1, 2 [1 + 1], 3 [1 + 1 + 1] and exhibited in November–December 1964 at the Green Gallery, exerted an enormous influence during the following months on the development of Minimal art, which became increasingly characterized by works conceived in series.

In March 1964, only a month after the Hartford exhibition, Flavin presented a group of his fluorescent light machines in New York at the downtown Kaymar Gallery. In his review of this show, published in *Arts Magazine* in April 1964, Judd singled out a work by Flavin now in the Elliott collection (pl. 8; cat. no. 45). A drawing documenting the exhibition (FR 31) indicates (as Judd's review does not) that Flavin had entitled this work *the alternate diagonals of March 2, 1964 (to Don Judd)*. In this regard, it seems significant that this piece consists of four red tubes and one long yellow one, colors then favored by Judd, who eventually acquired the piece. At his November–December 1964 Green Gallery exhibition, Flavin exhibited an identical structure, but with white bulbs (S 87). He later rationalized his will-ingness to repeat himself: "All my diagrams, even the oldest, seem applicable again and continually....

It is curious to feel self-denied of a progressing development if only for a few years."[17] Flavin often dedicated his projects to friends or to famous artists (S 80–81; FR 13, 29), and besides the piece dedicated to Judd, the Kaymar show in March 1964 included works dedicated to Sol LeWitt (S 86) and to art historians Robert Rosenblum (S 74) and Barbara Rose (S 67), who was then married to Frank Stella.

Flavin's show at the Kaymar Gallery was immediately followed at the end of March 1964 by a group show on the same premises, arranged by Flavin, of works by Jo Baer, Judd, LeWitt, Larry Poons, Robert Ryman, and Stella, among others.[18] Manufactured rather than handmade, Judd's work in this show was a metal-covered variation of the boxes he had exhibited only a few months before at the Green Gallery (DSS 47). It marked a turning point in his career, since henceforth all of his art would be fabricated by professionals from drawings that Judd supplied. The first of Judd's boxes to be installed cantilevered from the wall like a shelf, this iron-coated object amounted to a prototype, which Judd soon developed into similar works in a variety of metals, sometimes with sheets of Plexiglas for the top and/or bottom (DSS 63–64, 72–74). Some of these works were fabricated in small editions, providing the pieces from which, beginning in 1966 (DSS 78), he developed his stack pieces, such as the one of 1970 in the Elliott collection (pl. 13; cat. no. 64).

Mounted high up on a wall in the same exhibition, a white cube by LeWitt randomly perforated with little holes shared the installation premise of Judd's box.[19] Perhaps it was the accidental similarity between their works that led Judd to remove his wall box. Otherwise, given the significance of this box for Judd's immediate development, it comes as a surprise that after a week Judd decided to replace it with a different piece, albeit one just as full of implications for subsequent works. This was the first of his barlike horizontal wall sculptures (DSS 44); dating to 1963, it was apparently conceived as a response to the thin forms of Flavin's fluorescent-bulb wall pieces. Later in 1964 Judd began to extend the concept in a variety of related works, two of which, of May 7, 1970, and of 1984, respectively, are in the Elliott collection (pls. 12, 16; cat. nos. 63, 67). The second of LeWitt's pieces in the April 1964 Kaymar group show consisted of a table, its top painted in colored squares, supporting three movable, hollow wood cubes, each open on two facing sides. This anticipated yet another new group of works by Judd, the open-ended boxes that he would begin to make in 1968.

The give and take between these artists was fast paced at the beginning. LeWitt said that he wanted to "start where art left off last Wednesday."[20] For example, Judd's unique latticelike construction of plumbing pipes, exhibited at the Bird S. Coler Hospital grounds in the spring of 1964, may have suggested the open skeletal structures that LeWitt developed as a hallmark. And Judd's first fabricated box with Plexiglas sides, but without a bottom (DSS 53), reveals the floor as if it were a work in its own right protected under a vitrine, thus anticipating Andre's subsequent floor pieces.

The issue, already alluded to, of whether the floor should be considered the common base essential to all sculpture concerned Flavin no less than the others. Beginning at his November–December 1964 Green Gallery exhibition, he sometimes installed vertical wall pieces extending to the floor as if they stood on it. Perhaps as a result of this decision, he began to entitle some of the new pieces "monuments," or rather "pseudo-monuments," pointing out that, unlike conventional monumental sculptures in bronze or marble, his own were merely light bulbs with a life expectancy of 2,100 hours.[21] Already in August 1964, Flavin had made several drawings for a series of related works, each called "monument for V. Tatlin" (S 112-13; FR 37, 40, 42, 45). The Elliott collection contains one of the many works to emerge later from this series, *untitled (monument for V. Tatlin)* diagramed in 1970 (pl. 9; cat. no. 46).

Why Flavin chose to honor the founder of Russian Constructivism, Vladimir Tatlin, is unclear. He presumably learned about him from Camilla Gray's pioneering study *The Russian Experiment in Art, 1863-1922*, first published in 1962, and perhaps noted then a resemblance between his slender bulbs and the near vertical diagonal struts that are the supporting elements in Tatlin's 1919 project for *Monument to the Third International*.[22] Tatlin's *Monument* and the work of other Constructivists actually seem closer in generic visual terms to LeWitt's open lattice structures developed beginning in 1965. This is particularly true of Alexander Rodchenko's 1920 *Constructions* based on open circular or hexagonal shapes containing nests of similar shapes in smaller dimensions and of Naum Gabo's plastic linear constructions of the 1930s.

LeWitt, who had worked on and off as a commercial artist and architectural draftsman during the 1950s, had been making wall pieces in the early 1960s, most characterized by voids in, or projections from, the rectangular support and thus deriving, ultimately, like the works of Stella and Judd, from Johns's ideas about objectification of the painting surface. Like Judd's 1962-63 pieces, LeWitt's from the same years are handmade, hand painted, and severely geometrical. But unlike Judd's, many of LeWitt's were already composed in conceptual fashion from elementary mathematical progressions, the dimensions of the nested parts regulated by an impersonal logical system. Although LeWitt could not afford to pay assistants and fabricators until around 1966, as if to keep up with Judd, he decided to lacquer his surfaces to obtain a hard industrial look for a group of new works in 1964-65 as he began to exhibit more regularly.[23]

Quickly losing interest in the sort of pristine, planar surfaces that obsessed Judd, however, LeWitt decided to strip away the skin from his objects, thus arriving at his signature open-lattice structures based on a square module. Three-dimensional embodiments of the graph paper on which LeWitt plotted his relentlessly regular modules, these inert structures are full of surprises. From no matter what point of view, the lattice parts intersect along perspectival webs as dizzying as any of Pollock's abstract, allover composition paintings, and each module is like an empty window frame opening onto a multiplication of identical window frames, as if in a play of mirrors all over the surrounding room.

Despite superficial formal similarities, increasing disparities of attitude seem evident from the works these artists submitted to the "Primary Structures" exhibition presented in late April 1966 at the Jewish Museum, New York, to survey the new movement. LeWitt contributed his first cube module lattice sculpture; Judd's pieces (one on the wall, one on the floor), like LeWitt's, consisted of evenly spaced boxlike shapes, albeit closed ones, interconnected by a sort of cornice-bar (DSS 85-86).[24] Andre too was represented by a structure of aligned rectangular solids, in his case a row of industrially manufactured bricks extending across the floor. Flavin contributed a brand new corner monument dedicated to victims of an ambush. Like Flavin's, Andre's piece had a precise title (*Lever*), whereas Judd's were both (as always) "untitled." As if sensitive to the potential for humor in Minimal gesture, LeWitt went Judd one better and gave his piece no title at all. Andre submitted a concrete poem as a catalogue statement; Judd submitted a theoretical statement addressed to incompetent art critics; Flavin and LeWitt opted to do without statements.

Later that year, however, LeWitt published a full description and diagrams of his most important project to date, his *Serial Project No. 1 (ABCD)*, thus extending the serial art premise that Flavin had introduced with his pieces dedicated to William of Ockham and Tatlin. "I like everything about Dan's work," LeWitt pointed out to Mel Bochner at the time, "except the lights."[25] For this project, LeWitt likened the artist's thought process to that of a logical machine: "The serial artist does not attempt to produce a beautiful or mysterious object but functions merely as a clerk cataloguing the results of the premise."[26] LeWitt's premise in this case — to place one form within another, realizing all the variations in two and three dimensions, would involve the construction of four sets of works, each consisting of nine structures, each structure developed from a one-unit square contained in the middle of a three-by-three-unit square. Each set exhausts one of four possible relationships between contents and container: open inside/open outside, open inside/closed outside, closed inside/open outside, and closed inside/closed outside. LeWitt made a model of these sets for the Dwan Gallery's "Scale Models and Drawing" exhibition in early 1967. Slightly altering the scale, perhaps because of his unwillingness to make editions of his works, LeWitt made a second fabrication of this same model in 1972. Among the highlights of the Elliott collection is *Serial Project, Set D* of 1966 (closed inside/closed outside) (pl. 17; cat. no. 82). In 1967 at the Los Angeles Dwan Gallery, LeWitt presented a full-scale rendition of *Serial Project, Set A* (open inside/open outside), filling all of the exhibition space with maniacally systematic logic. From a narrow path around the room's perimeter, spectators could ponder more than an earnest demonstration of Modernist theory. Carried out at its intended enormous full scale, *Serial Project* amounts to the sort of Surrealist gesture of antilogic familiar in René Magritte's painting of an oversized apple filling a room; or to a sort of Warholian parody of fashionable installation art.[27]

Like LeWitt's model for *Serial Project, Set D*, Andre's *Zinc-Lead Plain* of 1969 (pl. 4; cat. no. 5) is one distinct set from a group of series variations intended initially as a vast installation piece. Aligning square, industrially manufactured plates of various metals in gridded rows on the floor beginning in 1966,[28] Andre made minimal sculptures as rugs, entitling these *Plains* to suggest the planar flatness of an infinitely extending landscape. For his 1970 retrospective at The Solomon R. Guggenheim Museum, Andre arranged thirty-six of his square "plains," each a checkerboard of thirty-six alternating metal planes, into one large square to cover the lobby floor. The Elliott piece is one of the thirty-six works that constituted what Andre then entitled *37 Pieces of Work*, visible from all along the museum's downward-spiraling ramp.

Unlike Andre, LeWitt, and Flavin, who presented variations on a theme together as installations, Judd, who fabricated multiple variations of each of his structure types, would choose to exhibit only one variation at a time. For Judd the notion of making an exhibition of all his horizontal wall pieces, for example, or of all his so-called "stacks," would evidently have resulted in a merely decorative approach to an environmental art situation. In nineteenth-century terms, Judd's variations could be called "repetitions." Successful artists, including J.A.D. Ingres and Gustave Courbet, willingly painted multiple versions of the same salable subject, each "repetition" slightly different, well before Claude Monet decided to exhibit versions of the same motif together as a series.

This is true, for instance, of Judd's nearly ten-foot-long horizontal wall piece of May 7, 1970, in the Elliott collection, which, as noted earlier, belongs to a type first developed in 1963. This early work consists of two colored horizontal pieces: an L-shaped construction and a hollow open-ended square bar of the same length that fits along the ledge of the L. In May 1965, Judd exhibited the first of his many related elaborations of the idea, replacing the single lower L-shaped component with L-shaped segments of different lengths, which still serve as a bracket for the single, hollow bar component. Despite the simple geometrical vocabulary, these works defy verbal description. In terms of shape, color, and position, the pieces in Judd's structure fit together, conundrumlike, for no seeming reason. Only apparently arbitrary, however, the placement of the shapes and the intervals between them obey a hidden logic based on the Fibonacci progression (0, 1, 1, 2, 3, 5, 8…), each new number the sum of the two preceding numbers. As the brackets diminish in length from left to right, the widths of the spacing intervals increase in inverse proportion, creating a balance based on an unbalancing mathematical progression, a balance based on logic rather than on visible symmetry. The overall length and the choice of colors for the brackets and bars are what Judd varies from object to object.

From 1964 until 1970, Judd determined the essential configurations of approximately a dozen different structural types, fabricating multiple variants of each as circumstances permitted.[29] Because of this approach, it is pointless to discuss the evolution of Judd's work after the mid-1960s, when he essentially devoted himself, somewhat like Mark Rothko and Adolf Gottlieb, to variations on a perfected format.[30] Given Judd's Modernism, to alter an essential configuration would be to detract from the idea, whereas to repeat it as a variant was to reassert it. It would be left to younger artists, such as Robert Smithson and Richard Serra, to elaborate on Judd's types starting already in the mid-1960s, infusing them with a wide range of poetic ideas that Judd himself studiously avoided.

LeWitt's work, like Judd's, evolved in distinct types, each explored like a musical theme with variations, but, unlike Judd, LeWitt placed increasing emphasis on the parity between language and visual statement. Symptomatic of LeWitt's interest in verbal-visual equivalents are the "illustrated" books that he began to produce in 1968 in lieu of ordinary exhibition catalogues. These were later developed as photographic studies of LeWitt-like structures observed by the artist in everyday life, from aerial views of urban grids to the various stamped patterns used for man-hole covers, suggesting the modern poetics to which all of his diagramatic structures allude.

One of these early book projects led the artist to introduce in 1968 a completely new type, the wall drawing, an influential decorative concept developed with astounding variety ever since. The Elliott collection boasts two of these, numbers 311 and 358 (pls. 18, 20; cat. nos. 83, 85), each of which exists in an unprecedented way for a work of art: as a plan and a certificate from the artist with a careful verbal description from which the wall drawing can be executed at the owner's discretion. Since an owner's installation possibilities are likely to change, requiring the removal, temporary noninstallation, or eventual reinstallation of a wall drawing, the permanent component of each of these works is the verbal certificate; depending on the wall chosen for installation, as well as on the unique talents of the draftsperson(s) commissioned to execute LeWitt's instructions, the visual component will vary every time it is made, just as each performance of a given musical score will vary. "Each person draws a line differently and each person understands words differently," LeWitt pointed out in a 1971 article published to explain the principles of this new genre.[31]

Drawing 311, for example, completed as a set of directions in April 1978, consists of the following verbal proposition: "The wall is divided vertically into three equal parts, one red, one yellow and one blue. 1st part: On the red part, a black outline of a square; 2nd part: On the yellow part, a black outline of a circle; 3rd part: On the blue part, a black outline of a triangle." Rendered for viewing, the equal baseboard-to-ceiling red, yellow, and blue sections might call to mind, for a historian, the sort of polemical purity introduced by Rodchenko in 1919 when he exhibited three monochromatic canvases asserting, "for the first time in art the three primary colors are declared."[32] They also recall the theoretical interests of Wassily Kandinsky, in his capacity as Form Master for the Wall-Painting Workshop at the Bauhaus in 1923, who equated the primary colors with the triangle (yellow), square (red), and circle (blue).[33] In a more immediate historical context, of course, drawing 311 could be understood in relationship to Newman's series of four *Who's Afraid of Red, Yellow and Blue* paintings, begun in 1966.

None of these possible antecedents, however, is about the recognition of the unpredictability inherent in any logical verbal idea when an attempt is made to render it visually, which is the conceptual foundation of LeWitt's wall drawings. In wall drawing 358, theoretically infinite options are established by the simplest sort of visual instructions to be executed in white on black according to the work's subtitle: *A 12" (30 cm) Grid Covering the Wall. Within Each 12" (30 cm) Square, One Arc from the Corner. (The direction of the arcs and their placement are determined by the draftsman)*. But any of the options provides a patterned field of arabesques as lyrical and unfathomable as the surfaces of Monet's famous decorative *Water Lilies* murals or Pollock's large abstract drip paintings. Monet considered his large canvases to be the result of intense visual concentration verging on spiritual meditation. Similarly, LeWitt pointed out in 1969 that "Conceptual artists are mystics rather than rationalists. They leap to conclusions that logic cannot reach."[34] Unthinkable without the example of Stella's Modernism or Alfred Jensen's paintings based on ancient mathematical symbolism, the ultimately decorative visual appearance of LeWitt's wall drawings seems most indebted to Andy Warhol's extraordinary gallery installation of *Cow Wallpaper* of 1966, or to Rauschenberg's electronically activated *Soundings* wall piece of 1968, based on a single photographic image of a chair printed on Plexiglas in a variety of different spatial orientations and illuminated at random. The environmental release of Minimal art's compacted energies, LeWitt's wall drawings, with their obsessive clarity and regularity predicated on simple verbal instructions made visible, provide a fascinating glimpse of the thought process, including coincidence and error, still a mostly uncharted world that increasingly obsesses our systemic, computerized, mass-circulation culture.

Although LeWitt, unlike Flavin and Judd, never issued his modular structures in editions, he has continued ever since 1964 to fabricate new lattice variations, such as *1-2-3-4-5* of 1980 in the Elliott collection (pl. 19; cat. no. 84). Considered in relationship to the wall drawings, these structures can now be more easily understood as machines to superimpose at once logical and whimsical patterns on the surrounding environment, constantly changing patterns depending on an observer's position in the exhibition space. Just as Duchamp's famous *Bicycle Wheel* readymade of 1913 transforms the background seen through it into Cubist-like segments, LeWitt's structures transform their immediate environment into related little segments comparable to the patterns in his grid-based wall drawings.

Whereas most artists who emerged in the 1950s and 1960s, including Rauschenberg, Stella, and Warhol, abandoned Minimal stylization in their works of the 1970s and 1980s, Andre, like Judd, has not, and his recent works appear little different from his early ones. Indeed Andre's *Arcata Pollux* of 1983 in the Elliott collection (pl. 5; cat. no. 6), like so many of the artist's structures, is directly related to drawings made in his notebooks around 1960, prior to the onset of his career as a gallery artist. Already then, Andre anticipated what he calls the "element series" of works made from segments of stock lumber, beginning around 1970. These structures, each identified with a poetic title,[35] are assembled according to Andre's longstanding premise that nails, glue, or other binding agents are inessentials for an art at odds with illusionism of any sort, including the illusion of geometric pieces held by force in unnatural compositional balance. It is, most of all, Andre's uncompromising rejection of binding agents that distinguishes works like *Arcata Pollux* from such antecedents as Rodchenko's Constructivist works made forty years before from unpainted stock lumber; Andre was apparently unaware of Rodchenko's works when he first developed his idea as notebook projects in 1960.

Of greater interest is the apparent correlation between Andre's efforts in the 1970s to realize his earlier ideas for unpainted lumber structures and Judd's decision by 1972 to fabricate constructions in unpainted plywood. Consisting of four boxlike elements installed on the wall, the plywood piece of 1983 in the Elliott collection (pl. 15; cat. no. 66) is an extension of the metal box wall structures that Judd first made around 1964. Although Judd began to install open box units frontally against the wall like empty picture frames by the late 1960s, it was not until 1977 that he began to divide the interiors of his boxes with diagonal planes like those in the Elliott piece. With these diagonal planes, Judd in effect "carves" three-dimensional interior space along two-dimensional planar surfaces. The resulting pictorial effect of the sharp shadows cast across the irregular slices of void adds an immaterial dimension to these structures; their abstract beauty recalls the geometric complexities of wood pattern and shadows in Cubist collages by Braque and Picasso that Greenberg understood as the original breakthrough to Modernist art about dimensionality as an essential pictorial condition.

The two fine sculptures by Richard Serra in the Elliott collection (pls. 29–30; cat. nos. 157–58), both from the 1980s, are predicated on the same sparse vocabulary developed by the artist in the late 1960s. Serra's twenty-year-long obsession with the elemental units and concepts of his signature style relates his output as a whole to Judd's, Andre's, and Flavin's. Moreover, Serra's debt to the example of their early works and the fact that he has limited himself almost exclusively to square or rectangular plates of lead or steel, occasionally in tandem with tubes of rolled steel, seem sufficient to categorize his works as Minimal. But, and it is a big "but," the blatant drama of Serra's structures is antithetical to the decorative, emotionless spirit characteristic of the classic phase of mid-1960s Minimalism. Serra's *One Ton Prop (House of Cards)* of 1969 (G 36) is essentially a Judd box opened at the seams and reconstructed in Andre fashion without welds, joins, or adhesives. But whereas for Andre part-to-part structural relationships must conform to the flattening exigencies of gravity, for Serra they must taunt the very laws of physics to which they are subject. Propping one another in position, the heavy planar sides of Serra's structure literally define the precarious-appearing flash point between erection and collapse. The weighty parts in Serra's sculpture strain to hold their own with a regimented logic as delicate as a dancer extended on tiptoe. *Five Plate Pentagon* of 1988 in the Elliott collection is identical in concept to this earlier piece. When it is arranged in place by a team of professional riggers, the five five-foot-square plates of Corten steel stand ready to fall, each shifting its heavy lateral thrust onto the next in a rotational transference—an abstract monument to the awesome rudiments of engineering.

Similarly, Elliott's *Another Look at a Corner* of 1985 harks back to works such as *Equal* of 1969 (G 42), in which Serra commemorated the structural logic of a room's corner by standing a plane on its edge along an imaginary line marking the center axis that bisects the right angles where walls meet. Serra pinned the standing plane's unbalanced weight in place with a heavy rolled element that would fall if not for its structural context, perpendicularly balanced at three points against the walls and the top corner of the standing plane. Mirroring the site's own interlocked architectural loads and supports, Serra's piece is indivisibly integrated into real space as an intensification of its defining essentials. Replacing the tubelike upper element in *Equal* with a metal plane placed perpendicular to the standing planar element like a tabletop, Serra developed a group of related corner pieces in the mid-1980s, exemplified by the one in the Elliott collection.[36]

Whereas nothing arbitrary detracts from the focused force of Serra's sculptures, LeWitt's most recent structures are predicated on the sort of arbitrary abstract logic that has always inspired him. Beginning around 1985, LeWitt decided to extend his method of generating wall drawings from a set of simple directions and began to compose instructions for bizarre three-dimensional objects. Providing fabricators with drawings of dots that might be connected by lines to create a polyhedron to a specified height, LeWitt instigated eccentric crystalline forms, the surprising three-dimensional projections from a given apex point in space along linear struts to meet the floor plane. By 1987, when LeWitt agreed to exhibit a group of these antimonuments without any particular structural rationale at the Donald Young Gallery in Chicago, he had decided to have them fabricated as solids rather than as lattices, their white skins thus obscuring the Kandinsky-like point-to-line-to-plane mechanics at issue. Encountering one of these, like the tilted, irregularly sided pyramid of 1986 in the Elliott collection (pl. 21; cat. no. 86), however, hardly amounts to a didactic experience. From the outset less earnest than his colleagues, LeWitt devises simple rules to explore what can be, rather than what has to be or what theoretically should not be. The principles of Modernism notwithstanding, for LeWitt Minimal art has become a license to visualize the elemental stuff of improvisation from which all meditations begin to take their fantastic shapes.

DSS Dudley Del Balso, Roberta Smith, and Brydon Smith, "Catalogue Raisonné of Paintings, Objects, and Wood-Blocks 1960–1974," in The National Gallery of Canada, Ottawa, 1975, *Donald Judd.*

FR The St. Louis Art Museum, 1973, *drawings and diagrams 1963–1972 by Dan Flavin*, text by Dan Flavin and Emily S. Rauh.

G Ernst-Gerhard Güse, ed., *Richard Serra* (New York, 1988).

S The National Gallery of Canada, Ottawa, 1969, *fluorescent light, etc. from Dan Flavin*, text by Brydon Smith.

1. Maurice Denis (as Pierre Louis), in *Art et critique*, Aug. 1890, reprinted in Linda Nochlin, *Impressionism and Post-Impressionism, 1874–1984, Sources and Documents* (Englewood Cliffs, NJ, 1966), p. 187.

2. Clement Greenberg, "'American Type' Painting," *Partisan Review* 12, 2 (Spring 1955), reprinted in his *Art and Culture* (Boston, 1961), p. 208.

3. Carl Andre, in The Museum of Modern Art, New York, 1959, *Sixteen Americans*, p. 76.

4. Donald Judd, *Complete Writings 1959–1975* (Halifax and New York, 1975), pp. 17, 27. By 1963, however, such corner-to-corner relationships were something that Judd avoided as too compositional; see John Coplans, "An Interview with Don Judd," *Artforum* 9, 10 (June 1971), pp. 41–43.

5. Judd (note 4), p. 178.

6. Ibid., p. 91.

7. For Judd's thinking about texture as an index of flatness at this time, see Coplans (note 4), p. 41.

8. Ibid., p. 43.

9. Ibid., p. 41; and Michael Ennis, "The Marfa Art War," *Texas Monthly*, Aug. 1984, p. 142.

10. Coplans (note 4), p. 44. Of course, given their institutional liabilities both to works of art and to spectators, museums have usually needed to modify and thus distort these artists' original intentions by installing floor pieces on platforms or behind barriers. At first art galleries showed similar concern. Installation photographs of Rauschenberg's late 1961 exhibition at the Leo Castelli Gallery show

that *193466*, a weathered bucket inside a crude wooden box with chicken wire sides, was initially installed directly on the floor and subsequently moved onto a platform. Such a platform was also necessary when the Sidney Janis Gallery included one of Andy Warhol's *Dance Diagram* floor paintings in its October–December 1962 "New Realists" exhibition.

11. Enno Develing, in Haags Gemeentemuseum, The Hague, 1969, *Carl Andre*, p. 39.

12. David Bourdon, "The Razed Sites of Carl Andre," *Artforum* 5, 2 (Oct. 1966), p. 15.

13. Judd (note 4), p. 117.

14. Ibid., p. 119.

15. Robert Smithson, "Donald Judd," in Institute of Contemporary Art, Philadelphia, 1965–66, *7 Sculptors*, p. 13.

16. This is the translation included by Flavin in a letter to Mel Bochner dated November 1, 1966, and excerpted in The National Gallery of Canada, Ottawa, 1969, *fluorescent light, etc. from Dan Flavin*, text by Brydon Smith, p. 206, no. 96; Mel Bochner, "Less is less (for Dan Flavin)," *Art and Artists* 1, 9 (Dec. 1966), p. 25, retranslated the phrase: "No more entities should be posited than are necessary."

17. Cited in Bochner (note 16), p. 25.

18. Lucy Lippard, "The Structures, the Structures and the Wall Drawings, the Stuctures and the Wall Drawings and the Books," in The Museum of Modern Art, New York, 1978, *Sol LeWitt*, p. 29, n. 17.

19. While the holes in LeWitt's structures herald the lattice structures that he would begin to make in 1965, they may be indebted to the holes punched by Judd into the surface of his untitled 1963 relief in the Elliott collection (pl. 11; cat. no. 62).

20. Quoted in Lucy Lippard, "The Third Stream: Constructed Paintings and Painted Structures," *Art Voices* 4, 2 (Spring 1965), p. 48.

21. The National Gallery of Canada (note 16), p. 218, no. 102.

22. According to Robert Morris, "Tatlin was perhaps the first to free sculpture from representation and establish it as an autonomous form both by the kind of image, or rather non-image, he employed and by his literal use of materials" (Robert Morris, "Notes on Sculpture, Part I," *Artforum* 4, 6 [Feb. 1966], p. 43).

23. See the artist's commentary in The Museum of Modern Art (note 18), p. 53.

24. Judd's pieces seem to counter the assertion Robert Morris made at the time: "an object hung on the wall does not confront gravity; it timidly resists it....The ground plane, not the wall, is the necessary support for the maximum awareness of the object" (Morris [note 22], p. 43).

25. Bochner (note 16), p. 27.

26. *Aspen Magazine* 5–6 (Fall–Winter 1966), n. pag.

27. The instructions included in the drawing that LeWitt reproduced for the announcement of his 1967 exhibition stipulate that "All sets seen together represent the completion of the plan."

28. David Bourdon, *Carl Andre, Sculpture 1959–1977* (New York, 1978), p. 31.

29. "All I want is more money—to make more pieces," Judd explained in 1968; see Grace Glueck, "A Box Is a Box Is a Box," *The New York Times*, Mar. 10, 1968, p. D23.

30. James R. Mellow, "Everything Sculpture Has, My Work Doesn't," *The New York Times*, Mar. 10, 1968, p. D26.

31. Sol LeWitt, "Doing Wall Drawings," *Art Now: New York* 3, 2 (June 1971), n. pag.

32. Camilla Gray, *The Russian Experiment in Art, 1863–1922* (1962; rev. ed., New York, 1986), p. 250.

33. See Clark V. Poling, *Kandinsky's Teaching at the Bauhaus* (New York, 1986), pp. 72–73.

34. Sol LeWitt, "Sentences on Conceptual Art," *Art-Language* 1, 1 (May 1969), p. 11.

35. *Arcata Pollux* means the arcade of Pollux; in Greek mythology, Pollux and his twin brother Castor are the semidivine children of Leda with whom the god Zeus, disguised as a swan, had mated.

36. These include *T with Two* (G 103), *Melnikov* (G 139), and *The Dead Egyptians (from Torino)*. This last piece is illustrated in The Museum of Modern Art, New York, 1986, *Richard Serra/Sculpture*, fig. 100. Exhibited in an art gallery in Milan in 1985, *The Dead Egyptians (from Torino)* is identical in scale with *Another Look at a Corner* in the Elliott collection. Serra, who seldom duplicates his works, made an exception in this case, realizing that *Dead Egyptians* would probably remain in Europe and yet concerned that an American audience should be able to see it (Richard Serra in conversation with the author, May 1989).

Plate 2. *Blue Wood Chain*, New York, 1964
  Painted wood
  26½ x 6 x 5½ in. (67 x 15 x 14 cm)
  Cat. no. 4

CARL ANDRE

Plate 3. *Untitled*, 1963
Text on paper
11 x 8½ in. (28 x 22 cm)
Cat. no. 3

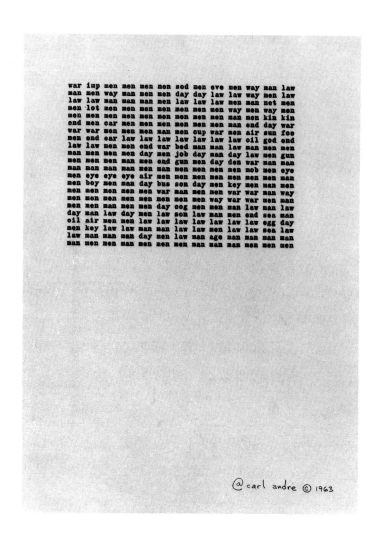

Plate 4. *Zinc-Lead Plain*, New York, 1969
  Zinc and lead
  Thirty-six units, overall ⅜ x 72 x 72 in. (1 x 183 x 183 cm);
  each ⅜ x 12 x 12 in. (1 x 31 x 31 cm)
  Cat. no. 5

Plate 5. *Arcata Pollux*, Atlanta, 1983
   Western red cedar
   Seven parts, overall 48 x 36 x 36 in. (122 x 91 x 91 cm);
   each 12 x 12 x 36 in. (31 x 31 x 91 cm)
   Cat. no. 6

Plate 6. *Atoll*, 1983
 Oil on canvas
 108 x 83½ in. (274 x 212 cm)
 Cat. no. 13

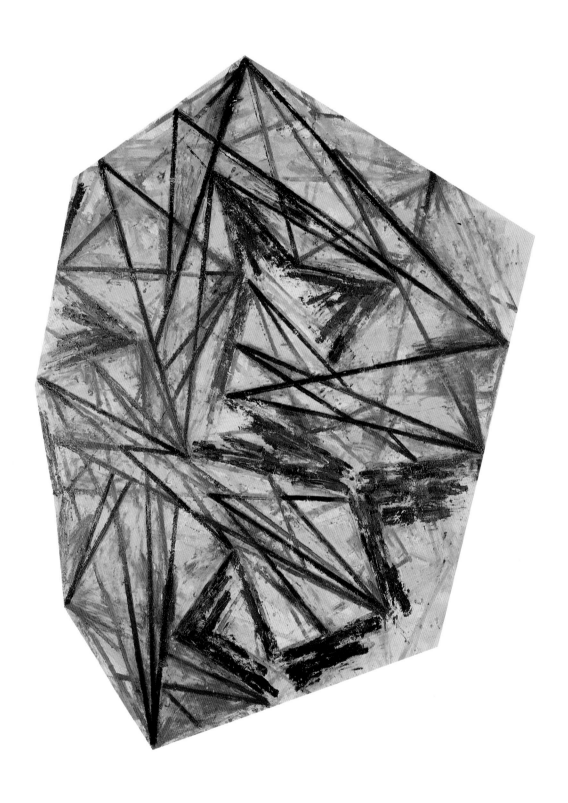

Plate 7. *Fjord*, 1984
    Oil on canvas
    93 x 94 in. (236 x 239 cm)
    The Art Institute of Chicago, gift of Gerald S. Elliott, 1985.1119
    Cat. no. 14

Plate 8. *the alternate diagonals of March 2, 1964 (to Don Judd)*, 1964
Red and yellow fluorescent light
145 x 12 x 4 in. (369 x 31 x 10 cm)
Cat. no. 45

DAN FLAVIN

Plate 9. *untitled (monument for V. Tatlin)*, 1970
   Cool-white fluorescent light
   96 x 31½ x 4 in. (244 x 80 x 10 cm)
   Cat. no. 46

Plate 10. *Untitled*, 1962
  Light cadmium red oil on Liquitex and sand on Masonite with yellow Plexiglas
  48 x 96 x 2½ in. (122 x 244 x 6 cm)
  Cat. no. 61

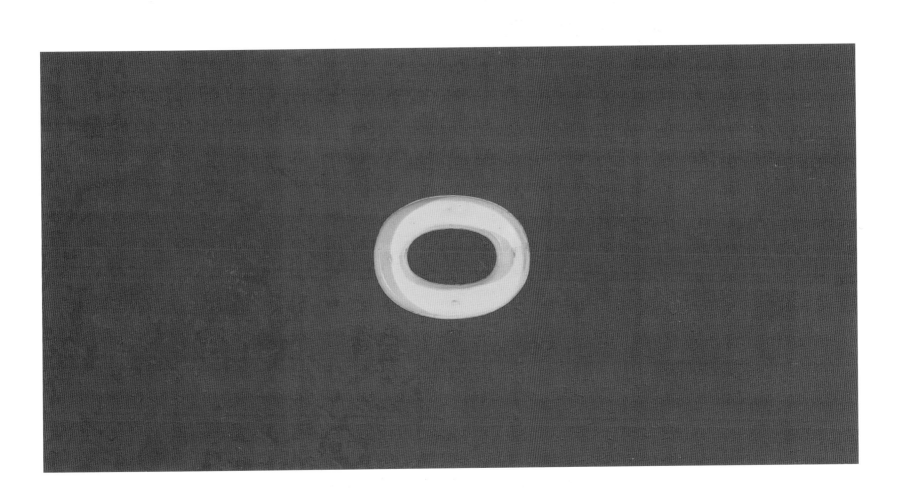

Plate 11. *Untitled*, 1963
Black enamel on aluminum and raw sienna enamel and galvanized iron on wood
52 x 42⅛ x 5⅞ in. (132 x 107 x 15 cm)
Cat. no. 62

Plate 12. *Untitled*, May 7, 1970
Anodized aluminum
6 x 110¾ x 6½ in. (15 x 280 x 17 cm)
Cat. no. 63

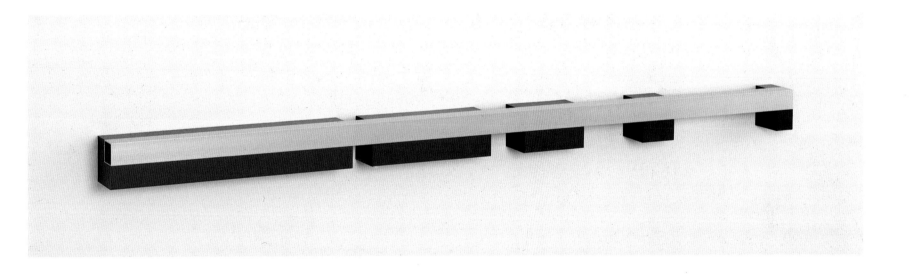

Plate 13. *Untitled*, August 28, 1970 (detail)
    Stainless steel and green Plexiglas
    Ten parts, each 6 x 27 x 24 in. (15 x 68 x 61 cm), with 6-inch intervals
    Cat. no. 64

Plate 14. *Untitled*, 1978
Red paint on plywood
19½ x 45 x 30½ in. (50 x 114 x 77 cm)
Cat. no. 65

Plate 15. *Untitled*, 1983
    Plywood
    Four parts, overall 39 x 216½ x 19⅝ in. (99 x 550 x 50 cm);
    each 39 x 39 x 19⅝ in. (99 x 99 x 50 cm)
    Cat. no. 66

Plate 16. *Untitled*, 1984
    Painted aluminum
    11⅞ x 70⅞ x 11⅞ in. (30 x 180 x 30 cm)
    Cat. no. 67

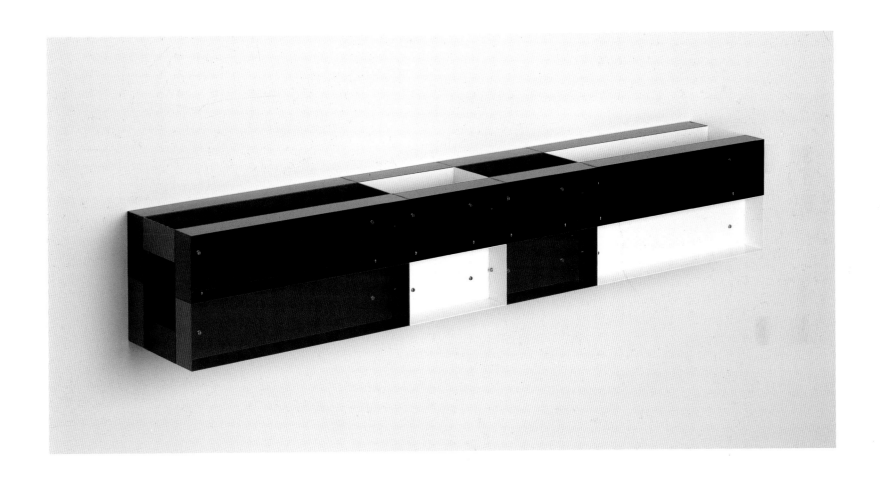

SOL LE WITT

Plate 17. *Serial Project, Set D*, 1966
Painted steel
15½ x 55½ x 55½ in. (39 x 141 x 141 cm)
Cat. no. 82

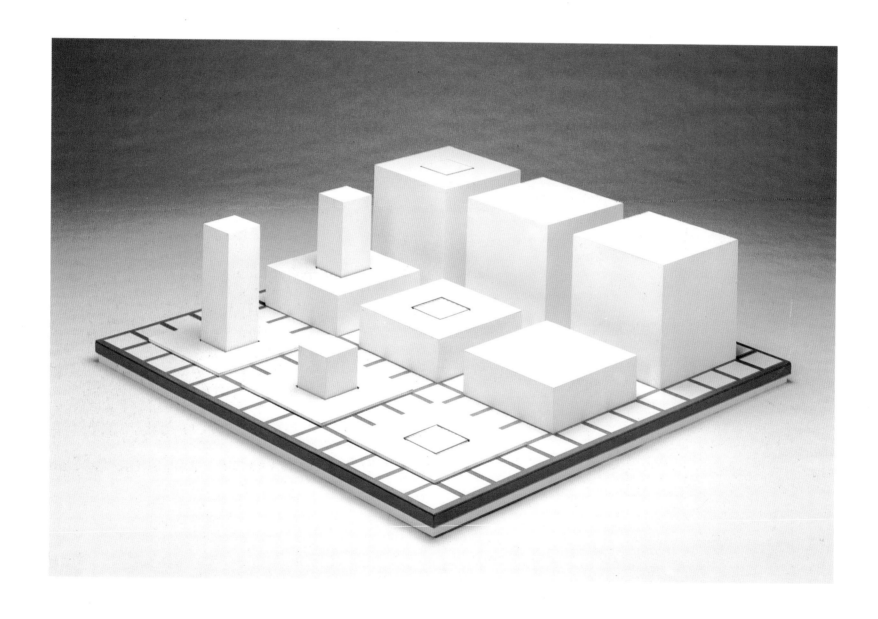

Plate 18. *Wall Drawing No. 311: Square, Circle, and Triangle on Red, Yellow, and Blue,*
1978
Wall drawing
Dimensions variable
Cat. no. 83

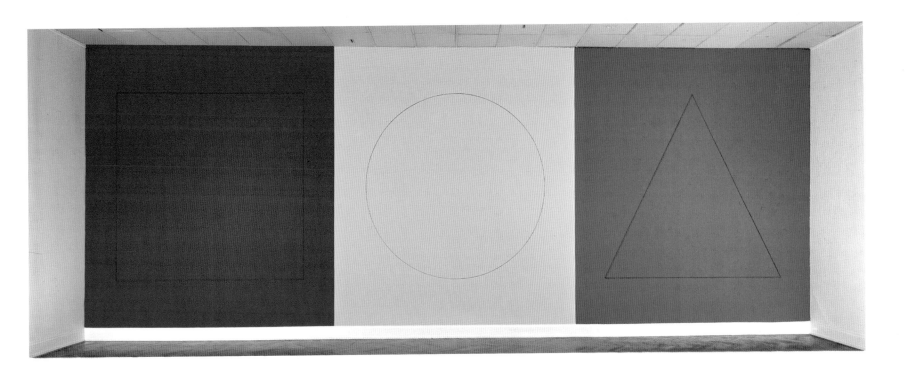

Plate 19. *1-2-3-4-5*, 1980
  Painted aluminum
  25¼ x 99¼ x 32¾ in. (64 x 252 x 83 cm)
  Cat. no. 84

Plate 20. *Wall Drawing No. 358: A 12" (30 cm) Grid Covering the Wall. Within Each 12" (30 cm) Square, One Arc from the Corner. (The direction of the arcs and their placement are determined by the draftsman.)*, 1981
Wall drawing
Dimensions variable
Cat. no. 85

Plate 21. *Untitled*, 1986
       Painted wood
       H. 78 in. (198 cm)
       Cat. no. 86

Plate 22. *V Series: Central Section (Vertical)*, 1968
Acrylic on Masonite
48 x 48 in. (122 x 122 cm)
Cat. no. 92

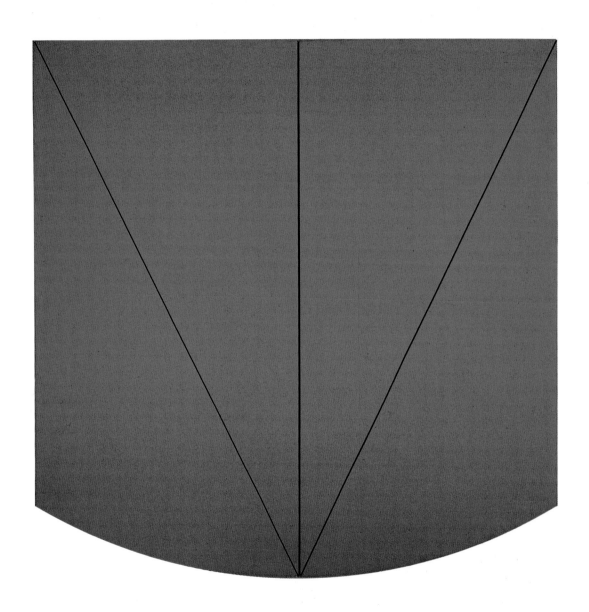

Plate 23. *Circle Painting No. 5*, 1973
　　　　　Acrylic and pencil on canvas
　　　　　Dia. 72 in. (183 cm)
　　　　　Cat. no. 93

Plate 24. *Four Color Frame Painting No. 6*, 1984
Acrylic and pencil on canvas
99 x 72 in. (251 x 183 cm)
Cat. no. 94

Plate 25. *Tour IV,* 1972
    Oil and wax on canvas
    96 x 48 in. (244 x 122 cm)
    Cat. no. 95

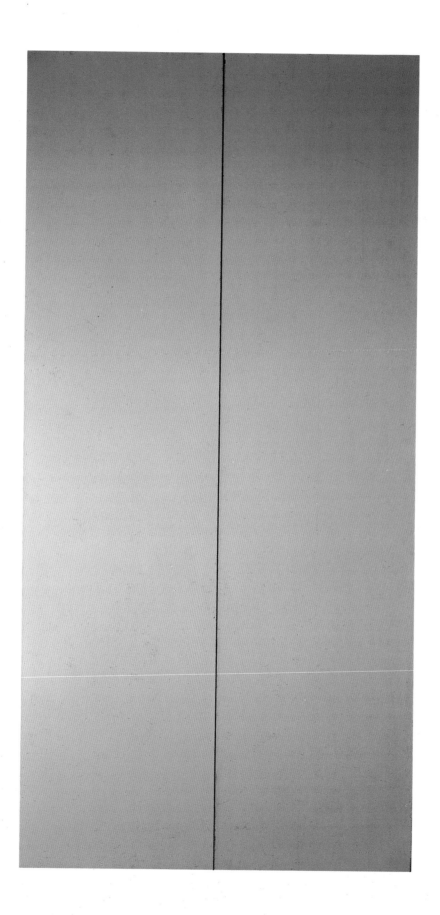

Plate 26. *Grove Group V,* 1976
Oil and wax on canvas
72 x 108 in. (182 x 274 cm)
Cat. no. 96

Plate 27. *8*, 1987–88
        Oil on linen
        84 x 60 in. (213 x 152 cm)
        Cat. no. 97

Plate 28. *Untitled*, 1988
Dolomite
86½ x 45½ x 12 in. (220 x 115 x 31 cm)
Cat. no. 142

Plate 29. *Another Look at a Corner*, 1985
Steel
55½ x 54 x 106½ in. (141 x 137 x 271 cm)
Cat. no. 157

Plate 30. *Five Plate Pentagon*, 1988
Corten steel
Five parts, each 60 x 1½ x 60 in. (152 x 4 x 152 cm)
Cat. no. 158

Empowering Space: Notes on the Sculpture of Bruce Nauman

NEAL BENEZRA

Bruce Nauman's process of making art has involved rigorous analysis and a willingness to lay bare a problem in testing new ideas. The results of this approach are best viewed in Nauman's sculpture, which began as both an analysis of the tradition of the solid, cast object, and as a commentary on the artist working alone in the studio. Nauman's early investigations have resulted in a body of sculpture in which space is endowed with profound psychological power and moral purpose.

Nauman's seriousness—an uncommon combination of intellectual rigor and moral commitment—derives from the artist's experience as a student at the University of Wisconsin, Madison, in the early 1960s. As an undergraduate, Nauman studied mathematics as well as art; the conjunction had a lasting impact on his sensibility.

> When I was in school I started out as a mathematician. I didn't become one, but I think there was a certain thinking process which was very similar and which carried over into art. The investigative activity is necessary.[1]

Nauman recalled that his painting instructors at Madison were artists who had formerly worked for the Works Projects Administration; their approach to art influenced his own.

> They were socialists and they had points to make that were not only moral and political, but also ethical.... So there were a lot of people who thought art had a function beyond being beautiful—that it had a social reason to exist.[2]

Although Nauman began as a painter, who "loved moving the paint and the manipulation of materials," soon after entering the graduate program at the University of California, Davis, in 1964, he decided that painting was a "lush solution." He abandoned painting, believing that it was not enough to develop and refine a style within a particular medium; it was necessary to address the larger issue of art and its possibilities. As he has noted, "I was interested in what art can be, not just what painting can be."[3]

By 1965 Nauman had immersed himself in sculpture, particularly casting, and he questioned several of the assumptions that have attended to the process throughout its history. His investigations were guided, in part, by his fascination with Gödel's Proof, a mathematical theory advanced in 1931 that holds, "if a system is consistent then it is incomplete."[4] In practice such a notion suggests that the logic underlying any structure or accepted practice, regardless of the discipline, might profitably be turned against itself. The artist applied this reasoning in his earliest sculptures, rejecting the traditional use of a mold in the production of a technically perfectable cast object. The results are seen in his earliest extant sculptures of 1965: a group of eleven elongated, vaguely anthropomorphic fiberglass works (see pl. 31; cat. no. 102). These untitled sculptures involved "making a mold, taking the two halves and putting them together to make a hollow shape and turning it inside out."[5] In these early works, Nauman was testing the notion of sculpture as a medium of solid, durable forms, and thus was "stepping outside" the traditional logic of the medium,[6] turning the assumptions of sculpture, as well as the form, inside out.

When complete, several of the sculptures revealed plaster remnants from the casting process. Nauman recalled the objections that were raised about his seeming carelessness concerning finish: "It would never occur to me to do that [clear the plaster off] as I wasn't trying to make a perfect object, I was trying to make a point. It seemed to me that when the point was made clear you could just quit, you didn't need to belabor it."[7] Beyond Nauman's logical outlook, these words reveal the freedom which the artist claimed for himself regarding the appearance of his work. If these early fiberglass sculptures are the product of a fresh mind reassessing the nature of sculpture, in their composition and degree of finish they are remarkably casual and open-ended.

While Nauman's discipline came naturally and was reinforced by his study of mathematics, the unburdened character of his early work owes a great deal to his experience at Davis. Although Nauman's work bears only a trace of the Funk art that predominated in the San Francisco Bay Area, beginning in the mid-1960s his relationship with William T. Wiley, whose teaching philosophy predominated at Davis during these years, was of great consequence. A remarkably intuitive teacher, Wiley was open to new approaches while offering great freedom and encouraging self-trust in his students.[8] This atmosphere certainly suited Nauman's solitary temperament and precocious talent. Although he was only twenty-four years old when the fiberglass pieces were made, the artist was remarkably mature and almost immediately became an influence on his fellow students and even his teachers.[9] The relationship between Nauman and Wiley was indeed symbiotic, for although their approaches were very different and their subsequent work diverged radically, there was an important interaction between 1964 and 1968. This is particularly evident in their shared interest in employing language and puns, and their parallel investigations into the meaning and implications of being an artist. In contrast to Nauman's ethical stance, Wiley considered art a highly personal form of exploration beyond the boundaries of moral imperative. Wiley believed that artists should develop their work "without having to set up a commitment in any way — to trust themselves enough to believe their commitment will grow out of their relationship to it."[10] For Nauman's part, the Funk art of Wiley and Robert Arneson, a canny, punning, more personal form of Pop art, offered a model of how an artist might free himself of limitations posed by existing attitudes and styles. Although his rigorous outlook always kept him at arm's length from its more humorous side, Nauman has noted that "Funk art allowed one to make things and not worry how they looked."[11]

An example of Nauman's relationship to Wiley and his Davis colleagues, which would have important consequences for his later sculpture, was the "Slant Step" episode of 1965–66. While exploring a salvage

Figure 1. The original *Slant Step.* Wood, linoleum, rubber, and nails, 18¾ x 15 x 12¼ in. (48 x 38 x 31 cm). The New York Society for the Preservation of the Slant Step.

Figure 2. Bruce Nauman, *A Cast of the Space under My Chair*, 1966–68. Concrete, 17½ x 15⅜ x 14⅝ in. (46 x 39 x 37 cm). Collection Geertjan Visser, Retie, Belgium, on loan to the Rijksmuseum Kröller-Müller, Otterlo, The Netherlands.

shop near his home in Mill Valley, Wiley discovered an object of peculiar shape and no apparent function (fig. 1). Wiley puzzled over the small, linoleum-covered wooden object and, as Nauman recalled, "He used to go and look at it alone, sometimes. He took me there and showed it to me when I was visiting, and then a couple of months later I asked him to buy it for me. I was going to take it to a carpenter shop and have an edition of copies made."[12] Nauman kept the object, which came to be called a "Slant Step," in his studio in Davis for nearly one year. It became an object of considerable interest among Bay Area artists, particularly since no one could pinpoint its purpose. Interest grew to the point where artists such as Wiley, Nauman, Arneson, William Allan, Robert Hudson, and Stephen Kaltenbach, among many others, made their own Slant Steps, reinterpreting the original to fit their preferred medium and fantasies. After many conversations and several casual meetings, an exhibition of the original and its spin-offs was organized and held at the Berkeley Gallery in San Francisco in

September 1966. During the course of this informal show, the Slant Step was playfully "stolen" by Richard Serra, who took it to his New York studio. Subsequently it has been transported surreptitiously across country on several occasions, and to this day it remains an object of fascination, speculation, and fun among Bay Area artists.[13]

Despite Nauman's role in the Slant Step affair, it would be altogether incorrect to characterize him as a Funk artist. While the mood surrounding the episode was humorous and high-spirited, and all the objects created for the exhibition unfailingly witty, Nauman's enterprise was characteristically solitary and serious. Recalling the importance of the Slant Step several years later, Nauman described it as:

> problematic and useful. What I was trying to do was find a way to make objects...that appeared to have a function...but in fact they didn't have any function and, in fact, the design of the pieces was arbitrary or invented. The Slant Step was such an example of that because it was something that everybody thought had a function until you really tried to use it...and so it was sort of like when you are thinking about something and then you read about it...and then it reinforces, makes it possible to go on. It reinforces ideas you have or validates them.[14]

In effect, the Slant Step experience encouraged Nauman to press Wiley's dictum to "trust yourself" to its logical if extreme end, and to make sculptures without worrying "how they look." After first seeing the object, Nauman made a drawing of it from memory; later, after obtaining it from Wiley, he made another, more finished study.[15] Rather than having the intended edition of copies made, Nauman conceived a "modernized version," constructing a new Slant Step and then covering it with plaster. He then removed the wooden "armature," cutting the plaster mold in two parts in the process. The *Mold for a Modernized Slant Step* (pl. 32; cat. no. 103), made early in 1966, and exhibited in the Slant Step show later that year, is, in fact, not a sculpture in the traditional sense at all. The object was discarded and the mold and surrounding space were presented as the finished work, thus setting the stage for much of Nauman's future exploration of the potential power of sculptural space.

In 1966 Nauman conceived or completed several more works that investigate space. Among these is *A Cast of the Space Under My Chair* (1966–68), a concrete sculpture whose solid mass measures the dimensions of the space beneath an actual chair, complete with voids representing legs and crosspieces (fig. 2). The resulting work, which in form and scale loosely resembles the sculpture of the Belgian Constructivist Georges Vantongerloo, reveals Nauman's continuing fascination with contradicting the function of standard objects, in this case by removing the object completely. The chair would appear often in Nauman's later sculpture as a highly expressive surrogate for the human figure, yet at this early stage it served as a vehicle for the artist's critique of the reductive aesthetics of Minimalism. Formally, he had pressed sculpture to the brink of immateriality, offering up a solid form which, in essence, simply measured negative space. Rather than presenting additional definitions of space, from this point on Nauman would endow space first with psychological, and eventually with political, meaning.[16]

Nauman's interests began to shift in late 1966. In June of that year, he completed his graduate degree at Davis and moved to San Francisco where he established a studio in a grocery storefront. That fall

Nauman assumed a part-time teaching position at the San Francisco Art Institute, thus beginning a period that would prove psychologically difficult if ultimately highly productive. Nauman was feeling extremely ambivalent about art and the meaning of being an artist; his Spartan existence in a studio devoid of the expensive materials required for making sculpture offered no solace.[17] Nauman was suffering from what he described as "the normal artist's paranoia ... kind of cut off, just not knowing how to proceed at being an artist."[18] Rather than filling his studio with objects, Nauman analyzed his situation with simple yet profound logic:

> That left me alone in the studio; this raised the fundamental question of what an artist does when left alone in the studio. My conclusion was that I was an artist and I was in the studio, then whatever I was doing in the studio must be art ... at this point art became more of an activity and less of a product.[19]

Feeling somewhat trapped in his studio and questioning his role as an artist, in 1966–67 Nauman transformed his self-doubt into works that focus explicitly on his activity in the studio. These works, in such diverse media as neon, photography, video, performance, dance, and sculpture, mix sophisticated humor with an unsparing critique of his own sometimes mundane activities. For example, after seeing a Man Ray retrospective at the Los Angeles County Museum of Art in the fall of 1966, Nauman became interested in photography and he subsequently made a series of eleven color images (pls. 34–44; cat. nos. 105–15). Finding himself drinking massive amounts of coffee and pacing his studio floor by the hour, in self-consciously mocking fashion Nauman devoted a pair of images to this subject (pls. 40–41; cat. nos. 111–12). Although he had recently considered the possibility of making outdoor sculpture, Nauman ultimately rejected the notion as foolish and vain,[20] and he disparaged the traditional ambitions of public sculptors by humorously proposing himself as a self-generating fountain (pl. 35; cat. no. 106). Nauman's double-edged humor — the parody of self-doubt — is perhaps clearest in *Bound to Fail* (pl. 44; cat. no. 115), a photograph of an anonymous, bound surrogate for the artist, who is "bound to fail," both literally and figuratively.

Bound to Fail became the source for one of Nauman's most important early sculptures, in which the back shown in the photograph was cast in wax, then plaster, and finally in iron (pl. 45; cat. no. 116). Although iron is a very unusual casting material, it was entirely appropriate to Nauman's purposes, since it accentuates the weightiness of the ties that bind the artist, again, both literally and figuratively. More surprising than the appearance and material of the sculpture is the title: *Henry Moore Bound to Fail*. Although Nauman occasionally referred to other artists in the titles of his works of this period, the choice of Henry Moore seems particularly curious given his concurrent rejection of monumental public sculpture — a tradition which the English sculptor personified. And yet, Moore had been the first modern sculptor to incorporate space with solid form, which was precisely Nauman's endeavor in the early sculptures of 1965. In addition, in his readings on Moore, Nauman learned that the English sculptor kept his plasters, left from the casting process, strewn about outside his studio. This, of course, appealed to Nauman, who had incorporated his own plaster in *Mold for a Modernized Slant Step*.[21]

Perhaps more important, however, was the psychological support that Nauman gained from Moore's "Shelter Drawings," studies made in the London underground during the German aerial attack on

Britain during World War II. Interestingly, it was the difficulty which Nauman perceived in these drawings that linked him to the older sculptor:

> Moore didn't have a light touch in any of them, neither the ones in crayon and wash nor the ones in pen and ink. All of them were very heavily worked; it seemed as though he didn't have much facility in his drawing—at that time anyway....But I liked that about those drawings, that he had to struggle to get them right. My drawings have always been like that—I've always had to beat them into shape as much as anything else.[22]

It was Nauman's affinity for what he perceived to be Moore's struggle that motivated the younger artist—a willingness to admit a lack of facility into a finished work—that encouraged Nauman to align himself with Moore. Ironically, while Nauman could reject the tradition of monumental public sculpture that Moore represented, he could nonetheless embrace the English artist on the basis of works that he considered imperfect. Ultimately, this unusual attitude allowed Nauman to shelter his own feelings of doubt at that time, while remaining open to as many artistic sources as possible.

Although the artist's own body was a recurring if not predominant theme during these years, Nauman generally disguised explicit self-expression, either through the incomplete nature or ambivalent identity of the form, or by his choice of titles. Nauman's indirectness and his disdain for excessive autobiographical reference appear often in his words as well. "I will tell you about myself...but I will only tell you so much."[23] This notwithstanding, the "bound artist" motif is perhaps Nauman's most revelatory and compelling image of the period, for it is as close as he has ever come to self-portraiture or a commentary on the psychological paralysis he felt in the studio. One can only agree with Jane Livingston, who, writing as early as 1972, described *Henry Moore Bound to Fail* and two other early sculptures, *Untitled (Folded Arms)* and *From Hand to Mouth*, all of 1967, as "images of the artist in states of incompletion, of constrictedness and paralysis so drastic as to imply a negation of the hand of the artist."[24]

The two themes that I have traced in Nauman's early sculpture—the activation of sculptural space and the "bound artist" motif, however disguised—came together in 1969 in a single remarkable work. Nauman made a number of short films and videos at this time; one of them, *Walk with Contrapposto* of 1969, depicts the artist seen from behind and walking in an exaggerated fashion in a narrow, twenty-foot-long hallway open at one end only. As in *Self-Portrait as a Fountain*, Nauman here parodies the tradition of heroic, classical sculpture by virtue of his peculiar pose.

> I walked very slowly toward and away from the camera, one step at a time. My hands were clasped behind my neck, and I used a very exaggerated contraposto [*sic*] motion....The way you saw it, the camera was placed so that the walls came in at either side of the screen. You couldn't see the rest of the studio, and my head was cut off most of the time.[25]

In the summer of 1969, the corridor itself, a pair of freestanding plywood panels abutting a wall at one end, was included in "Anti-Illusion: Procedures/Materials," an important exhibition held at the Whitney Museum of American Art, which included works by Nauman, Serra, Eva Hesse, Robert

Morris, Joel Shapiro, and Keith Sonnier, among others. It was this exhibition that signaled the shift in American sculpture away from Minimalism and toward a more open attitude toward form, materials, and the subjective presence of the artist. In his review of the exhibition, Peter Schjeldahl emphasized the work of Nauman and Serra, noting the similarities between *Performance Corridor* and Serra's *One Ton Prop* (fig. 3). Schjeldahl presciently described Nauman's work as a "somber corridor" that induced "claustrophobic discomfort," and the experience of Serra's sculpture as "precarious" and "threatening to the viewer."[26] In employing the clear, rational geometry of Minimalism, and infusing it with a bewildering and even frightening human presence, Nauman and Serra had turned the seemingly unassailable logic of that movement against itself. These two works, seen in close proximity at the Whitney in 1969, foretold the shift toward a subjective human presence in the sculpture of the 1970s.

Together, *Walk with Contrapposto* and *Performance Corridor* culminate Nauman's ambivalent attitude toward the history of sculpture and his obsession with his existence in the studio. The self-referential aspect in Nauman's work would now be stilled; the "bound artist," walking monotonously back and forth in a narrow corridor, hands clasped behind his head, suggests imprisonment rather than artistry, with the figure shackled and coerced into performing a single, repetitive task. Nauman's shift from personal to social concerns developed in the sculpture of the 1970s, a body of work dedicated to uninhabited, enclosed spaces that abound in psychological tension. While these include a number of additional corridor pieces—some filled with colored light, some with sound, and some with video monitors—Nauman also conceived new and even more intimidating spaces which induce anxiety and discomfort in the viewer.

It is noteworthy that in 1969 Nauman moved from northern California to Pasadena. Whereas Funk art continued to prevail in the San Francisco Bay Area, in southern California artists such as James Turrell and Robert Irwin were creating pivotal environmental works, manipulating color, light, form, and space in attempts to expand human perception. Nauman employed these same formal means in his sculpture of the 1970s, yet his work yielded compelling psychological as well as perceptual results. Although comparison of the work of these artists suggests certain similarities, particularly around 1970, the increasingly emphatic nature of Nauman's expression over the course of the 1970s would prove a crucial distinction.

For example, in 1974 Nauman completed his *Floating Room*, a square room whose walls are raised several inches off the ground. As in the corridor pieces, Nauman shaped the experience by strictly controlling the effects of light; in this case the impact is greatly enhanced by the perception of the floating walls. Upon crossing the raised threshold, one immediately feels manipulated and entrapped. The experience, as Nauman has said, "has to do with fear, but it also has to do with the way we normally control space, or fill up space."[27]

Nauman pursued the individual's inability to control his or her own environment in a number of tunnel pieces, conceived on paper as early as 1972, but not realized as sculpture until the late 1970s. These hollow, reinforced plaster structures are models for much larger, potentially inhabitable environments. Although the early examples were conceived as circular, open-air trenches, *3 Dead-End Adjacent Tunnels, Not Connected* of 1979 (pl. 47; cat. no. 118) is a complex shape intended for construction under ground. Whereas the *Floating Room* was planned for a single individual and a personalized response, the tunnels imply the control of large numbers of people:

> they were really about a certain type of frustration and anger—creating uncomfortable spaces and shapes even on a very large scale for lots and lots of people.... There is a Beckett book called *The Lost Ones* which describes a large number of people in a strange, very accurately and clearly described space...but they're stuck in it. A greenish yellow light, circular space with no top to it, just black and then greenish light and walking around and around in a circle. When I read this, a very powerful connection to a lot of the work I had done before encouraged me in the direction of the tunnels and the kind of oblique comment they make on society.[28]

Whereas social criticism remained implicit in Nauman's tunnel sculptures—indeed, in most of his works of the 1970s[29]—it has become far more direct and biting in the works of the past decade. For example, *Rats and Bats (Learned Helplessness in Rats) II* (pl. 51; cat. no. 122), a recent sculpture and video installation of 1988, follows the theme of physical entrapment, but now with much more graphic results. Although enclosed in a small room, this work is first experienced from afar, as we hear an unidentified, muffled, pounding sound on approach. Once inside the room, we see that the sound is actually that of a well-muscled man striking a heavy suspended sack with a baseball bat. Even more disturbing is the sight of a multilevel, Plexiglas maze, a second video which shows a rat desperately seeking freedom from his tortured imprisonment, and an additional video made with an ongoing video camera, which results in the superimposition of the viewer himself within the maze. While the earlier tunnel pieces implicitly suggested physical and psychological entrapment, *Rats and Bats* makes these notions inescapably real by incorporating sound (who or what is in the bag, one wonders), the videos, the viewer, and the overriding implication of torture throughout. Beyond this, the space of the installation is so fraught with tension as to redefine contemporary sculpture in more theatrical terms.[30]

If the tunnel and maze pieces constitute one direction in Nauman's recent sculpture, works involving suspended chairs and carousels form a second. For example, *Diamond Africa with Tuned Chair, D.E.A.D.* of 1981 (fig. 4) is an enormous diamond-shaped sculpture with an overturned chair hanging in the center. Nauman's desire to make spaces uncomfortable led to the use of diamonds and triangles at this time. In particular, he considered "triangles really uncomfortable, disconcerting kinds of spaces. There is no comfortable place to stay inside them or outside them. It is not like a circle or square that gives you security."[31] Whereas the corridors and tunnels are enclosed spaces from which one cannot escape, the iron diamond in *Diamond Africa* hangs low, thereby thwarting entry. Because the space within the diamond cannot easily be traversed, the chair, overturned and suspended plaintively, has the psychological impact of a surrogate human presence. As a result, the chair, which appeared in the late 1960s as a subject of Nauman's formal measurement of sculptural space in *Cast of the Space under My Chair* (fig. 2), now

> becomes a symbol for a figure — a stand-in for the figure. A chair is used, it is functional; but it is also symbolic. Think of the electric chair, or the chair they put you in when the police shine the lights on you. Because your imagination is left to deal with that isolation, the image becomes more powerful, in the same way that the murder off stage can be more powerful than if it took place right in front of you.[32]

The chair as an implement of torture, within an interior space in which such acts occur, was reinforced once again by Nauman's readings. In 1981 Nauman read Jacobo Timerman's *Prisoner Without a Name, Cell Without a Number* (1981), an autobiographical account of Argentine government torture. In this book the author described being tied to a chair and given waves of electric shock of such intensity that, "[I] kept bouncing in the chair and moaning as the electric shocks penetrate my clothes. During one of these tremors, I fall to the ground, dragging the chair."[33] Nauman has also noted that V.S. Naipaul's "Michael X and the Black Power Killings in Trinidad," made a particularly important impression on him at that time, for it "clarified things for me and helped me to continue. It helped me to name names, to name things."[34] The Naipaul essay is an account of the activities and eventual downfall of a Trinidadian paramilitary cult; it includes detailed descriptions of a number of murders committed by the group, culminating with an excruciatingly powerful passage in which a woman member is hacked

Figure 4. Bruce Nauman, *Diamond Africa with Tuned Chair,*
D.E.A.D., 1981. Steel and cast iron, 60 x 285 x
138¼ in. (152 x 724 x 351 cm). The Art Institute of
Chicago, Mr. and Mrs. Frank G. Logan Prize Fund
Income, 1982.407.

to death in a ready grave. While the account focuses on the murder, Naipaul also concentrated on the men who surround the scene, some of whom participate in the act while others are paralyzed by their own thoughts and do not enter the arena.[35] The physical and psychological distance separating viewer and victim in this passage is analogous to the effect which the iron diamond has in barring anyone who might hope to approach the chair.

While the writings of Timerman and Naipaul are helpful in understanding this work, the specific reference to Africa in the title has to do both with the diamond form—South Africa is the leading producer of diamonds—and with sound. In planning works such as this, Nauman intended that the chair swing like a pendulum and actually strike the iron framework. When this proved impractical, Nauman, who considered sound integral to the piece, actually tuned the legs of the chair to sound the notes D-E-A-D. He then inscribed each leg accordingly, invoking the pattern of notes in conjunction with the title as a personal protest against apartheid.[36]

In one of Nauman's most recent works, the suspension of objects from above has taken on a yet more direct and vigorous expression. *Hanging Carousel (George Skins a Fox)* of 1988 (pl. 50; cat. no. 121) consists of a series of slowly rotating beams which form a cruciform armature. Hanging beneath each of the four arms is a polyurethane animal fragment, precisely the kind of object used by taxidermists in rendering stuffed animals. As has been noted, these rubberized forms lack anatomical detail and thus each animal appears embryonic as well as lifeless.[37] In the center of the sculpture is a video monitor that displays an ongoing interview with a taxidermist in the process of skinning a fox. The overall effect is so graphic, so unnerving, as to send the viewer fleeing from the room. At a time when many young sculptors have chosen to critique the current obsession with collecting consumer and luxury goods, Nauman's work stands as a brilliant commentary on both hunting and the notion of animals as trophy prizes, and on the sometimes self-indulgent art of the 1980s. Ultimately, while *Hanging Carousel* employs the same mechanisms as does *Diamond Africa*—the suspension of objects from above, the impenetrable space, etc.—the more recent work is far more direct and unnerving.

In works such as *Diamond Africa* and *Hanging Carousel*, Nauman employed several images that have long concerned him: chairs, sound, and impenetrable spaces all resonate in various forms and at various times throughout the artist's career. Nauman began by investigating space and its enclosure, a formal approach that soon constituted a rejection of Minimalism. By the late 1960s, Nauman moved toward a more personal, psychological approach, in which various surrogates for the artist became the focus. If the figure, in the form of the "bound artist," revealed his concerns around 1970, soon the self-imposed oppression of the studio was superceded by external, more universal feelings of despair and discontent in the form of empty rooms and tunnels. By the early 1980s, Nauman's concern for socio-political issues had come directly to the fore, providing the focus for a more public investigation of the implications of sculptural space. In works such as *Diamond Africa with Tuned Chair, D.E.A.D.* and *Hanging Carousel (George Skins a Fox)*, Nauman created large-scale sculpture in which space is empowered as an expressive component with explicitly public purposes.[38] Nauman's position in the history of sculpture since Minimalism is thus unique; by activating and employing space as an integral element in his work, the artist established himself, along with James Turrell and Robert Irwin, in the forefront of those sculptors employing space as a predominant formal element. Yet, while Turrell and Irwin have done so as a means of expanding our perceptual faculties, Nauman has pressed enclosed space into service as a conveyor of potent ethical and even political meanings. It is this combination of avant-garde form and humanist content that distinguishes the sculpture of Bruce Nauman.

My preparation of this essay depended in no small measure on the assistance and suggestions of Price Amerson, Robert Arneson, Kathy Halbreich, Maria Makela, Mary Murphy, Angela Westwater, and Donald Young.

1. Ian Wallace and Russell Keziere, "Bruce Nauman Interviewed," *Vanguard* 8, 1 (Feb. 1979), p. 16.

2. Joan Simon, "Breaking the Silence: An Interview with Bruce Nauman," *Art in America* 76, 9 (Sept. 1988), p. 143.

3. The above comments by Nauman are drawn from Coosje van Bruggen, *Bruce Nauman* (New York, 1988), pp. 7–8.

4. Nauman cited Gödel's Proof in his "Bruce Nauman: Notes and Projects," *Artforum* 9, 4 (Dec. 1970), p. 44. See also Marcia Tucker, "Bruce Nauman," in Los Angeles County Museum of Art, 1972, *Bruce Nauman: Works from 1965–1972*, pp. 45–47.

5. Willoughby Sharp, "Nauman Interview," *Arts Magazine* 44, 5 (Mar. 1970), p. 24.

6. Simon (note 2), p. 143.

7. Van Bruggen (note 3), p. 107.

8. I am grateful to Robert Arneson for his comments on Wiley's teaching. See also Thomas Albright, *Art in the San Francisco Bay Area, 1945–1980* (Berkeley, 1985), p. 120, and Brenda Richardson, "I Am My Own Enigma," in University Art Museum, University of California, Berkeley, 1971, *Wizdumb: William T. Wiley*, p. 10.

9. This has been described to me by Arneson, with whom Nauman studied ceramic sculpture, and by several other individuals familar with the program at Davis in the 1960s. Wiley has described Nauman's work and influence on him: "Those [Nauman's] ideas were bubbling in my head and he had figured out how to get it out there. There were certain appreciations and sensibilities we shared. And then there was all that anti–form work developing and I felt very touched and moved, just watching that happen" (John Perreault, "Wiley Territory," in Walker Art Center, Minneapolis, 1979, *Wiley Territory*, p. 9). See also Cindy Nemser, "An Interview with Stephen Kaltenbach," *Artforum* 9, 3 (Nov. 1970), pp. 47–53. It is also important to note that Nauman's work was so troublesome to some members of the Davis faculty that, without the support of Wiley and Arneson, he might not have received his graduate degree (Robert Arneson in conversation with the author, Dec. 5, 1988). See also Tucker (note 4), p. 34.

10. William T. Wiley, in Berkeley (note 8), p. 10.

11. Jane Livingston, "Bruce Nauman," in Los Angeles County Museum of Art (note 4), p. 10.

12. Frank Owen and Phil Weidman, "Bruce Nauman Interview," in Phil Weidman, *The Slant Step Book* (Sacramento, 1969), p. 6. For a thorough history of the Slant Step, see Richard L. Nelson Gallery, University of California, Davis, 1983, *The "Slant Step" Revisited.*

13. The Slant Step and the activities surrounding it are perhaps the quintessential example of Bay Area Funk. The focus of attention, the Slant Step itself, is a latter-day Dada sculpture, a found object that served as a catalyst to imaginative fantasy. The object's simple, rustic appearance and unexplained function placed it squarely in the tradition of Man Ray, whose work Nauman admired precisely because of its open-ended "unreasonableness." For the Funk artists, with their shared antipathy for the Minimalism then current in New York, the Slant Step manifested the freewheeling approach to form to which they all subscribed. Beyond this, the Slant Step became the focus of group rather than individual activity, another characteristic

of both the Bay Area art scene and its Dada predecessor. With their rejection of formalism, these artists shared new ideas, keeping pride of authorship and petty jealousies to a minimum.

14. Nelson Gallery (note 12), p. 9.

15. Both drawings, in the Öffentliche Kunstsammlung, Basel, are illustrated in Museum für Gegenwartkunst, Basel, 1986, *Bruce Nauman Drawings: 1965–1986*, nos. 4–5, figs. 6–7.

16. Nauman has related this work to a statement attributed to Willem de Kooning: "If you want to paint a chair, don't paint the thing, but paint the space between the rungs of the chair." Coosje van Bruggen has subsequently linked this to Jasper Johns, whose *Painted Bronze* of 1960 is similarly indebted to an offhand remark by de Kooning, concerning Leo Castelli's ability to sell anything as a work of art— even two beer cans. See van Bruggen (note 3), pp. 114–15. Nauman has also traced his interest in chairs to another monument of contemporary art, Joseph Beuys's *Fat Chair* of 1964. See Simon (note 2), p. 147.

17. See Livingston (note 11), p. 14.

18. Sharp (note 5), p. 25.

19. Wallace/Keziere (note 1), p. 18.

20. See Joe Raffaele and Elizabeth Baker, "The Way-Out West: Interviews with 4 San Francisco Artists," *Artnews* 66, 4 (Summer 1967), p. 75.

21. Van Bruggen (note 3), pp. 110–11.

22. Ibid., p. 111.

23. Wallace/Keziere (note 1), p. 16.

24. Livingston (note 11), p. 14.

25. Sharp (note 5), p. 23.

26. Peter Schjeldahl, "New York Letter," *Art International* 13, 7 (Sept. 1969), p. 70.

27. Jan Butterfield, "Bruce Nauman: The Center of Yourself," *Arts Magazine* 49, 6 (Feb. 1975), pp. 54–55.

28. Bob Smith, "Bruce Nauman Interview," *Journal: A Contemporary Art Magazine* 4, 2 (Spring 1982), p. 36.

29. The most important exception is *Double Steel Cage* of 1974 in the collection of the Museum Boymans-van Beuningen, Rotterdam. Nauman has described this work, an enormous cage that unmistakably

suggests imprisonment, as "the earliest piece that was really overt....I didn't do anything like that for a long time after because I was scared to really focus on these loaded subjects" (ibid., p. 36). The *Double Steel Cage* is illustrated in van Bruggen (note 3), p. 58.

30. Robert C. Morgan, "Jasper Johns, David Salle, Bruce Nauman at Leo Castelli," *Flash Art* 144 (Jan.–Feb. 1989), p. 123.

31. Simon (note 2), p. 147.

32. Ibid.

33. Timerman, in van Bruggen (note 3), p. 21.

34. Simon (note 2), p. 147.

35. V. S. Naipaul, "Michael X and the Black Power Killings in Trinidad," in *The Return of Eva Peron with The Killings in Trinidad* (London, 1980), particularly pp. 80–86.

36. As early as 1968–69, Nauman made a videotape, *Violin Tuned D E A D*. In this work Nauman played the notes indicated in the title on a violin as quickly as possible. Visually, the artist once again turned his back to the camera, at times filming with the camera on its side. The combination of the sequence of notes and the pose personalizes the artist's circumstances in the studio while simultaneously seeking to retain his anonymity.

37. See Patricia C. Phillips, "Bruce Nauman at Sperone Westwater," *Artforum* 27, 4 (Dec. 1988), p. 115. It is noteworthy that Nauman has lived in Pecos, New Mexico, since 1979, and that he is an avid outdoorsman.

38. *Hanging Carousel* was particularly effective when exhibited at the Sperone Westwater Gallery in 1988, because the dimensions of the room in which it was shown barely exceeded those of the work itself. The tightly constricted surrounding space and the unnerving character of the video imagery, combined with the slowly rotating sculpture itself, invested the work with an almost unbearable intensity. The combination of these elements was lacking in a variation of this work, *Carousel (Stainless Steel Version)*, which was exhibited in the 1988 Carnegie International in a vast space and without the video element. See Pittsburgh, 1988, *Carnegie International*, suppl., 1989, p. 185.

Plate 31. *Untitled*, 1965
Fiberglass
83 x 8 x 83 in. (211 x 20 x 211 cm)
Cat. no. 102

Plate 32. *Mold for a Modernized Slant Step*, 1966
Plaster
22 x 17 x 12 in. (56 x 43 x 31 cm)
Cat. no. 103

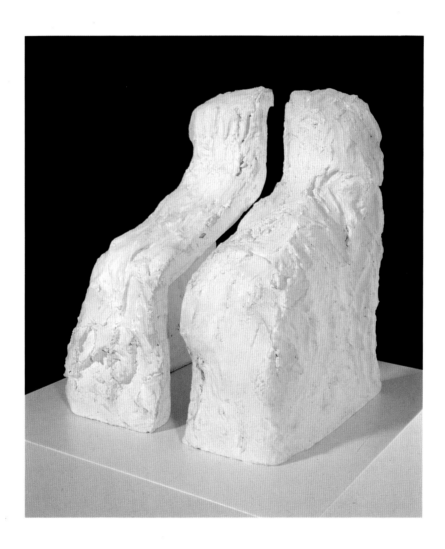

Plate 33. ½ *or* ¾″ *glass or plastic templates of my body separated by grease*, 1966
Watercolor and ink on paper
19 x 24 in. (48 x 61 cm)
The Art Institute of Chicago, gift of Gerald S. Elliott, 1988.555
Cat. no. 104

Plate 34. *Untitled*, 1966–67
Color photograph
20 x 23⅞ in. (51 x 61 cm)
Cat. no. 105

Plate 35. *Self-Portrait as a Fountain*, 1966–67
Color photograph
19¾ x 23¾ in. (50 x 60 cm)
Cat. no. 106

Plate 36. *Drill Team*, 1966–67
    Color photograph
    20 x 23⅞ in. (51 x 61 cm)
    Cat. no. 107

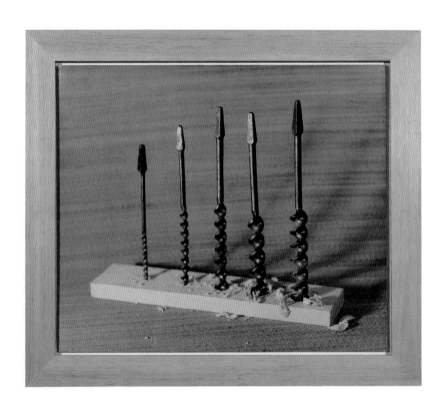

Plate 37. *Feet of Clay*, 1966–67
  Color photograph
  22½ x 23½ in. (57 x 60 cm)
  Cat. no. 108

Plate 38. *Waxing Hot*, 1966–67
Color photograph
19¾ x 20 in. (50 x 51 cm)
Cat. no. 109

Plate 39. *Finger Touch with Mirrors*, 1966–67
Color photograph
19¾ x 23¾ in. (50 x 60 cm)
Cat. no. 110

Plate 40. *Coffee Spilled Because the Cup Was Too Hot*, 1966–67
Color photograph
19¾ x 23¾ in. (50 x 60 cm)
Cat. no. 111

Plate 41. *Coffee Thrown Away Because It Was Too Cold*, 1966–67
Color photograph
19½ x 23 in. (50 x 58 cm)
Cat. no. 112

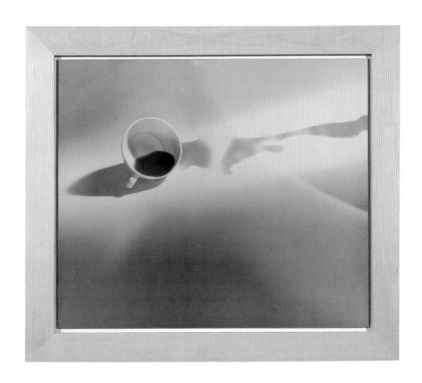

Plate 42. *Finger Touch Number 1*, 1966–67
Color photograph
19¾ x 23½ in. (50 x 60 cm)
Cat. no. 113

Plate 43. *Eating My Words*, 1966–67
Color photograph
19¾ x 23¼ in. (50 x 59 cm)
Cat. no. 114

Plate 44. *Bound to Fail*, 1966–67
Color photograph
19¾ x 23¾ in. (50 x 60 cm)
Cat. no. 115

Plate 45. *Henry Moore Bound to Fail*, 1967
Cast iron
25½ x 23 x 3½ in. (65 x 58 x 9 cm)
Cat. no. 116

Plate 46. *Run from Fear, Fun from Rear*, 1972
Neon
Two parts, 7½ x 46 in. (19 x 117 cm); 4¼ x 44½ in. (11 x 113 cm)
Cat. no. 117

Plate 47. *3 Dead-End Adjacent Tunnels, Not Connected*, 1979
Plaster and wood
21 x 117 x 106 in. (54 x 297 x 268 cm)
Cat. no. 118

Plate 48. *Life, Death, Love, Hate, Pleasure, Pain*, 1983
Neon
Dia. 70⅞ in. (180 cm)
Cat. no. 119

BRUCE NAUMAN

Plate 49a. *Chambre d'amis*, 1985 (detail)
Videotape installation: videotape (*Good Boy/Bad Boy*),
audiotape (*Live and Die*), and neon (*Hanged Man*)
86⅝ x 55⅛ in. (220 x 140 cm)
Cat. no. 120

Plate 49b. *Chambre d'amis*, 1985 (detail)

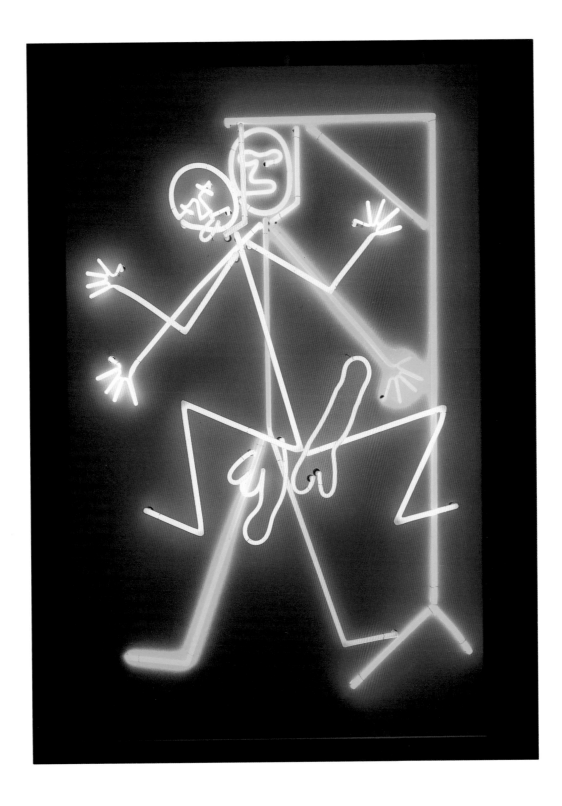

Plate 50. *Hanging Carousel (George Skins a Fox)*, 1988
Steel, polyurethane foam, and television monitor
Dia. 204 in. (518 cm); 74½ in. (189 cm) from floor
Cat. no. 121

Plate 51. *Dog Biting Its Ass*, 1989
Foam
35 x 30 x 34 in. (89 x 76 x 86 cm)
Cat. no. 129

Plate 52. *Rats and Bats (Learned Helplessness in Rats) II*, 1988
    Three ¾-inch U-matic videotapes, six television monitors,
    one projector, one live camera, and Plexiglas
    Dimensions variable
    Cat. no. 122

Plate 53. *Above Yourself* (Study for "Elliott's Stones"), 1989
Graphite on paper
26¼ x 40 in. (67 x 101 cm)
Cat. no. 123

Plate 54. *After Yourself* (Study for "Elliott's Stones"), 1989
Graphite on paper
26¼ x 40 in. (67 x 101 cm)
Cat. no. 124

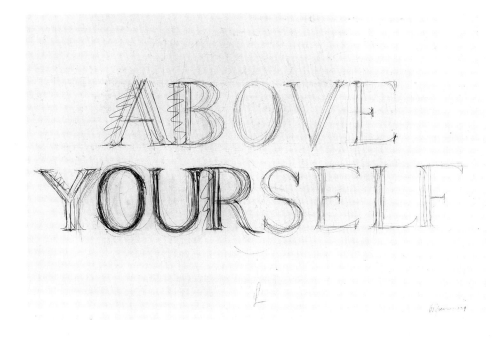

Plate 55. *Before Yourself* (Study for "Elliott's Stones"), 1989
 Graphite on paper
 26¼ x 40 in. (67 x 101 cm)
 Cat. no. 125

Plate 56. *Behind Yourself* (Study for "Elliott's Stones"), 1989
 Graphite on paper
 26¼ x 40 in. (67 x 101 cm)
 Cat. no. 126

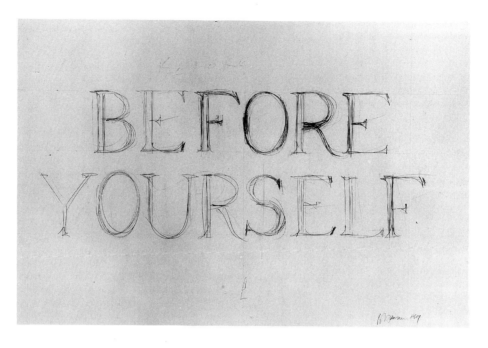

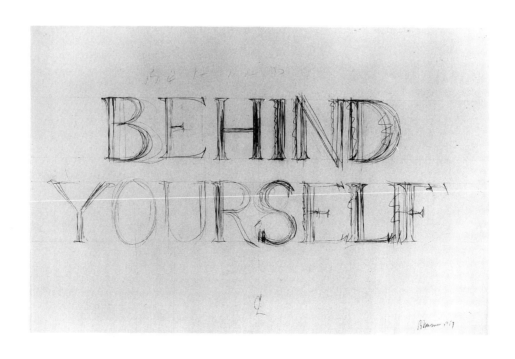

Plate 57. *Beneath Yourself* (Study for "Elliott's Stones"), 1989
Graphite on paper
26¼ x 40 in. (67 x 101 cm)
Cat. no. 127

Plate 58. *Beside Yourself* (Study for "Elliott's Stones"), 1989
Graphite on paper
26¼ x 40 in. (67 x 101 cm)
Cat. no. 128

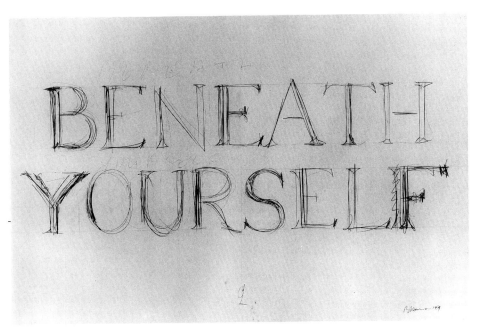

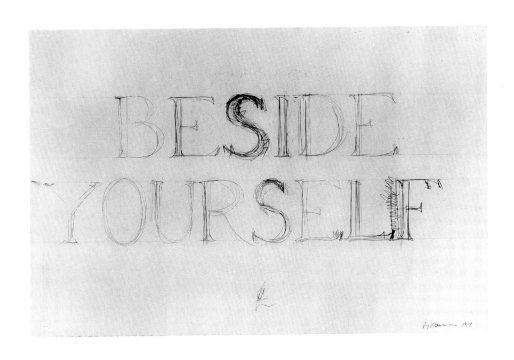

Robert Ryman: *The Charter Series*
A Meditative Room for the Collection of Gerald S. Elliott

NEAL BENEZRA

During the past twenty-five years, Robert Ryman has taken great care to eliminate information and incident from his painting. He has intentionally restricted himself to the color white, and to abstract and measured fields of carefully considered brush strokes. Eloquent and assured, these paintings consistently convey Ryman's ability to achieve compelling visual effects through radically reduced means. Ryman's discretion holds particular meaning for a culture accustomed to the constant assault of superficial audio and visual insult. His clear, silent, and authentic surfaces induce a contemplative moment for weary urban eyes.

Ryman's paintings bear certain unmistakable characteristics. As noted, he not only eliminates all incident from his paintings, he also works exclusively in white, a color devoid of drama but rich in its reticence. Although white is usually considered a "noncolor," it is actually the most subtle of hues, capable of revitalizing the senses for those whose visual awareness and concentration are acute. Beyond its sensuous aspect, the color white enables Ryman to bring other painterly elements — particularly brush stroke and supporting surface — to the fore as equal partners in his paintings. "The use of white in my paintings came about when I realized that it doesn't interfere. It is a neutral color that allows for clarification of nuance in painting."[1]

Among the nuances with which Ryman is concerned is the delicate but crucial relationship between the painted surface, the underlying structure of the painting, and the wall plane itself. Most of his recent works have been painted on thin sheets of metal — generally aluminum or fiberglass — and these are affixed to the wall by a variety of small, thoughtfully placed but always visible fasteners. By carefully selecting the fashion in which the works are mounted, Ryman incorporates the means of installing his paintings into the composition of the work itself. Furthermore, the artist also maximizes the interaction between wall and painting, successfully creating a visual dialogue between these elements as well as between individual paintings. Ryman's best paintings tend to fill their surrounding space both perceptually and psychologically, evoking a profound sense of calm or even euphoria.

It is this interest in creating expansive works of art, paintings that communicate impressions and emotions exceeding the limitations of the means employed, that links Ryman with several of the great geometric painters of the century. Integral to the work of Kasimir Malevich, Piet Mondrian, and, more recently, Barnett Newman, Mark Rothko, and Ad Reinhardt is a will to translate the orderly poetry of their painting to the daily lives of viewers. In their work, painted forms implicitly extend beyond the existing boundaries of the painted plane, and each artist intended this expansion of form to be emblematic of a world in greater spiritual and formal harmony than our own.

The work of all these artists, Ryman included, is most successful when the artist's aesthetic is allowed to dominate an entire space. Painters of restrained forms have often strived to control environmental conditions, occasionally making exacting demands on exhibitors of their work in order to ensure the purity of the viewing experience. To this end, many modern artists have dictated the lighting levels or the color of gallery walls, and some have refused to participate in group exhibitions or have required that their works be shown in separate galleries. Superior expressions in this vein have occurred when artists have created series of paintings for specific circumstances, as in Barnett Newman's *Stations of the Cross* (1958–66), and the fourteen paintings Mark Rothko was commissioned to complete for a chapel designed by Philip Johnson in Houston (1971).

It was the example of Rothko and Newman that provided the inspiration for Ryman's *Charter Series*. The series was conceived during the course of conversations held in May 1985 between Ryman and Gerald S. Elliott. Long an admirer and collector of Ryman's painting, Elliott asked Ryman to consider painting a series of works that might eventually be exhibited together in a single room, apart from other works of art, in order to evoke a meditative mood. A student of modern collectors as well as modern art, Elliott was inspired both by the work of Rothko and Newman, examples of which he had once owned, and by the model of John and Dominique de Menil, who had commissioned the Rothko chapel in 1971. Although Ryman has consistently rejected the existence of any spiritual intent in his work and has never made excessive demands in terms of installation, he was fascinated by this challenge and agreed.[2]

The point of departure for the series was a painting that Elliott already possessed, *Charter* of 1985 (pl. 59; cat. no. 145). Although Ryman has generally worked in a square format, *Charter* is emphatically vertical, composed of two evenly painted white panels, with the upper projecting inches beyond the plane of the lower. The two fields are divided by the shadow that the upper casts on the lower and by a thin aluminum strip. Wider aluminum bands bracket the painted fields, top and bottom, with the lower large enough to balance the projecting upper panel. *Charter* is among Ryman's most successful paintings, both because of the formal tension produced by the contrasting surfaces and because of the allusive, perhaps totemic, quality of the stacked fields of white color. Ryman was so pleased with the finished work that he decided it should serve as the basis for the four additional paintings that would compose the series.

A large measure of the creativity in Ryman's work resides in the inventiveness with which the artist attends to practical matters. Despite the success of *Charter*, for the four additional works Ryman decided to return to his accustomed square format. This created a problem, because the fiberglass/ aluminum laminate that he employed in *Charter* was not available in the square, six-to-eight-foot lengths he projected for the new paintings. Unwilling simply to abut two metal sheets to create these larger surfaces, after much investigation Ryman employed an "H" channel, an element that would perform the necessary structural function, while adding a horizontal design element. In the process, each painting was divided into upper and lower registers, corresponding to the similar composition of *Charter*, while retaining the overall square configuration.

Yet, on superficial inspection, the four subsequent paintings seem unrelated to *Charter* and remarkably similar to one another. Besides being square, they all share the horizontal band, a matte painted surface, and a few discretely placed fasteners. Only after sustained, even repeated, examination do subtle formal distinctions and shifts in impact and mood become apparent.

Charter V (pl. 63; cat. no. 149), the largest of the later paintings, is eight feet square. It is also the most rigorously composed, for although it was not required for structural reasons, Ryman divided the upper panel vertically, the only work in the series so handled. The emphatic partitioning of the whole and the exclamatory feel of the painting are further enhanced by Ryman's handling of the aluminum, which is only partially painted. While the public, emblematic character of *Charter V* links it to *Charter*, its square format and compositional disposition connect it with the other three paintings.

Charter II, III, and *IV* (pls. 60–62; cat. nos. 146–48) are all slightly smaller than *Charter V* and, to a varying degree, they share an intimacy that enhances their allusiveness. This effect also results from Ryman's decision to reduce the formal weight of the strips by painting several segments white. While the aluminum disciplines the white fields of *Charter* and *Charter V*, the other three paintings read as quiet white planes, their compositions only gently punctuated by additive forms.

Charter II is only inches smaller than *Charter V*, yet by painting over much of the horizontal band, Ryman significantly reduced the compositional weight of the aluminum. *Charter IV* is handled similarly, as the aluminum remains visible only at the lateral edges of the painting and at the foot. This latter element links it to the original painting, which has a large aluminum band at its base. *Charter III* is perhaps the most poetic of the series. Here the aluminum has been painted away almost entirely and the composition is structured largely by four black fasteners, which implicitly divide the whole into quadrants. In comparison to *Charter* and *Charter V*, the other three paintings are less conspicuous in their subdivisions, and this encourages their reading as unspoiled, meditative fields of color.

Ryman's achievement in the *Charter* paintings lies in the range of impressions expressed within a rigorously circumscribed set of possibilities. In establishing a compositional framework and then exploring it in all its permutations, Ryman demonstrated the potential for freedom that self-imposed discipline holds, a lesson not commonly understood in our time. More specifically, the series reveals that rigor can yield poetic calm, an impressive accomplishment given such frugal means.

Viewed in the context of Ryman's previous work, the series is an inspired, if logical, step in the artist's continued exploration of the outer boundaries of painting. Although without formal training as an artist, Ryman worked in the mid-1950s as a guard at The Museum of Modern Art, New York, where he became enthralled with the modern masters Paul Cézanne and Henri Matisse. "What interested me in Matisse was not so much what he was painting but how he was doing it.... He was sure, it was immediate. With Cézanne it was more the way he could work with paint...the building up, the structure, the complicated composition."[3] Ryman's fascination with these artists' techniques led to his eventual mastery of the means of painting. Methodical and probing by nature, he acquired these skills and then developed alternatives to traditional craft. By the early 1960s he was employing a wide variety of paints, brushes, and surfaces, developing unusual means for adhering his work to the wall, and working only in white.

It is in the nature of Ryman's work that each painting is both a new discovery and a summary of past experience. The *Charter* paintings, for example, were prefigured as early as 1965, when Ryman began systematically to devote groups of works to the exploration of a particular paint surface. This series owes rather directly to the `Standard* paintings of 1967, in which enamel paint was washed in translucent brush strokes over thin sheets of cold rolled steel. This was the first occasion in which Ryman aligned painting and wall plane so closely, an element fundamental to the current series. "The thinness of materials interested me because my painting has a lot to do with the wall plane. Thinness of materials allows clarity of working with the wall plane and the environment."[4]

Yet, despite the similarities linking the two series, they differ in subtle but significant ways. Whereas the *Standard* paintings are thinly washed and evidence a delicately veiled surface, the *Charter* paintings are evenly brushed, and their matte finish enhances the imposing formal presence of the group as a whole. This distinction attests to Ryman's determination to press beyond previous solutions, an aspiration aided by the extensive record of past paintings that the artist keeps visible in his studio at all times. Because he has generally worked in series, producing groups of works that share a related size, support, and paint surface, Ryman has found it useful to fill a large wall with a photographic log of black-and-white images that document the history of his work. Although many contemporary artists maintain such records, or ask assistants or dealers to do so, few artists care to be constantly reminded of their past efforts in such a fashion. The implications are telling, for even though Ryman has reduced his creative options almost beyond reason, he is utterly unwilling to admit repetition into his work.

If creative discipline and a will to invent characterize Ryman's endeavor, they also link the artist to the great tradition of Modernist abstraction. Ranging from Malevich and Mondrian early in the century, to Newman, Rothko, and Reinhardt following World War II, these artists shared a commitment to the unity of mind and spirit. Accepting of the modern world, each in his own way attempted to rejuvenate the human spirit through painted forms.

Modest by nature, Ryman has never made expansive claims for his work. Throughout his career, he has preferred to concentrate on formal problem-solving rather than on postulating meanings for his paintings. Yet, he has long since established working mechanisms for the creation of an extremely impressive and often magnificent body of work. Born of the ongoing confusion of contemporary culture, Ryman's endeavor to translate his forms into environments demonstrates both his confidence in the importance of his work and a faith in the power of art to shape experience in a productive manner. In his steady search for new visual expression, Robert Ryman has assumed this Modernist commitment as his own.

This essay was originally published as a brochure to accompany the 1987 exhibition of *The Charter Series* at The Art Institute of Chicago.

1. "The '60s in Abstract: 13 Statements and an Essay," *Art in America* 71, 9 (Oct. 1983), p. 123.

2. Ryman subsequently noted his debt to Elliott in this regard, commenting that the series, which required eighteen months to complete, would not have been attempted without the collector's encouragement. See Judith Neisser, "A Magnificent Obsession," *Art & Auction* 10, 2 (Dec. 1987), p. 113.

3. "The '60s in Abstract" (note 1), pp. 123–24.

4. Quoted in Nancy Grimes, "White Magic," *Artnews* 85, 6 (Summer 1986), p. 91.

Plate 59. *Charter*, 1985
Oil on aluminum
82 x 31 in. (108 x 79 cm)
Cat. no. 145

Plate 60. *The Elliott Room: Charter II*, 1987
Acrylic on fiberglass with aluminum
93¾ x 93⅝ in. (238 x 238 cm)
Cat. no. 146

Plate 61. *The Elliott Room: Charter III*, 1987
Acrylic on fiberglass with aluminum
84¼ x 84 in. (214 x 213 cm)
Cat. no. 147

Plate 62. *The Elliott Room: Charter IV*, 1987
Acrylic on fiberglass with aluminum
72⅜ x 72 in. (184 x 183 cm)
Cat. no. 148

Plate 63. *The Elliott Room: Charter V,* 1987
Acrylic on fiberglass with aluminum
95½ x 95½ in. (243 x 243 cm)
Cat. no. 149

New Image Art Revisited

MARK ROSENTHAL

When the exhibition "New Image Painting" opened at the Whitney Museum of American Art in 1978, it surveyed a fresh vision that had emerged in the New York art world during the 1970s.[1] Richard Marshall, the curator of the exhibition, wrote that the tendency linking the artists in the show was the representation of familiar things but "isolated and removed from associative backgrounds and environments," and depicted in a "drastically abbreviated or exaggerated" fashion. This description still applies, although a broader context can now be defined. The unifying characteristic mentioned by Marshall is part of an approach fundamental to late nineteenth- and early twentieth-century art, one which was addressed by many artists, including, for example, Philip Guston, Neil Jenney, Robert Moskowitz, Susan Rothenberg, and Joel Shapiro to be discussed in this essay.

The harmonization of a subject with an abstract pictorial structure lies at the heart of modern art, starting with Cézanne and the Cubists. Many subsequent artists have employed this essential procedure, refining and simplifying a recognizable theme so as to render it a manifestation of formal qualities. Neither the subject nor its pictorial definition takes precedence; rather, there is an attempt to form a fragile, delicate interaction, resulting in a drama of ambiguity. Mediating between the poles of nonobjectivity and figuration and relishing the interplay, the artist fuses the two poles, thereby implying that each requires the other to complete itself and become art. By structuring the subject in this way, the artist often shields his or her feelings with regard to it and keeps the theme at a psychological distance. In effect, the modern artist makes the manipulation of the motif the subject of the work of art.[2]

After considerable elaboration, this crucial strategy evolved into pure abstraction and finally into Minimalism, as the last barely recognizable traces of the subject disappeared. Yet it was Minimalism that provided the most direct stimulus for New Image work. In Minimalist sculpture, the complete form of each object—its composition, structure, and dimensions—is quickly perceived and comprehended. An elemental quality reigns, as the artist eliminates any detail that might be considered extraneous. The New Imagists, too, created depictions that were emphatically simplified so as to be essential in concept. But even while adopting this outlook, they rebelled in a fundamental way against Minimalism. By giving to their compositions a human content, the New Imagists transformed Minimal into what Neil Jenney termed "Maximal" art.[3] In other words, despite an admiration for Minimalism, these artists envisioned a corrective action to integrate their work with the mandate of Pop art and its emphasis on subject matter. In this regard, Jenney proclaimed, "Pop is the father of us all."[4]

Reviewing the work of Guston, Jenney, Moskowitz, Rothenberg, and Shapiro, it is possible to observe that, while all five individuals reacted to the stranglehold of formalist, subjectless art, not all broke equally with the tradition on which this art is based. Guston, Jenney, and to some extent, Rothenberg, all pursued a similar course, making formalist concerns subservient to emphatically stated, easily accessible subject matter. Embracing a primitivizing style and eschewing specific locales, they sought themes having a universal quality, and approached these with varying degrees of emotion and analysis. In the context of general aesthetic inquiry, they were investigators on the trail of worthwhile subject matter for art.

Even if Pop helped bring about their breakthrough, in no sense did Guston, Jenney, and Rothenberg embrace the occasional cynicism, irony, or parody of that movement, nor its specifically and completely American iconography. Whereas banality was an important component of Pop, these New Imagists were utterly committed to their imagery. Moreover, in place of the machine-made look of much Pop art, Guston, Jenney, and Rothenberg favored a coarse, unfinished surface. The rebellious crudity characterizing their paintings suggests that only the stated image is of importance; the skills of the artist can best be gauged by the degree to which the depiction is sufficiently riveting to its viewers.

Whereas the approach of Guston, Jenney, and Rothenberg has a hot boldness about it, that of Shapiro and Moskowitz has the character of a cool hipster. Seemingly unconcerned whether their subject matter is immediately accessible, the latter even play with the viewer's ability to recognize it. If some degree of political concern underlies the work of Guston and Jenney, little of that appears in the art of Shapiro and Moskowitz. They evince less of the exhaustion with modern (and Modernist) art values; for instance, Shapiro exhibits the influence of Minimalism's hard edges and machine-made aesthetic, and Moskowitz repeatedly presents icons of modern society and art. Their work is full of nuance and indirectness; yet, while subdued and dispassionate, they are nonetheless cunning and provocative with regard to viewers' responses.

Philip Guston was the first to prefigure New Image art in the works resulting from the artistic crisis he experienced around 1960. During the 1950s he had studied and then manifested the strengths of formalist art, painting canvases that were celebrated for their refinement and delicacy. These works had given Guston a position at the forefront of the New York School, yet a native restlessness led him to become gradually dissatisfied with the values of abstraction:

> There is something ridiculous and miserly in the myth we inherit from abstract art.... That painting is autonomous, pure and for itself.... But painting is "impure." It is the adjustment of impurities which forces painting's continuity. We are image-makers and image-ridden.[5]

Expressed in 1960, Guston's statement foreshadowed a more radical change in his thinking and the slow unraveling of his style. Throughout the decade, in part motivated by the changing political conditions in the United States, he underwent an artistic metamorphosis.[6] Although he never mentioned Pop art, Guston's embrace of recognizable subject matter could hardly have occurred in isolation from this tremendously influential change in the artistic climate. Thomas Hess, Guston's friend, described the situation in this way: "He said that Pop was blasphemous, unclean ... like feasting on pork after Yom Kippur service. Shortly thereafter, he succumbed."[7] In effect, Guston returned to the themes and representational style of his youth, but in an altogether more raucous, hell-bent fashion. Starting in the late 1960s with images of Ku Klux Klansmen and various objects isolated on neutral backgrounds in prototypical New Image fashion, Guston gradually expanded his range of subjects throughout the 1970s.

Night Room of 1976 (pl. 64; cat. no. 51) is typical of Guston's paintings from the mid-part of the decade, in which pink and red tonalities appear against black backgrounds. In this case, a cat-o'-nine-tails is shown whipping a group of emaciated legs with prominent shoes and soles. Guston had employed most of these elements in works of the 1930s and 1940s, but now imparted to them a less narrative, more hallucinatory quality. Throughout the 1970s, he frequently painted huddled masses of humanity, variously referring to an apocalyptic deluge, to a concentration camp, or to the victims of Klan activity. While the worn shoes recall those of Vincent van Gogh, Guston may also have been playing on an obvious verbal pun with his emphasis on soles, which can be interpreted as the souls inhabiting the shoes. Furthermore, the nails that stud the bottoms of the shoes echo those in the bodies of murdered individuals in earlier images by Guston.[8] In an ironic demonstration of his artistic metamorphosis, Guston rendered the soles/souls as the most frontal plane of the painting, thus parodying much academic, formalist art of mid-century and its stress on that aspect of the picture.

At the same time that Guston was arriving at his subject-oriented imagery, Neil Jenney was turning from color-field paintings and earth and process sculptures to his style of 1969–70. Working independently of and apparently unknown to one another, Guston and Jenney became exemplars of a new attitude and style in the New York art world. Both were exhausted with abstraction and possessed a deeply felt need to bring about a rapprochement between art and life, including the anxious upheavals in contemporary society. At the time, their emphasis on subject matter appeared virtually anachronistic; they seemed to revel in the images and offer them for profound contemplation. While Guston painted nightmares, and Jenney analytically investigated a range of human and physical situations, the two shared a similarly absurd, Beckett-like world view, in which optimism is found only in black humor. Thus Jenney's figurative, "high emotion" paintings have a cartoonish character,[9] yet are filled with a staggering depth of feeling. In *Vexation and Rapture* of 1969 (pl. 67; cat. no. 59), his rendering of the relationship between the sexes (their differences as well as similarities typified by the juxtaposition of hand gestures), ought to be compared to the unitary structure of a Minimal sculpture. That is, in both cases a completeness of depiction is sought, whether a vision of humanity or a geometrical form.[10]

Jenney heightens the content of an ostensibly trivial situation by painting the title in block letters at the bottom of each frame. His use of these weighty designations to add significance to the scene exemplifies the New Imagists' emphasis on subject matter. Yet, as in Guston's paintings, evidence of a Modernist outlook remains. For example, both artists stress the brush strokes that delineate the images rather than choosing an illusionistic style, and both manifest a primitivistic quality, following a practice that goes back to the early moderns. Furthermore, Jenney's frames contribute to the sense that his works are physical objects.

Throughout his paintings of 1969–70, Jenney inventoried and explored mundane and/or archetypal human situations, one general thematic category being survival. In *Man and Thing* of 1969 (pl. 66; cat. no. 58), which is part of a series showing human beings threatened by sea creatures, Jenney's interest is the natural fear, aggression, and violence that may occur between species. A third class of subject matter during this period, in addition to "high emotion" and survival, concerns basic aspects of work. Whether indicated by farm situations or technological advances (for example, tools or airplanes), human endeavor is generally celebrated in these paintings, as for example in *Implements Intrenchments* of 1970 (pl. 68; cat. no. 60). Typically, Jenney has created a simple yet forceful compositional arrangement to reinforce the elemental character of the subject.

After a series of paintings in which she created a scaffolding of directional and divisional lines on neutral fields, Susan Rothenberg came to prominence in 1974 with canvases of expressionistically painted horses. Apparently partly inspired in these renderings by Neil Jenney, Rothenberg isolated the animals on large, brushy fields of color. The depictions have the character of primitive cave paintings rather than contemporary graffiti, for the horses appear to be revered or the object of an exalted state of mind. Rothenberg's animals variously exhibit a brute strength, vitality, and abandon that recall the imagery of Franz Marc; but whereas Marc, despite compositional subtleties, almost always presented nature in its untouched state, Rothenberg has depicted domesticated animals or ones that have clearly been subjected to structural definition or enclosure by her hand, as in *Kelpie* of 1978 (pl. 71; cat. no. 140). While her handling stresses the almost fetishistic or obsessive presentation of the motif, the horse still retains a quality Rothenberg described as follows: "I identify the content of my work strongly with spirituality, with a universal religious impulse."[11]

Following about five years of painting only horses, as if working with a mantra in which a crucial theme is endlessly repeated, varied, elaborated, and characterized anew, Rothenberg turned to a series of new subjects. In these exceedingly rich paintings, for example, *Up, Down, Around* of 1985–87 (pl. 72; cat. no. 141), the figure has become, compared to the horse, elusive, seemingly engaged in a struggle to survive on the pictorial ground on which it is situated. Each of the energetic individuals—either leaping upward, downward, or spinning—is barely present. In this frenetic atmosphere, composition occupies a secondary role. Instead, Rothenberg's effort is spent creating a sense of gravity battled, impossible physical actions undertaken, and the artist's struggle at representation made manifest.[12] If a religious impulse is for Rothenberg still an issue with regard to the subject matter, it is held at arm's length; she reveals that motion, both on the part of her subject and as exhibited with her brush stroke, remains at the center of her concerns.

Like Rothenberg and Jenney, Robert Moskowitz places subjects on large fields of color, but unlike the other two artists, his figure and ground are usually rendered with a highly flat finish. This handling, along with the sharply defined edges of the forms, places Moskowitz's version of New Image art in close proximity to Minimalism. His choice of subjects recalls Pop art, in that they are typically well known to most viewers, as is true, for example, for *Empire State* of 1984–86 (pl. 69; cat. no. 100). In the spirit of New Image art, however, and in contrast to Pop art—for instance, Andy Warhol's film titled *Empire* of 1964—Moskowitz's motifs are presented in an isolated fashion that discourages an anecdotal or transitory reading. Selected for personal reasons, the subjects are elevated to the status of objects for contemplation and celebration, that is, once an image is recognized, for Moskowitz often makes it difficult to perceive it — *The Razor's Edge (for Bill Murray)* of 1985 (pl. 70; cat. no. 101), for instance, is virtually indecipherable. The title of the latter is borrowed from a film based on a story by Somerset Maugham concerned with World War I devastation.[13] The painting appears as an apocalyptic but ambiguous land – or cityscape, outlined against a red sky. It is an epic vision that is surprisingly similar to a luridly colored Walt Disney animation.

Since the late 1960s when he made white paintings that could be read only with considerable study as showing the corner of a room, Moskowitz has been absorbed with one of the central strategies of modern art: the process of abstracting from recognizable subjects. Like *Bird in Flight* of around 1924 by Constantin Brancusi, Moskowitz's paintings offer an exquisite union of the subject and structure; indeed, even when a shape by Moskowitz relies on an objective source, it assumes a new, almost subjective, existence on the picture plane. Variously aggressive, dynamic, or static, Moskowitz's forms have the potential to become icons of abstract art. Reinforcing the stark monumentality of a recently hatched shape, Moskowitz creates epic expanses of color, each of which is chosen, the artist reports, with a "metaphorical" intention.[14] Robert Rosenblum related Moskowitz's efforts to those of artists associated with sublime traditions,[15] an observation that is apt since the viewer is dwarfed by the scale of the paintings, and the usual absence of a ground or horizon line enhances the sense of infinity.

The New Image phenomenon is not found exclusively in painting. Since the early 1970s, Joel Shapiro has produced diminutive sculptures in which houses, horses, and figures have been rendered in exceedingly abbreviated, hard-edged form. As in discussing Moskowitz, a comparison of Shapiro's work to that of Brancusi is revealing. All anecdotal detail is removed, and the representation is at one with the geometrical forms that describe it. In effect, form and subject are fused. Shapiro's sculptures throughout the 1970s were filled with a constricted yet pulsating vitality. Though seemingly bound within small objects, this tremendously energetic quality seemed to possess the possibility of expanding outward into the viewer's space. When Shapiro turned more consistently toward figurative themes, about 1980, he still managed to convey that same quality but in altogether more complex structures, the energy extending outward through the splayed body parts. Furthermore, movement, as opposed to the stasis of the 1970s, became a central issue of the figurative works of the 1980s.

Untitled of 1981–84 (pl. 73; cat. no. 159) typifies the new direction in Shapiro's oeuvre. A figure, its arms and legs askew, appears to have been thrown, or to have dived, into the floor. When speaking of this and related sculptures, Shapiro said that his particular interest was "motion or dislocation,"[16] qualities that can be understood in either purely abstract or figurative terms. That is, *Untitled* is both an extremely dynamic abstract sculpture in which the symmetrical parts are asymmetrically composed or an abstracted figure whose motion has caused the depicted disarray. *Untitled (Arching Figure)* of 1985 (pl. 74; cat. no. 160) is reminiscent of Shapiro's earlier work in its stolidly static construction. This anthropomorphic sculpture evokes an appendageless, slightly comic character leaning forward in order to hear better. In *Untitled (for G. S. E.)* of 1986–87 (pl. 75; cat. no. 161), Shapiro returned to the energetically posed figure in motion, but amplified its human anatomy. A second "head" of lumpy bronze balances the first, and a protuberance has been added to serve as a crude hand. These startling additions make certain that the figure, like most in Shapiro's dramatis personae, will lack lithe movement or a perfect physique.

New Image art is less a movement than an approximately accurate designation for a number of artists working at about the same time. Still, if their differences are glossed over for a moment, certain generalizations might be proposed. New Image art has been an almost exclusively American phenomenon, a reaction to the commanding position that formalism held in this country, unlike Europe. In a sequential sense, it synthesized Minimal form with Pop subject matter and served as the premise for subsequent, more emotional, kinds of expression. Although the latter may also be found in New Image art, an air of refinement often distinguishes this type of work because of its fusion of abstraction and figuration. In this regard, New Image art might even be described as at times epitomizing a late form of Modernism, a description that grows more apt as the mid-career developments of many of these artists unfold.

Because of its renewed engagement with subject matter, New Image art may be said to belong most of all to those individuals whose experience was shaped by the dramatic events of the 1960s.[17] In general younger than the Pop artists, the New Imagists were therefore more sympathetic to calls for "relevance," and for the need to break with or modify the implications of a self-satisfied, modern era. Thus an embrace of themes meaningful to them was in keeping with the mandate of their formative years. If, as it now appears, New Image art has had little influence on most younger artists, the reason may be found in its close tie to a specific cultural and historical situation.

---

1. Richard Marshall, in Whitney Museum of American Art, New York, 1978, *New Image Painting*, p. 7. The exhibition comprised paintings by Nicholas Africano, Jennifer Bartlett, Denise Green, Michael Hurson, Neil Jenney, Lois Lane, Robert Moskowitz, Susan Rothenberg, David True, and Joseph Zucker.

2. For more discussion of this approach, see Mark Rosenthal, "The Structured Subject in Contemporary Art," *Bulletin, Philadelphia Museum of Art* 79, 340 (Fall 1983), pp. 3–24.

3. This term was used by Neil Jenney. See Mark Rosenthal, "From Primary Structures to Primary Imagery," *Arts* 53 (Oct. 1978), p. 107.

4. Mark Rosenthal, in University Art Museum, Berkeley, California, 1981, *Neil Jenney: Paintings and Sculpture 1967–1980*, p. 12.

5. Musa Mayer, *Night Studio: A Memoir of Philip Guston by His Daughter* (New York, 1988), p. 141.

6. See Mark Rosenthal, "La Metamorfosis de Guston: Cueston de Consiencia," in Ministerio de Cultura, Madrid, 1989, *Philip Guston*, pp. 48–59.

7. Thomas B. Hess, "The Abstractionist Who Came in from the Cold," *New York Magazine* 7 (Dec. 9, 1974), p. 102.

8. For example, *Drawing for Conspirators* (1930) in the collection of the Whitney Museum of American Art, New York.

9. The expression "high emotion" was used by Jenney. See Rosenthal, *Jenney* (note 4), p. 10.

10. See Rosenthal, "Primary Structures" (note 3).

11. Peter Schjeldahl, "Putting Painting Back on Its Feet," *Vanity Fair*, Aug. 1983, p. 85.

12. Unpublished interview with the author, Feb. 1989.

13. I thank Ned Rifkin for kindly supplying me with this information.

14. Marshall (note 1), p. 50.

15. Robert Rosenblum, in Blum Helman Gallery, New York, 1983, *Robert Moskowitz*, p. 6.

16. Cited in Whitney Museum of American Art, New York, 1982, *Joel Shapiro*, p. 101.

17. See Mark Rosenthal, "The Ascendence of Subject Matter and a 1960s Sensibility," *Arts* 56 (June 1982), pp. 92–94.

Plate 64. *Night Room*, 1976
Oil on canvas
80 x 69 in. (203 x 175 cm)
Cat. no. 51

Plate 65. *Portrait of Gerald Elliott*, 1980
   Pastel and gouache on paper
   30 x 22 in. (76 x 56 cm)
   Cat. no. 57

Plate 66. *Man and Thing*, 1969
Acrylic on canvas
74 x 44½ in. (188 x 113 cm)
Cat. no. 58

Plate 67. *Vexation and Rapture*, 1969
     Oil on canvas
     62½ x 96½ in. (159 x 244 cm)
     Cat. no. 59

Plate 68. *Implements Intrenchments*, 1970
Acrylic on canvas on wood
75½ x 63½ in. (192 x 161 cm)
Cat. no. 60

Plate 69. *Empire State*, 1984–86
Oil on canvas
96 x 32 in. (245 x 81 cm)
Cat. no. 100

Plate 70. *The Razor's Edge (for Bill Murray)*, 1985
Oil on canvas
30⅛ x 72 in. (76 x 183 cm)
Cat. no. 101

Plate 71. *Kelpie*, 1978
Acrylic and flashe on canvas
76¾ x 109 in. (198 x 280 cm)
Cat. no. 140

Plate 72. *Up, Down, Around*, 1985–87
Oil on canvas
89 x 93 in. (226 x 236 cm)
Cat. no. 141

Plate 73. *Untitled*, 1981–84
Bronze
47¼ x 46⅞ x 46½ in. (120 x 119 x 118 cm)
Cat. no. 159

Plate 74. *Untitled (Arching Figure)*, 1985
Bronze
38½ x 28½ x 14 in. (98 x 72 x 36 cm)
Cat. no. 160

Plate 75. *Untitled (for G.S.E.)*, 1986–87
Bronze
64½ x 69½ x 49 in. (164 x 176 x 124 cm); base 26½ x 34¼ x 48⅜ in. (67 x 87 x 123 cm)
Cat. no. 161

American Neo-Expressionism

ROALD NASGAARD

When Cindy Sherman casts and photographs herself acting out the roles of women who, in turn, consciously or innocently, are picturing themselves in the images of stereotypical characters from magazines, the movies, television, or everyday life (see pls. 90–94; cat. nos. 162–66), she is engaged in demythologizing the power of mass-media representations to construct the self-images that we all display. This common interpretation of her work would make it a mere exercise in knowing mockery, were it not that each of her characterizations is so intensely felt that her undoing of the surfaces of being is at once also the painful exposure of deeper layers of the self. It is on this basis—because her photographs, although they negotiate the maze of social representations, also finally travel inwards into the shifting recesses of the uncertain subject—that we may call Sherman's work Neo-Expressionist. Thus Sherman can be aligned with the other artists gathered here under that label— Eric Fischl, Robert Longo, David Salle, and Julian Schnabel—even though the term is more usually applied to painters and to work associated with subjective indulgence.

These five artists form a somewhat amorphous group. Their work ranges from the straight, if staged, photography of Sherman to the material and painterly extravagances of Schnabel, with the other three staking out territory somewhere in between these two poles. Yet at some point all the painters (if that is the correct description for Longo) refer to images that derive from photographs (including reproductions of paintings), while Sherman is usually described as working with the scale, color, and career ambitions of painters. All five are realist artists, interested in images, especially the freely circulating and recyclable images of mass culture. They even engage in some kind of narrative structure, although coherence and continuity of development may break down if their art is to be true to life experience. This discontinuity has also predicated their common resort to a strategy of montage or collage to make discernible the breaks they encounter in the realm of meaning. But if these are some of their shared means, we must also take care not to blur the individuality of their respective strategies. We must finally note that if they explore cultural codes, their common test of meaning is to process their interrogations of the world through their emotional and artistic selves.

Accordingly, Fischl proclaimed a shift in emphasis in the 1980s when art has become a personal rather than simply an epistemological matter; his remark, that "The whole struggle for meaning since the 1970s has been a struggle for identity...a need for self,"[1] was no doubt intended to redress the imperatives of Conceptual art of the 1970s that prevailed at both the California Institute of Arts where he was a student (along with David Salle) and the Nova Scotia College of Art and Design where he subsequently taught. It is, of course, not their obsession with images, especially those flowing from the paroxysm—à la Baudrillard[2]—of media-derived representations, nor the unfolding of the hidden ideological content of images and the defusing of their propagandistic power, that is a problem for the opponents of Neo-Expressionism. Growing out of earlier Conceptual art, these are common epistemological practices for artists in the 1980s. On the contrary, what is troubling is that the reevocation of the terrible persuasive power of images should devolve from *personal* reenactments in art. If, as has been said, Schnabel's (like Fischl's) undertaking constitutes a "private enquiry of the artist,"[3] and he proceeds by reviving now retrograde ego-based styles, he, like the other painters (Sherman by virtue of being a photographer has gained some exemption), has merely recentered the idea of the self at the heart of art; he has thereby resurrected not only the myth of the sovereign subject, but also the tired avant-garde cliché of the individual pitted against a philistine and hostile society. Now that the self has been exposed to be "largely an instrumental category," long decentered by impersonal socio-economic forces, the warring discordancies of the unconscious, the universality of language, and other intrapersonal codes, these ideas are held to be bankrupt. So understood, Neo-Expressionism operates in bad faith, or is at best a naively pathetic response to the loss not only of the subject but also of our relation to the real and to history, because of its attempts to restore these false notions, or even merely to simulate, too often cynically, their restoration.[4]

From such a critical standpoint, Schnabel (see pls. 85–89; cat. nos. 152–56), perhaps more than any of the artists discussed here, has been held up as a regressive purveyor of "reified expressionism," as a mere poseur spectacularly manipulating his confectioner's pastiche of images by the "modernist practice of critical collage" in what is no more than an obfuscating overlay to a dead pursuit. In the end, presumably, all he has achieved is the reaffirmation of the traditional discipline of painting and "the old sovereignty of the ... artist as expressive origin of unique meaning," failing to question the integrity of his multiple references and borrowings when he, also presumably, wraps them up in the unifying package of a signature style.[5]

Schnabel has widely protested that his art is not about ego, but directed outwards towards the world; not about the self, but how the self fits into the world.[6] This is an ambiguous differentiation, but one that may be inherent to the multivalent work of the Neo-Expressionists. By being less painterly, Longo has escaped some of the more militant prejudice against the 1980s resuscitation of painting; as well, despite the often exaggerated pitch of his voice, he engages the rhetoric of *public* presentations, simulating the scale of monuments and other formal symbols and clichés (see *Rock for Light* of 1983, pl. 79; cat. no. 90). But also Longo bifurcates his work both towards the needs of the self and towards his responsibilities as social guardian. He is the "policeman ... who blows the whistle ... on the visual mechanisms of culture," who simultaneously implicates his work in extreme expressionist modalities that, were they not so cooly tuned in the works, threaten sentimental overkill: "I'm real interested in that feeling that happens when someone you love leaves you, that kind of feeling pushing up under your diaphragm. I want a gasp or almost a cry. To find that kind of joy and sadness, it's a weird desire, a longing."[7]

Again Sherman provides a helpful example, as an exemplary deconstructor of the myth of the originative self and of the "expressionist fallacy" (the belief that one can speak independently of socially constructed codes). The smooth surface of her staged photographs is in actuality as complexly collaged a structure as that of the painters, if more conceptually than physically conceived. Her final image is as much a palimpsest as Schnabel's plate or velvet paintings, its play through depth operating as a series of ironic inversions of identification and reference to the effect that our reading of it must go something as follows: "We are to know (and she is to know that we know that she knows, in the spiraling complicity of the theatrical) that she is acting an actress acting a part."[8] Peter Schjeldahl's head-spinning unraveling of the ironic space of viewer-work interaction in Sherman's photographs finds a remarkable parallel in Umberto Eco's description, in his *Postscript to the Name of the Rose*, of how irony is useful and inevitable in both the personal and the social spheres of the Postmodern world. Eco portrayed the Postmodern condition as that of a man in love with a very cultivated woman; he wants to tell her so, but knows he cannot say to her outright, "I love you madly,"

> because he knows that she knows (and that she knows that he knows) that these words have already been written by Barbara Cartland. Still, there is a solution. He can say, "As Barbara Cartland would put it, I love you madly." At this point having avoided false innocence, having said clearly that it is no longer possible to speak innocently, he will nevertheless have said what he wanted to say to the woman: that he loves her, but he loves her in an age of lost innocence. If the woman goes along with this, she will have received a declaration of love all the same. Neither of the two speakers will feel innocent, both will have accepted the challenge of the past, of the already said, which cannot be eliminated, both will consciously and with pleasure play the game of irony.... But both will have succeeded, once again, in speaking of love.[9]

As in Eco's *Postscript to the Name of the Rose*, the name of the game in Neo-Expressionism is to succeed once again in speaking, whether of love or something else, with the resonance of personal commitment; to use irony in the face of the embarrassing cliché, to say perhaps the reverse, although not necessarily the reverse, and as often to say again a meaning lost by being said too often. To speak of "hope," said Longo: "It doesn't look good in print and I don't like the sound of it. But it's one of the most necessary words we've got."[10] "Irony," suggested Salle, with reference to the field of meaning his work deploys, "often denigrated in art as being not serious... is the most rigorous mechanism of natural selection because of its ability to admit complication and progress... progress in thinking."[11] The issues in Neo-Expressionism are finally not about an opposition of Modernist recidivisms and Postmodernist reform. Rather, by its interpenetrating overlay of cool, detached analysis and overt emotional tensions, Neo-Expressionism seeks to stage the field of ambiguities that are inherent to contemporary psychic life. It is nowhere given that because art can no longer deal in Modernist absolutes and its language for the moment is in crisis, it must remain silent to broad areas of subjective experience.

In 1990 it is hard to recall that not long ago we believed that images could be banned forever from painting and sculpture. When images began to reassert themselves in art in the late 1970s, it was in photographically based work, coming not from the tradition of art photography, but from the use of photography to document anti-object art of the 1970s,[12] such as earth art, performance, body art, etc. In this nonaesthetic application, photography was more comparable to the images of the media, of magazines, of the movies, and of television, that were to become—under the influence of European critical theories—the subject of examination for the deconstruction of their ideological content. In this context the work of Gilbert and George, Jeff Wall, or Cindy Sherman, for example, was readily embraced.

As we have noted, imagery in painting had a harder go of it, especially when re-presented in a painterly way. Imagery had been the heart and soul of Pop, but there it was perceived as either a superfluous sugarcoating to the true values of high formalist art, or it was reproduced in a mechanical way that also underscored the obsolescence of traditional painting craft. The latter's historical dependence on imagery had in the mid-1940s finally submerged itself and disappeared in the overall drip paintings of Jackson Pollock, then hailed as the most abstract paintings the Modernist tradition had produced. By the mid-1970s, however, the monochromatic surface that had dominated Postpainterly Abstraction or Minimalism seemed to need to be cracked open to see where meaning had vanished, or where it had merely been repressed and could be recovered by a revitalized painting practice. Robert Morris's holocaust-obsessed painting constructions that began to appear in the early 1980s could indeed be read as wanting to reveal, as Carter Ratcliff put it, "the horrors suppressed by the blank surfaces and clean edges of his Minimalist geometry."[13]

For Julian Schnabel it was Brice Marden's matte oil-and-wax paintings that, on the one hand, had buried all of the information of the history of painting under them, and on the other, were "a tablet, a clean slate, a place to begin to reintroduce language into painting."[14] David Salle's paintings began in the late 1970s as monochromes reinscribed with images. At the same time Eric Fischl found himself confused at the reception given to his abstract paintings, in which his viewers would read only formal ambiguities, when he himself wanted to attribute personal desires, feelings, and meanings to his forms and colors, not irreducible essences (wanting to recover the literary resonance that, except in de Kooning's work, had disappeared by the 1950s).[15] His first contextless figurative glassine drawings of the late 1970s, collaged together in transparent overlays against a blank wall, in retrospect resemble in a telling way Salle's early single-paneled, monochrome-grounded paintings, also from the same time. Longo's *Men in the Cities* (see pl. 78; cat. no. 89) act out their disembodied postures in the limbo of the white field, while his stripped-down skyscraper shapes emerge from flat, monochrome grounds (reminiscent of Les Levine's furniture objects of the early 1970s futilely trying to push through blank gray urex panels that strain to maintain their cool planarity). And if finally Sherman did not enact her first movie-based characterizations against a blank canvas, she did so against a repertory of expressions, poses, and settings that seemed quite personally produced or naturally given until she exposed our reading of them as culturally predetermined.

When images did resurge in Neo-Expressionism, however, they tended not to be freshly invented, but to come in the form of appropriations, givens from the wealth of images of the everyday world dominated by mass media and pop culture, adopted for critical reuse and dissected for their supposed manipulative and seductive power. Neo-Expressionist works may give the impression that their selections were randomly made, their surfaces assuming the busy collaged proliferation of either a Rauschenberg or a Rosenquist, in which individual meanings tend to flatten out so that it is the virtuosity and glamour of their representation that holds our attention. The Neo-Expressionists, on the contrary, pick and choose with another kind of commitment. True, theirs is a greater image promiscuity, less burdened by an inescapable history of cultural icons that need to be confronted and exorcized than that of their European counterparts, the Transavanguardia or the German Neo-Expressionists. But if their subject matter is less heroic in a traditional historical sense, the Americans, like the Europeans, choose their subject matter passionately, with conscious fear and desire. Hopefully and sadly, they mine the layers of life in which brew the deep anxieties that pervade the everyday world of the middle-class America that has bred them, and are challenged by the aggressive presence and the ambivalent stereotypes of its visual communication. Like Schnabel, they are also drawn to vague spiritual and cultural recollections whose symbols, all but forgotten, or at best lifelessly exchanged, must be probed (the operation presumably already hopeless) at least once more for signs of lingering potency.

The Neo-Expressionists rarely present their images straight, but manipulate them in order to extract them from the conceptual network we have spun around them and reopen them to our sense of wonder. Nor do they give meaning (which finally may not be possible) as much as seek it, so that their works do not resolve but orchestrate their images to establish what Salle calls "a field of meaning."[16] This strategy may be the real reason that most of these artists are painters. Although Fischl's paintings seem to adhere to the traditional unities of time and place, their compositions are a collage of figures and backgrounds taken from photographs of disparate origins, their staging not predetermined, but jumbled for what will turn up, what will be disclosed in their interstices. This was the overt structure of Fischl's first suburban narratives, made by overlaying glassine drawings of individual figures and pieces of furniture. Fischl would subsequently disguise this working method by painting and repainting on single canvases as the phrasing of his narrative developed, striving to displace discontinuity from his formal structure into an ambivalent narrative structure. For Fischl, this shift is commensurate with the disjunction between the ideal visual harmony of the suburban scene and its underlying spiritual dilemma. The slowness and deliberateness of the act of painting serve to open up for him the instantaneousness of the traditional realist photograph, stretching the time of an image and poignantly inhabiting it with divergent readings. (Although Sherman works with photography, her staging methods comparably destabilize its conceptual unity, making her Fischl's closest counterpart in their shared concern with open-ended social narrative.) In the more recent work, for example, *The Evacuation of Saigon* of 1987 (pl. 77; cat. no. 44), where narrative has become increasingly contracted and contemplative, Fischl has inverted his method, as the anxiety of discordance resurfaces in collagelike structures of overlapping canvases that, similar to the glassine drawings of a decade ago, now formally disturb the visual unity of the image.

While Fischl and Sherman in most of their work present a facade of formal unity, Longo, Salle, and Schnabel fully exploit the discontinuities of collage, not only juxtaposing apparently unrelated images, but re-presenting them in a number of disparate stylistic manners. Image deployment is, however, neither immediate nor cursory; images are dwelt on. Longo blows up his stereotypes of life in the city to the scale of public monuments, pushing seductive belief over the edge into spectacular incredulity. Schnabel similarly aggrandizes, extravagantly sprawling his culturally imbedded iconography across heavily worked fields where it never quite takes root, the spiritual resonance of his crucified Christ

Figure 1. Gerhard Richter, *Birds*, 1982. Oil on canvas,
88½ x 115¾ in. (225 x 294 cm). Collection Susan
and Lewis Manilow, Chicago.

(see *Vita*, pl. 88; cat. no. 155) shattering on the reflective fragments of cracked, porcelain ground. Salle is more cooly objective, but equally nervous of easy consumption of what we may presume already to know well enough. Hence—like the German artist Gerhard Richter, who in the mid-1960s needed to repaint his archive of photographs in order to come to terms with what and how they were—Salle redraws and repaints, rescales and restages. The extreme postures and close-ups of his nudes, the aggressiveness of real objects projecting physically from the surfaces of illusionistic spaces, the labored vigor of the repainted Old Master borrowings, all serve as methods of deterrence, frustrations to slow down readings of a structure of information that metaphorically mirrors his sense of the make-up of our accessible world.

I mentioned Gerhard Richter with reference to Salle's reworking of received images. Richter may be neither American nor strictly a Neo-Expressionist, and he is now celebrated as a maker of abstract paintings (see fig. 1), but this, his most recent work, provides a model with which to illustrate the dynamics of image orchestration in American Neo-Expressionism. Richter's work of the 1970s was dominated by series of mechanically constructed paintings that are quite literal and anonymous in appearance: color charts, gray monochromes. Unlike American Minimalists, for whom literal objectivity was a virtue, for Richter, in retrospect, it seems to have been more a mask for embarrassment about imagery, for a (less than) secret wish that images of some sort would emerge regardless, if unexpectedly, out of the mechanically produced fabric of the paintings. The "formation of figuration" was to be the prize for looking well and hard. By the mid-1970s it began to dawn on Richter that if his minimal painting remained somehow impoverished, it was perhaps because he had downplayed the essential role of the viewers' needs and desires in discovering the promised image in those emotionally blank objects. The arena of inquiry had to be opened up to recuperate the play of affective responses that he had long ago rejected, along with Art Informel, in the early 1960s. In the so-called *Abstract Paintings*, which flowered in 1980, he discovered how to resurrect painterly gesture not only as image, but as emotional vector, and how to orchestrate it in a manner both charged with emotion and critically countercharged in complex and contradictory structures that succeed in establishing an expanded discursive field for art and viewer. Nominally abstract, but contaminated irrevocably with similitude to realistic forms and spaces, as well as evocative of sensations and moods, Richter's collage and palimpsest compositions, despite their "abstractness," closely parallel those of the Americans, Salle being perhaps his closest American counterpart.[17]

In Salle's *His Brain* (pl. 83; cat. no. 150), for example, there is no hierarchy of image importance or formal or stylistic allegiances. What we have are patterns of interference caused by see-through overlays, by radical juxtapositions of physical scale, by abstract painterly marks that illogically contradict deep illusionistic spaces. Speeds of perception vary from the slow to the instantaneous and different time frames overlap (is that the explanation for the relation between the nude woman with her buttocks thrust enormously towards us and the loosely superimposed female figure, her hand to her mouth—or is this a physical as against a psychological state of being?). How are we to respond intellectually or emotionally to these rebuslike clues whose precise meaning has no sure verification—the Lincoln head silhouettes cut from the yellow paint layer in the right panel seem, at least to me, to read like wounds revealing a deeper vulnerability. Even if we track down the sources of individual images, it is often secondary or tertiary references that apply as much as any original sense.

Just as important as the opening up of the individual image for critical scrutiny is the orchestration of the images in and across the painting: the formal against the literary, the abstract against the figurative, and so forth for the real and the illusionistic, the heavy and the transparent, the slow and the fast, the soft and the hard, the ugly and the beautiful, the hilarious and the tragic, the seductive and the forbidden. All of these circulate in an unstable flux of promised narrative fragments that provoke the intellect and the imagination, our memories and deepest emotions. But their closure is continually diverted and deferred, as they compose and decompose from one perspective to the next. As I have suggested elsewhere with reference to Richter but generally applicable here, "each focus, uncon-nected by a common plane, is a setting free of signs, another a retrieval of them, their elusive identity reiterating the arbitrariness of our memory projections on them."[18]

But if Neo-Expressionist painting distrusts centralized, hierarchic, ideologically closed systems, it is not as if the artists resign themselves forever to chaos. As important as their destruction of hierarchized order is their urge to speak with precision, to reconstitute an order (even if it is only where you find it), because such structure is an inescapable human quest. This order, like meaning, like the self, is also only a human construct, provisionally useful and bearing with it nothing of the absolute.[19] In its tenuousness it reflects an image that Salle finds interesting in Karole Armitage's dance: "as though all four limbs are working in contradictory ways, but also with complete visual harmony."[20] Theodor Adorno expressed more absolutely art's necessary tolerance of ambiguity:

> Art is true to the extent to which it is discordant and antagonistic in its language and in its whole essence, provided that it synthesizes those diremptions, thus making them determinate in their irreconcilability. Its paradoxical task is to attest to the lack of concord while at the same time working to abolish discordance.[21]

The strategies of conscious and deliberate reenactment of the contingencies of our place in a world characterized by randomness and multiplicity account for the pervasive element of theatricality in the work of the Neo-Expressionists. Abstract art was intended forever to fend off the theatrical, but theatricality would out in Minimalism and all that followed, when art first performed, then the artist, and simultaneously the spectator, changing forever the equation between art and audience. Meaning has fled from within the work of art to the act of reception and completion in the participating spectator, sometimes by overtly physical action in the 1970s, and by a discursive interplay of critical and emotive responses in the 1980s.

1. Donald Kuspit and Eric Fischl, "An Interview with Eric Fischl," in *Fischl* (New York, 1987), p. 62.

2. Jean Baudrillard, French sociologist, has in the 1980s been especially influential on American art and art criticism because of his analysis of the dominant role of the media in shaping mass culture and, to some extent, high culture: "Although the media interfere and are being endemically, chronically and panicky present like a virus, they cannot be considered any more isolated in their consequences…we are not subject to the penetration and the pressure, to the violence and the blackmail of the media and models, but instead subject to their inductions and infiltrations, their invisible and illegible power" (Jean Baudrillard, *Agonie des Realen* [West Berlin, 1978], pp. 48–49, cited in Städtische Kunsthalle, Düsseldorf, 1986, *A Different Climate: Women Artists Use New Media*, p. 80).

3. Denys Zacharapolous, "Julian Schnabel, Galerie Daniel Templon," *Artforum* 22, 8 (Apr. 1984), pp. 90–91.

4. See, for example, Hal Foster, "The Expressive Fallacy," in *Recodings: Art, Spectacle, Cultural Politics* (Port Townsend, WA, 1985), pp. 59–77.

5. See Hal Foster, "(Post)Modern Polemics," in ibid., p. 131.

6. See, for example, Julian Schnabel, *C.V.J., Nicknames of Maitre D's & Other Excerpts from Life* (New York, 1987), p. 205; Julian Schnabel, "The Patient and the Doctors," *Artforum* 22, 6 (Feb. 1984), pp. 54–59.

7. See Robert Hobbs, in University of Iowa Museum of Art, Iowa City, 1985, *Robert Longo Dis-Illusions*, pp. 4, 11.

8. Peter Schjeldahl, in Whitney Museum of American Art, New York, 1987, *Cindy Sherman*, p. 11.

9. Umberto Eco, *Postscript to the Name of the Rose* (New York, 1984), pp. 67–68, cited in Charles Jencks, *What Is Post-Modernism?* (London, 1986), p. 18.

10. Paul Gardner, "Longo: Making Art for Brave Eyes," *Artnews* 84, 5 (May 1985), p. 65.

11. Peter Schjeldahl, "An Interview with David Salle," in *Salle* (New York, 1987), p. 39.

12. Lisa Phillips, in Whitney Museum (note 8), p. 13.

13. Carter Ratcliff, *Robert Longo* (New York, 1985), p. 23.

14. Schnabel, *C.V.J.* (note 6), p. 27.

15. Gerald Marzarati, "I Will Not Think Bad Thoughts: An Interview with Eric Fischl," *Parkett* 5 (1985), p. 13.

16. Schjeldahl (note 11), p. 72.

17. See Roald Nasgaard, in Museum of Contemporary Art, Chicago, and Art Gallery of Ontario, Toronto, 1988, *Gerhard Richter: Paintings*, pp. 106–10.

18. Ibid., p. 110.

19. Kevin Power, in Fundacion Caja de Pensiones, Madrid, 1988, *David Salle*, p. 33.

20. Schjeldahl (note 11), p. 44.

21. Theodor Adorno, *Aesthetic Theory*, trans. C. Lenhardt (London, 1984), p. 241.

Plate 76. *Mother and Daughter*, 1984
Oil on canvas
84 x 204 in. (213 x 518 cm)
Cat. no. 43

Plate 77. *The Evacuation of Saigon*, 1987
Oil on linen
Three parts, overall 120 x 142 in. (305 x 361 cm)
Cat. no. 44

Plate 78. *Untitled*, 1982
    Charcoal, graphite, and ink on paper
    96 x 48 in. (244 x 122 cm)
    Cat. no. 89

Plate 79. *Rock for Light*, 1983
Acrylic on paper, lacquer on wood, and acrylic on aluminum and copper
98 x 216 x 36 in. (249 x 549 x 91 cm)
Cat. no. 90

Plate 80. *Now Is the Creature (The Fly)*, 1986
Acrylic, graphite, and charcoal on linen and steel
82 x 140 x 26 in. (208 x 356 x 66 cm)
Cat. no. 91

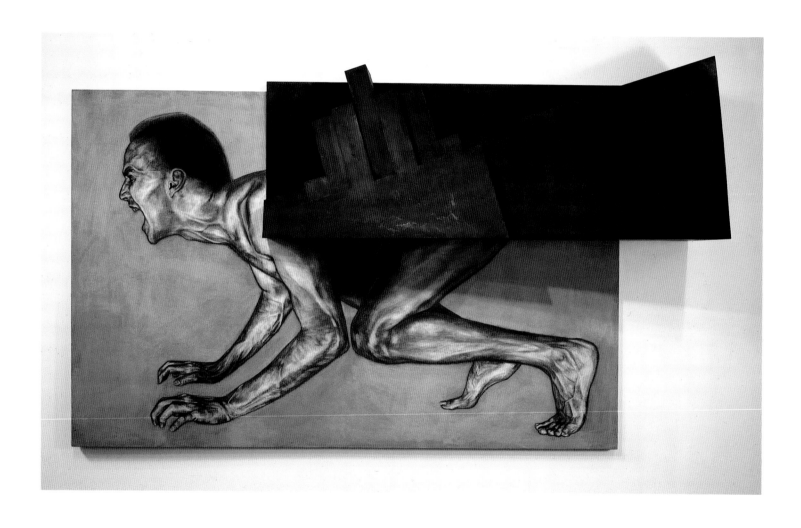

Plate 81. *Untitled*, 1984
  Painted Hydrocal and oil on canvas
  69½ x 86½ in. (177 x 200 cm)
  Cat. no. 99

Plate 82. *The Doors*, 1985
   Pressed wood and bronze
   95½ x 60 x 5 in. (243 x 152 x 13 cm)
   Cat. no. 130

Plate 83. *His Brain*, 1984
   Oil and acrylic on canvas and fabric
   117 x 108 in. (279 x 274 cm)
   Cat. no. 150

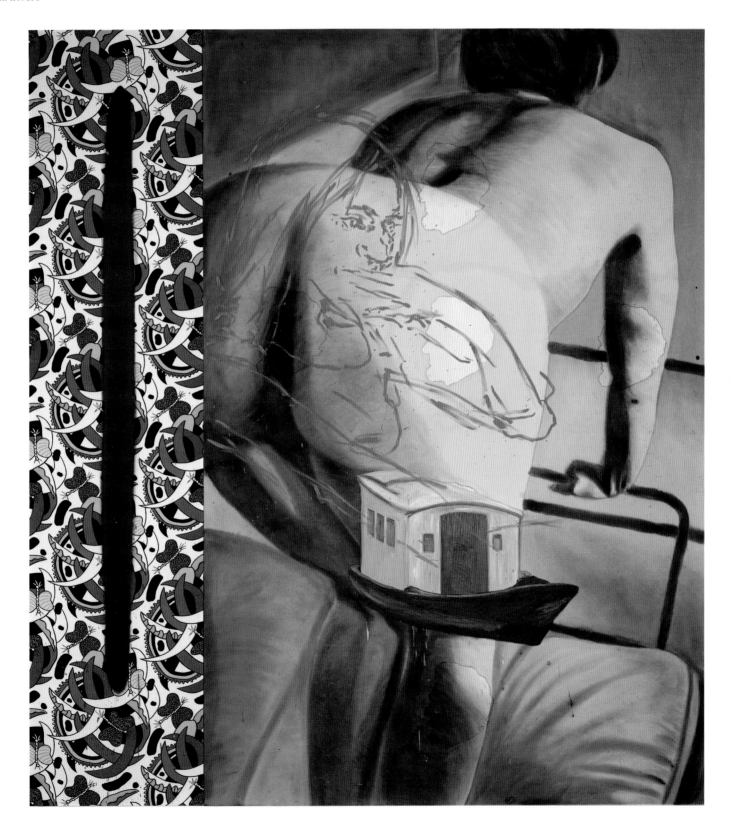

Plate 84. *Dusting Powders*, 1986
Acrylic and oil with wooden chair parts on canvas
108 x 156 in. (274 x 396 cm)
Cat. no. 151

Plate 85. *Conversion of St. Paul*, 1980
Oil on canvas
96 x 84 in. (244 x 213 cm)
Cat. no. 152

Plate 86. *Aorta*, 1981
    Oil on sisal rug with wooden frame
    118 x 165¼ in. (300 x 420 cm)
    Cat. no. 153

Plate 87. *Private School in California*, 1984
Oil and modeling paste on velvet
120 x 84 in. (305 x 213 cm)
Cat. no. 154

Plate 88. *Vita*, 1984
Oil and bondo with plates on wood
120 x 120 in. (305 x 305 cm)
Cat. no. 155

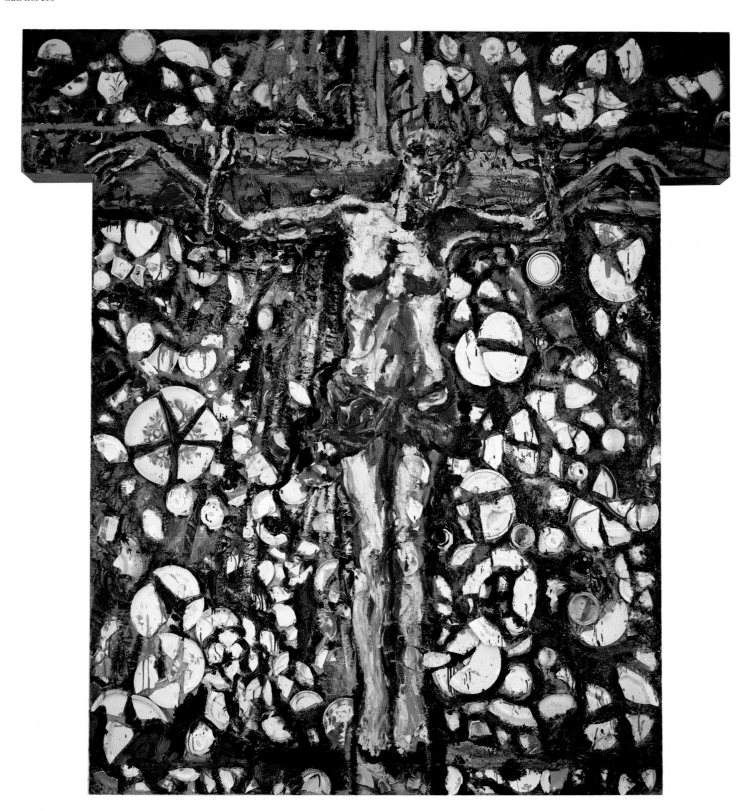

Plate 89. *Untitled*, 1988
Oil on tarpaulin
126 x 96½ in. (320 x 244 cm)
Cat. no. 156

Plate 90. *Untitled #88*, 1981
Color photograph
24 x 48 in. (61 x 122 cm)
The Art Institute of Chicago, gift of Gerald S. Elliott in memory of Ann Elliott, 1988.118
Cat. no. 162

Plate 91. *Untitled #137*, 1984
Color photograph
70½ x 47¾ in. (179 x 119 cm)
Cat. no. 163

Plate 92. *Untitled #147*, 1985
Color photograph
49½ x 72½ in. (153 x 184 cm)
Cat. no. 164

Plate 93. *Untitled #152*, 1985
Color photograph
72½ x 49⅜ in. (184 x 151 cm)
Cat. no. 165

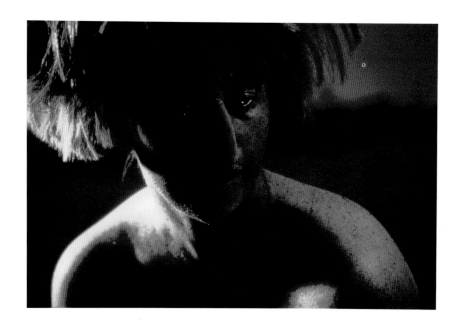

Plate 94. *Untitled #188*, 1989
Color photograph
45¼ x 67 in. (115 x 170 cm)
Cat. no. 166

Expanding the Possibilities for Painting:
Baselitz, Polke, Kiefer

NORMAN ROSENTHAL

The art world has always concentrated in centers, ever since the Renaissance and indeed long before that. For centuries Rome was the capital until, toward the end of the eighteenth century, it began to lose its prominence and Paris became the focus of activity. In 1940, with the outbreak of World War II and the imminent fall of Paris, many European intellectuals and artists fled to New York. This immigration launched New York as the new undisputed center of the art world. Style and the subversion of conventions now hailed from New York. Suddenly after 1945 art made in Europe was perceived to be provincial. Great collectors as well as museums in both the United States and Europe found themselves marginalizing European art, whether French, German, British, or Italian. But by the beginning of the 1980s, it began to appear that for once there might be no true center. German, Italian, and British artists, in particular—some of them quite young, others who had been engaged in art practice at least since the early 1960s—seemed to make a serious dent in those culturally subjective attitudes that had established New York as the only point of reference.

Gerald S. Elliott has assembled an outstanding and representative collection of much that is best in art today; his collection is still overwhelmingly American and above all New York centered. But whereas just over a decade ago virtually no European artist would have been perceived as "worthy" to stand as an equal to the great masters of Abstract Expressionism, Pop art, or the most significant practitioners of Minimal and Conceptual modes, serious attention has been paid in recent years to many European artists. Among these Europeans are three German painters, Georg Baselitz, Sigmar Polke, and Anselm Kiefer, who in their different ways have done much to break down barriers that even now sometimes threaten to resurrect themselves, perhaps partly as a result of overkill mediation on the part of certain propagandists. Art today cannot happily be explained with nationalistic bombast, even if place, language, and a common general culture do provide useful modes of categorization that help to join and place works of art within an appropriate context.

Much has been written on the historical condition of Europe after World War II, specifically on the near destruction of deep seated cultural traditions by Hitler, Stalin, Mussolini, and Franco, and on the unbelievably difficult task faced by artists in Europe to piece together their culture in a way that avoided banality. It is now understood that it is only through fragmentary perceptions that valuable and useful truths may be arrived at. Art made at the center, that is, in New York, after 1945, expresses little if any doubt concerning its own validity. However angst-ridden the Abstract Expressionists—Newman,

Pollock, Rothko, and Still—may have been, however cynical (using the strategy in a positive sense) the great artists of Pop—Johns, Rauschenberg, Warhol, etc.—their art is one of philosophic and aesthetic certainty. Even when we compare the Minimal/Conceptual artists of Europe with those from the United States, this lack of certainty in Europe contrasts with the positivistic certainty of the work of American artists. One need only compare Joseph Beuys's work in Germany with Robert Morris's work of the late 1960s and early 1970s; or the transitory, even nomadic, qualities of Mario Merz or Jannis Kounellis with the static, even immovable, positions of artists such as Carl Andre or Richard Serra. The real question for art at the end of the twentieth century is whether the expressive uncertainty of European artists may not be as central aesthetically as the overwhelming directness that characterizes American art—even in the case of artists such as Bruce Nauman, whose position and structures seem deliberate attempts to subvert existing modes of social and aesthetic behavior.

It might at first seem a bit strange to consider even in a nonpejorative sense the work of artists like Baselitz, Polke, and Kiefer as expressions of uncertainty. For too long and ultimately incorrectly their work has been characterized as heavy German Expressionism. German art has long suffered from the cliché of crudity, even barbarism, and accused of lacking subtlety and nuance. It was in fact the perception of this apparent brashness that made it so appealing to the art world at the end of the 1970s when Conceptual art was flourishing; the Duchampian position had talked itself into such refined forms of expression that it almost ceased to exist. "A New Spirit in Painting" suddenly appeared like a breath of fresh air.[1] New groups of artists from Europe began to bring art back to its senses and seemed to make the long-declared dead art of painting vital once again.

The misunderstanding involved in this revival of interest in painting, particularly that coming from Europe, was that it became mistakenly linked to the cause of Postmodernism, a stylistic nomenclature derived from architectural criticism (the return of the classical order) and that was fundamentally a search for traditions that some argued had been interrupted by the false gods of Modernism. If a useful term of architectural criticism, Postmodernism was and is a profoundly unhelpful way to describe art, a practice in which regression has no place and that can only lead to kitsch and aesthetically useless production. What needs to be emphasized is that there have been a number of German painters and also other artists working with more expanded media (above all the towering figure of Joseph Beuys), who have from their positions of "provinciality" made formidable contributions to the possibilities of art. Art from Europe is profoundly rooted in deep cultural traditions that refuse to disappear. Yet it can still propose forms of radical behavior and execution that convince us of the usefulness of the works of art that confront us.

Georg Baselitz was born in Deutschbaselitz in Saxony in January 1938 in an area today situated well into East Germany. His painting in the Elliott collection *Das Malerbild* of 1987–88 (pl. 96; cat. no. 7) represents for the artist a kind of summary—a statement on a very large scale of many of the artist's formal and ideological concerns. Resembling an enormous Byzantine iconostasis, the vast canvas is a composite work consisting of a series of images in blue windows, some of which are covered with mesh as though certain of the subjects were untouchable or even imprisoned. Many of the images appeared in earlier paintings. At the top right is a chair on which rests a bottle; to its left is an eagle, a symbol of freedom featured in a major group of paintings done by the artist in 1981, but it is an eagle that looks as though it could scarcely fly. At the bottom of the painting is a pig (a symbol of intelligence) seemingly entangled in yellow mesh. At the left of the canvas are two further motifs, a house and a tree. Significantly, the latter is the first motif that Baselitz chose to paint upside down in 1969 in the painting *The Forest on Its Head (Der Wald an den Kopf)*. Contrasting with these traditional motifs, to the extreme left of the painting is a small yellow window on which is delineated an airplane, which the artist has described as a threatening, sinister element. It is certainly the only foreign element in a repertoire of motifs that stand for the traditional, even conservative, sources that inform the artist's inspiration.

Das Malerbild is, however, primarily a painting of heads and full-length female figures, each staring out from the painting. For Baselitz each figure is associated with an admired artist and represents the muse of the artist or what Baselitz described as the female element in the artist's make-up: his sensibility (*Empfindsamkeit*). Baselitz's pantheon includes, among others, the little-known Swedish painter Carl Fredrik Hill and the Viennese painter Richard Gerstl, who committed suicide at the age of twenty-five and was a colleague of Gustav Klimt, Egon Schiele, and Oskar Kokoschka. Also represented in *Das Malerbild* are the composer-painter Arnold Schönberg, Ludwig Meidner, the Berlin Expressionist who painted "apocalyptic landscapes" on the eve of World War I, and some of the artist's friends and contemporaries, among them A.R. Penck and Jörg Immendorff. For the artist the very large figure at the center of the canvas is an amalgam of the spirits of Edvard Munch and Karl Schmidt-Rottluff. Munch, along with van Gogh, was very much the originator of the Expressionist style in modern painting. Schmidt-Rottluff, for Baselitz, was the most significant member of Die Brücke, the group of artists from Saxony who came together in 1905 to establish modern German art as we have come to understand it.[2]

Of course, unless instructed, there is no way that we could recognize Baselitz's spiritual heroes. The artist has always emphasized the fundamentally private nature of his activity as an artist. Ultimately the painter, the true artist, can work only for himself and must be profoundly uninterested in his audience. One ideal place for Baselitz to paint might be in a primitive cave where there is "no audience and no light, only hunger and yearning for love."[3] Baselitz gave a remarkable lecture-performance entitled "The Painter's Equipment" at the Royal Academy of Arts, London, in 1987. In a hermetic text emphasizing the private nature of art and the uselessness of an obsession with communication as such, he spoke of the artist's having

> traded the cave for some other place? Propagandizing about needs? He feeds upon a yearning for freedom and the fear of death and entices us into taking another way, off the painter's course. Painting became music. Surrealism won. Everything durable has been kicked out of painting but the colours in the cave are aglow. Light is superfluous. Everything is utterly different anyway. The paraphernalia of Venus, Zeus, the angels, Picasso were invented by the painters as were the bull, the roast chicken and the lovers.[4]

Baselitz's language is extravagant but in a world that demands a public face from the artist, the basic message is simple if not without contradiction. There is little need for Baselitz to explain why he should paint his motif upside down any more than Picasso need justify his Cubist strategy in depicting the world. Is Baselitz's portrait of Munch any less readable than Picasso's portrait of Kahnweiler? Analysis, research, and even deception can play a part in making art more diverting and interesting for the viewer. In the end it must be formal quality as well as ideological stance that give vitality to one art rather than another. But formal qualities require resolutions. Paradoxically, they are best invented at the edge of the world.

Baselitz lives and works in a romantic castle situated only a few miles from the East German border at the margin of our culture, which rightly or wrongly takes into account only Western Europe and the United States. Art, during this century in particular, has demanded that each artist invent for himself a private cosmos and an individual style. Baselitz's strategy is above all an abstract one — or at least as abstract as that of de Kooning, Pollock, or Newman. Baselitz has described how he arrived at the upside-down motif:

> Before I began painting pictures that involved the upside-down motif, much of my work contained elements that anticipated this type of painting but they were neither as explicit nor as crass. These were pictures where the little figures were fragmented and later moved freely on the canvas. When you pull your finger out and begin to create motifs and are still concerned to paint pictures, then the upside-down motif is the next best possibility. The hierarchy of the sky being above and the earth below is just a convenient understanding which we have all got used to but we do not have to believe this arrangement at all. I regard painting as an autonomous object, self-sufficient whether seen on a wall or carried around in your head.[5]

The strategy was visually brilliant, opening up endless possibilities for making new pictures.

Baselitz is a highly prolific painter but every now and then he makes a single work that seems to sum up a whole epoch in his oeuvre. *Die Grossen Freunde* of 1965 was one such painting. *Das Malerbild* once again asks the eternal question posed by Gauguin so dramatically in 1897: "Where do we come from? What are we? Where are we going?" As a result, Gauguin also made a painting that might be read as a series of windows of individual incidents each adding up to a private mythological system into which, nonetheless, we can enter if we choose. The German romantic castle is as far from New York as Tahiti is from Paris but it is in self-imposed exile that such questions are most appropriately posed.

Sigmar Polke was born in the town of Oels in Lower Silesia, now East Germany, in February 1941. In 1953 he moved with his family to West Germany and later entered the Düsseldorf Academy just at the time when Germany was at the height of the economic miracle that transformed it into a major consumer society. If Warhol ironized the United States consumer society to perfection, then Polke was to become the archetypal depictor of German-style consumerism. It is the world of the *Nierentisch* (the kidney table) — complete editions of Goethe, sausages and sausage eaters, biscuits, chocolate, and brightly colored plastic bowls. Polke's paintings have been done on a wide variety of grounds — blankets, tablecloths, colored sheets — whose patterns become as intrinsic to the paintings as the more or less precisely delineated motifs. During the 1960s, as Rauschenberg demonstrated so

well, it seemed that anything was capable of being transformed into an art object. Unlike Baselitz, whose outwardly serious stance is incredibly direct, Polke is a quixotic artist deliberately elusive and mysterious about his ways of working and always unorthodox in his use of materials. He is like a Faustian figure, always searching for the philosopher's stone that might turn dross into gold. If Pop irony was the driving force of his earlier work, then it is magic that seems to inform his most recent paintings.

The untitled triptych in the Elliott collection (pl. 99; cat. no. 134) clearly alludes to the trompe l'oeil frescoes painted by Francisco Goya in the church of San Antonio de la Florida in Madrid in 1798. Goya's brilliant group of Madrilenians witnessing the miracles of St. Anthony of Padua with all the concentration of a seance is palely reflected in Polke's painting. The painting, made primarily with synthetic resins mixed with strange inks, mostly sulphurous yellow and purple, that change color in response to changes in light and temperature, at first appears abstract. However, slowly one begins to perceive the figures that inhabit the fringes of each panel. Goya, for all his contacts with the Enlightenment, was an artist of the irrational, of the witch's sabbath, of the horror and fright of the Black Paintings. Polke sees in him a kindred spirit and one who came to share his secrets with him.[6]

Polke's position relates less obviously than Baselitz's or Kiefer's to the history of Western European culture but it transforms itself magically, and with maximum freedom and unconventionality, into a mysterious and highly aesthetic experience for the viewer who spends a long time with the works. They do not easily relinquish their secrets. Polke's earlier paintings reveal his connections with the dandified Dadaism of an artist such as Francis Picabia. More recently he has aspired to a mysticism and elusive sublimity that seem to relate to late Turner or the black magic world of Goya. Indeed, in his spectacular performance at the Venice Biennale in 1986, he seemed to find a contemporary affinity with the sfumato paradise of Tintoretto. His work seems to distance itself deliberately from normal bourgeois behavior, concepts, and obsessions, relating frighteningly or sometimes comically to a world that we know ought not to exist but does, inevitably exciting our curiosity and/or repulsion. Concentration camps and mine fields have been transformed by Polke into something mysterious, beautiful, yet still sinister and threatening, part of a cosmic strangeness that is impossible to explain. We are dealing with a representation of a firmament and with a spiritualistic dimension that in a way come close to Kandinsky and the strange mystical world of the Blaue Reiter rather than having any connection with northern German Expressionism. Paintings such as the untitled triptych of 1982 in the Elliott collection have much in common with the great compositions of Kandinsky, which were also an attempt to take us out of our world of perspective, and even perception, into a free cosmic space that exists in the mind and outside this world. In 1903 Kandinsky wrote,

> when I was young, I was often sad. I searched for something, something was lacking, I absolutely wanted to have something and it seemed to me that it is impossible to find this lacking thing. The feeling of this "lost paradise" I used to call this state of mind. Only much later did I get eyes which can sometimes peer through the keyhole of the gates of paradise. I am still searching too much on earth and he who looks down naturally sees nothing above.[7]

Compared to the perspectives of Baselitz and Kandinsky, Polke does not have his eyes trained to the ground but if sometimes he appears to see paradise he also has equally beautiful visions of hell. Maybe the grotesque figures that surround his canvas are looking into a void that has no moral overtones other than the changing beauty of the surface. Like Goethe's Faust, Polke presents himself as a magus who can make a pact with the devil and in return travel the earth, perhaps in search of eternal youth. Polke is indeed very much the magus rather than the shaman (Beuys) of German art. His world is a world of parapsychology, paraphysics, parachemistry, and above all para-aesthetics. The artist for Polke is not in the normal sense a free person. Rather he is at the command of the *hohere Wesen*, the higher force that compels the work of art. He is at best a medium and it is this that gives unity to the deliberate banality of his earlier subject matter and the more sublime subjects at the center of his more recent work. Yet we are not confronted with a surrealistic art, for the other aspects of Polke's art are its self-consciousness, alienation, and humor. The figures staring at us in the Elliott painting are laughing at us from the other side of the world. Already in 1966 Polke described how he "stood in front of a canvas wanting to paint a bunch of flowers" and then he received an order from a higher force: "Don't paint flowers, paint flamingos. First I just wanted to carry on and then I knew they meant it seriously."[8] Polke is a medium of our own times and to times past. His paintings describe common European as well as German dreams and nightmares. It is for us to draw conclusions if we so wish.

Each artist makes his own pact with perspective. Baselitz looks straight ahead even if deliberately standing the world on its head. Polke looks beyond perceptual reality and becomes a medium, as it were, for a world on the other side of life. Anselm Kiefer also looks at a world, rarely if ever inhabited by living human beings, but his perspective is consciously turned towards the ground and even if it looks up towards the sky, it does its best to come down to the surface of the painting. Kiefer was born in 1945 in Donaueschingen in southern Germany just before the end of World War II. The postwar scorched earth and ruined cities, which feature so strongly in his paintings, were a profound aspect of his childhood years. He has attempted, in a world after the Holocaust, to deal with the problem of culture and the continuity of a European, specifically German, world. Baselitz, Polke, not to mention painters such as Markus Lupertz, Penck, and Immendorff, and Kiefer's own teacher Beuys, have also addressed this theme. But few, if indeed any, postwar European artists born after 1940 have been so successful in communicating the necessary message that art and specifically painting in Europe are very possible and relevant.

Kiefer has done this from a position of maximum isolation. His studio in Hornbach is quite literally situated in the depths of the German forest. He never allows himself to be photographed and indeed makes himself as inaccessible as possible. His art is deliberately hermetic; his subject matter deals with obscure Nordic, classical, Early Christian, and, recently, Kabalistic texts. Few of us will have read such texts and Kiefer's paintings, with their unbelievably obscure references to texts all but lost from our cultural consciousness, are both a challenge and a commentary implying that perhaps we have entered a new cultural dark age. In an earlier such age, speculative philosophical concepts were preserved in manuscripts in distant monasteries on the fringes of civilization. Perhaps the task now is to preserve, in however fragmentary a way, culture through visual imagery.

Kiefer's paintings seem almost deliberately drained of color; indeed they seem to postulate the very absence of color itself. They are also densely collaged, the canvas weighted down by the widest possible range of heavy materials: paint (oil often dangerously mixed with acrylic), photographic imagery, and objects of various kinds, not to mention materials such as straw, lead, and steel. The untitled triptych of 1980–86 (pl. 98; cat. no. 70) in the Elliott collection contains most of these elements. But although technically it is a collage, it is not like one by Kurt Schwitters or even by Jasper Johns (an artist whom Kiefer in his recent work seems to challenge). For these artists, the collage is applied in a basically surreal, Dadaistic manner. Kiefer's triptych in no way looks surreal. It seems hardly to have been made by the artist himself, but rather to be an occurrence in nature. The boulders on the left-hand panel look as though they have fallen from the skies; they belong there not because the artist has chosen their position but because this is how they are situated within the cosmos. In this sense the painting resembles quite literally nature but not the nature of beautiful fields and flowers. Nor is Kiefer's vision one derived from science fiction. Rather it seems to evoke a three-dimensional world that exists either before or after man. At the bottom of the central panel lies a serpent. Mark Rosenthal has described Kiefer's deliberate use of ambiguity in the image, "Is it the seraphic angel, having just descended the ladder from heaven, or the Satanic creature writhing at the foot of the ladder used in Christ's crucifixion?"[9] Kiefer apparently is happy with either interpretation; indeed one might also be reminded of Aaron's rod that also changed into a serpent, or of the ladder in Jacob's dream that connected heaven with earth, which has often been interpreted by artists as well as theologians as a prefiguration of the coming of Christ. The lead funnel that dominates the panel on the right resembles a cosmic listening organ, or perhaps a musical instrument that seems to be disgorging lava onto the surface of the world picture that the painting presents.

Like all great paintings, this work is doing something that can be expressed in no other way. It is in one sense idle to reach for literary references, to listen to the "sound" of the painting, or to regard it as a form of theater. While all these aspects are relevant, the painting functions primarily as a visual object and through looking becomes intensely satisfying and abstract in implication. The spiritual message need not be clear ultimately even to the artist himself. Joseph Beuys tried in his work to solve the problems of the social organism through the therapeutic nature of art. For Kiefer, reality seems to go beyond the human condition; he describes a world situated within a universe in which human beings have no meaning. In a complex way, Kiefer's work deals with the enormity of the existential problem and tries philosophically to resolve it through the image.

At the center of Kiefer's work, both literally and metaphorically, lies the studio. It is thus not surprising that the second major painting by Kiefer in the Elliott collection, a work of 1984, is called *The Studio of the Painter* (pl. 97; cat. no. 71). This title, used frequently by Kiefer, generally describes paintings dominated by large 1930s classical buildings with Fascist overtones, in the center of which is often the artist's palette (in place of a flame). Here the artist has represented instead an endless field deeply furrowed and probably barren and burnt, occupied in the center by a small building with a tower, maybe a church. Is the studio the field itself or is it the small chapel? In fact the artist has indicated that the building represents the Neoclassical museum in Linz designed to house the Führer's collection.[10] All Kiefer's works pose riddles to which the answer in the end is immaterial, such is the power of their symbolism, whether ancient or modern, Jewish or Masonic, Egyptian or Christian, or even (which makes us very uncomfortable) Fascist; unlike speech or language, the visual appearance of things in themselves can give no answer. Like Cézanne's Mont St. Victoire, itself a repository of complex historic symbolism going back to Roman times, Kiefer's landscape is the perfect expression of the question. The work of art at its best always represents the unanswered question; German artists since the war have been perfectly positioned to make this the justification for their work. Baselitz, Polke, and Kiefer are each thinking practitioners of the art of painting, making it possible for it to be a meaningful activity today on both sides of the Atlantic.

---

1. "A New Spirit in Painting" was the title of the exhibition of new painting held at the Royal Academy of Arts, London, in 1981.

2. Georg Baselitz in conversation with the author, May 1989.

3. Georg Baselitz, "Painters' Equipment," *Burlington Magazine* 130, 1021 (Apr. 1988), p. 283.

4. Ibid.

5. Georg Baselitz in an interview with Walter Grasskamp, in *Ursprung und Vision—Neue Deutsche Malerei* (Madrid, 1984), p. 12.

6. "One day Goya the Lucretian came to me and said—/Quasuntarne/quasuratun/quasa tula/marquataquapa/marutuque/mirabile/ tabla tale/telepantuta/la tombola la tuque/ lateque laque te, laquet a,/leta que, e lat equ./Telque ta, Queta la, Qualte quelta/ taquel qualet,/queta ateque,/quelta quatel, qualet e, eque alt/que late, te quale/I asked him, how are you? And he wanted to know how I knew this. I told him that I remembered that he had once made a drawing of a monkey and how it had looked behind a mirror and…then he lit all the candles round about himself and became totally illuminated" (Museum Boymans van Beuningen, Rotterdam, and Städtischer Kunstmuseum, Bonn, 1983–84, *Sigmar Polke*, p. 64.

7. Letter from Kandinsky to Gabriele Münter, Oct. 11, 1903, quoted in The Solomon R. Guggenheim Museum, New York, 1982, *Kandinsky in Munich 1896–1914*, p. 57.

8. Sigmar Polke, *Hohere Wesen Befehlen* (West Berlin, 1968), n. pag.

9. Mark Rosenthal, in The Art Institute of Chicago and the Philadelphia Museum of Art, 1987, *Anselm Kiefer*, p. 138.

10. Anselm Kiefer in conversation with the author, June 1989.

Plate 96. *Das Malerbild*, 1987–88
Oil on canvas
110¼ x 177⅛ in. (280 x 450 cm)
Cat. no. 7

Plate 97. *The Studio of the Painter*, 1984
  Oil, straw, emulsion, shellac, and woodcut on canvas
  110 x 150 in. (279 x 381 cm)
  Cat. no. 71

Plate 98. *Untitled*, 1980–86
    Emulsion, oil, acrylic, shellac, and charcoal on photograph mounted on cardboard,
    lead objects, and steel wire mounted on canvas
    Three parts, overall 123 x 216 in. (312 x 548 cm); each 123 x 72 in. (312 x 183 cm)
    Cat. no. 70

Plate 99. *Untitled*, 1982
Synthetic resin and mixed media on canvas
Three parts, overall 118 x 236 in. (300 x 600 cm); each 118 x 78¾ in. (300 x 200 cm)
Cat. no. 134

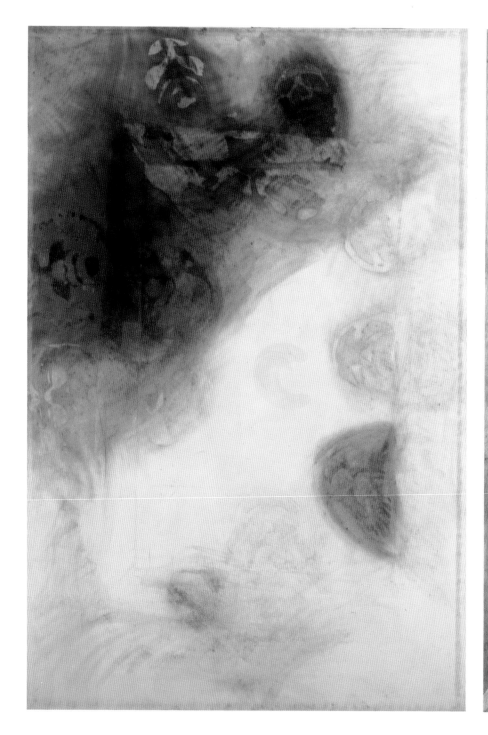
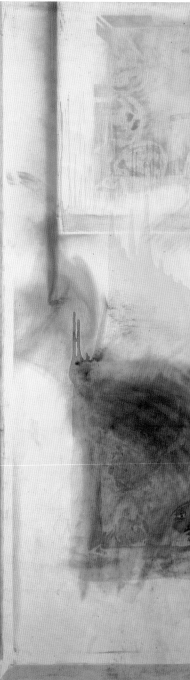

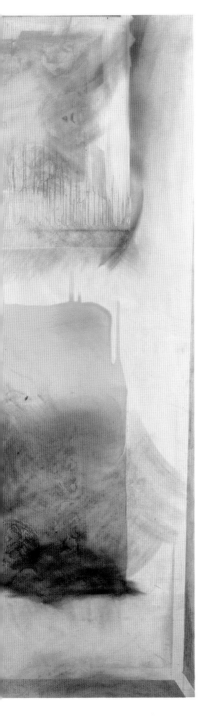

Primitive Decorum: Of Style, Nature, and the Self in Recent Italian Art

MICHAEL AUPING

The history of postwar Italian art balances on a curious edge between impeccable stylishness and brute expressionism. Indeed, for many of us it is this seemingly incompatible fusion that most fascinates, consistently attracting our attention, if not always our understanding. To be sure, this is a quality difficult to specify, though nonetheless apparent in the elegant but aggressively slashed canvases of Lucio Fontana; in Alberto Burri's sublimely rich and bloody "wounds"; in the delicate, urban primitivism of Mario Merz's glass igloos; in Michelangelo Pistoletto's classical Venuses buried in mountains of colored rags; and in Jannis Kounellis's impeccably arranged installations involving live animals, fires, rocks, and decaying building fragments. It is no less an aspect of the animated, at times scatological, self-portraits of the Neo-Expressionists Sandro Chia, Francesco Clemente, Enzo Cucchi, and Mimmo Paladino, whose works have come to represent Italian art in the 1980s.

Given this strange field of imagery—its lyricism, mordant irony, implied violence, and childlike wonderment turned melancholy—it is not surprising that we have difficulty rationalizing "the Italians." Yet these qualities, as varied as they are, act as a kind of theoretical umbilical cord between recent generations of Italian artists. Such qualities signal basic layers of content, not simply a sense of style. In unraveling these layers, we glimpse a desire for a more innocent, primitive self and an unmediated dialogue with nature. This is not a nostalgic yearning for arcadia, but a mythopoetic search for an essential, or primal self; an urge to strip experience of civilized superstructures in an attempt to achieve an aggressive purity. At the same time, for the Italians, style persists as an inherent aspect of these strategies, a means of coaxing this primal content into a poetic form.

Following World War II, Lucio Fontana and Alberto Burri established the mood of the Italian position. Fontana's precisely slashed monochrome canvases of the 1950s and 1960s possess a regal classicism while achieving an ominous surgical removal of the pictorial space of painting. Rather than building up the surface—as did Jackson Pollock, Willem de Kooning, and Clyfford Still—to establish the painting less as a visionary window than as a totemic presence, Fontana virtually cut into his pictures, revealing their fleshy vulnerability, what the Italian critic Germano Celant variously described as a "gaping wound" or "the inner folds of a sexual organ."[1] The works are not beautiful in the decorative sense, but as a result of the ironic coupling of primitive aggression and elegance. Such pristine violations suggest a human, physical presence. They become emblems of sorts, beings made of canvas skin over wooden bones. In the end, they operate as sacrificial bodies, the cuts uncovering a veiled and mysterious self.

Alberto Burri graduated in medicine from the Università di Perugia in 1940, subsequently serving in the Italian army medical core until 1943, when his unit was captured by the British in Tunisia. He began to paint while in a prisoner-of-war camp in Hereford, Texas. This experience reinforces the notion that the artist's rich black-and-red surfaces act, at least on one level, as metaphors for burned earth and flesh. At the same time, Burri's disparate materials—tar, living molds, burlap, pigments—create remarkably sensuous and tasteful surfaces, contrasting glossy and matte areas with lyrical cracks and encrusted pigment. Within this emphasis on the literal beauty of the painted surface, however, resides a disturbing subtext: a cathartic and primitive reenactment of a violated body. As with Fontana, the painting becomes a powerful metaphor for the self and all its human vulnerabilities.

Perhaps it was Piero Manzoni who forced to an extreme the notion of the primal self as the most elevated and charged form of art, packaging and selling as art his blood and excrement. Addressing what would appear to be the critical existential impulse in Manzoni's art, Celant has noted that after forming art from his own body, Manzoni "performed the miracle of the rebirth of the world: *The Base of the World* transformed everything animal, vegetable and mineral into a work of art. Art becomes a phenomenon in the purest of states; it neither speaks nor explains, but only is."[2] As strange as these visions strike us even now, Fontana, Burri, and Manzoni are critical to an understanding of the curious imagery and emotions that inform the work of the two succeeding generations of Italian artists.

With the advent of Arte Povera, or "poor art," in the late 1960s, the impulse towards an increasingly radical experimentation with materials and the concern with conferring on these materials a sense of spiritual power erupted in a theatrical explosion of symbols related to myth and nature. The term Arte Povera was interpreted, if not defined, by Germano Celant, whose book of the same title was published in 1968. Celant wrote of a new type of freedom in Italian art, one not identified with rational systems. He also alluded to an anthropological dimension and a position in which content is related to the self and nature in a primary way.[3]

Many critics have analyzed Arte Povera as an inspired outgrowth of the social and political unrest that had galvanized so many in Europe and the United States in the 1960s. Like related developments in Conceptual, Minimal, Performance, video, and Earth art in the United States, Arte Povera represented an attempt to bypass the art-commodity system with the creation of works that were not discreet objects per se and presumably could not be sold. Indeed, Arte Povera incorporated a remarkable constellation of highly unorthodox materials—dirt, glass, living animals, neon, plants, etc.—in an attempt to liberate art from its increasingly benign status as a commodity.

Beneath this questioning of the art market, however, existed a more profound content, one focused on critiquing the Modernist impulse toward autonomous and rational form. The exhibition "The Knot: Arte Povera at P. S. 1," which restaged many important installations in October 1985, offered Americans an opportunity to experience Arte Povera in a broad way, indeed, to compare it to American Minimalism to which it is so often thought to relate. While Minimalism essentially extended the rigorous formalist geometry of Piet Mondrian, the American Abstract Artists, and the geometric side of Abstract Expressionism (Barnett Newman and Ad Reinhardt), bringing it into an environmental arena, the Arte Povera artists seemed to gravitate toward a kind of content that transgressed the rational in a bold attempt to recapture a more fundamental language. In contrast to the sleek, modern character of American Minimalism, Arte Povera appears not so much "poor" but hyper-primitive. It is in effect anti-Minimalist and antidesign, predicting the ritualistic presence of American Earth art, in which enigmatic monuments project a profound, almost mystical, presence. Like site-inspired works by Robert Smithson and Michael Heizer, Arte Povera could not be adequately described by American formalist criticism. Beyond surface, color, line, and composition, these artists were reaching for a powerful recovery of myth, folklore, and, more basically, man's place in nature.

Michelangelo Pistoletto's "mirror" paintings throw the viewer's image back on himself, dryly hammering home the point that we, as the perceiving self, remain the seeds of all content. We are, as Jackson Pollock had said a decade earlier, nature itself.[4] Pistoletto's well-known *Venus of Rags* of 1967–68 elicits, on the one hand, a powerful and ironic contrast between ancient classical beauty and cast-off clothing. It is unclear, on the other hand, whether Venus is being buried in these rags or is caressing them in a sensuous ritual. For Pistoletto, this work is not to be interpreted strictly as a matter of art and politics, as referring to an idealistic historical style overwhelmed by a poor and garish urban reality. It is, rather, "like a ritual of nature. The rags are like leaves, falling over the world. They ferment into a mountain of rags. It is a kind of burial rite or birth, if you see her emerging from this mountain."[5]

One of the elder statesmen of the Arte Povera movement, Mario Merz may be considered the poet primitive of postwar Italian art. Both his art and his endearing persona provide the model of a nomadic visionary balancing on a precarious mental bridge between intellect on the one hand and intuition and passion on the other. Like that of his German contemporary Joseph Beuys, Merz's work forms an explosive fusion between fragments of nature and the scraps and detritus of urban culture. The result is often a kind of poetic meltdown in which nature envelops culture. Delicate sheets of glass form igloos, baroque paintings depict wild animals and immense vegetable forms in an elaborate and mysterious cross-referencing. Merz's works and his statements evoke the belief that nature and creativity have reciprocal and ultimate power; they are in effect the fundamental elements of existence. He has related his work to primal and organic forces and holds that a work of art is itself like an organism, evolving endlessly in relation to external conditions, a strategy related to Merz's concept of the nomad and the primitive. Although this primitive self is not "illustrated" in Merz's art, the artist has constructed a portable architecture for it, the igloo (see pl. 116; cat. no. 98), which has become the artist's leitmotif. Merz and his igloo are nomadic, continually adjusting to new locations and imperatives. His architecture conjures the image of a hunter and wanderer, reminding us of a lost past and unity with the land. There is, after all, something pure and authentic about the nomad, who moves across the surface of the planet as a part of nature, as opposed to the builder who colonizes and takes possession of new territories.

Basic to Merz's philosophy (and overlayed on many of his images) is a numerical system for the proliferation of forms based on the findings of the medieval monk Leonardo Fibonacci of Pisa. The progression in this system —1, 1, 2, 3, 5, 8, 13, 21, 34, 55, etc.—requires that each term be the sum of the two preceding numbers. The growth pattern of pine cones, sunflowers, antlers, and the growth rate of leaves, reptile skins, and shells all follow this progression. The series can also be used to define proportion and spatial logic in architecture. Speaking of the natural order discovered by Fibonacci, Merz has remarked that "This parabolic, deep breathing whole is the real subject of art."[6]

Since the late 1980s, Merz has also made numerous paintings, using mixed media on raw canvas. His subjects have primarily involved vegetable forms and exotic, archetypal beasts, such as the tiger and crocodile. Speaking about an exhibition of his work at the Albright-Knox Art Gallery in Buffalo in 1984, the artist noted, "Nature is the subject, not the depiction. The animal is nature. It is the essence of who we are, or were, or should be."[7] Merz's comment points up an empathy that surfaces in other recent Italian painting and sculpture: an identification with the animal presence in nature.

Jannis Kounellis came into prominence in 1969 with an installation presented in the Galleria L'Attico in Rome. Kounellis exhibited a group of live horses, literally transforming the gallery into a "stable," the term often used to describe the group of artists represented by a particular gallery. Beyond an art-world pun, however, Kounellis was confronting his visitors with the living (and smelling) presence of archetypal beasts. Richard Serra had also presented caged animals at the Galleria La Salita in Rome in 1966. However, while Serra's caged animals seemed to refer primarily to man's imprisonment (and perhaps to the imprisonment of art in a given political system), Kounellis's horses celebrated the simple beauty of contained primal energy. An important prelude to this powerful installation took place in 1967, also at the Galleria L'Attico, when Kounellis presented a live parrot perched in front of a painted sheet of steel, the intense natural colors of the bird paling the artifice of the decorated pictorial plane. As with much of Kounellis's work, nature or the organic overcomes artifice and the man-made.

Live animals have played less and less of a role in Kounellis's art as it has developed, yet nature in a broad sense remains a cornerstone of his subject matter. In an untitled etching done at Crown Point Press in 1979, a rich, aqua-tinted black square is surrounded by photoetched flowers printed in blue. An imposing void is given life by a delicate and fragile element of nature. In recent years, Kounellis's work has involved the convergence of hard, industrial structures and organic, unstructured, agricultural elements. Kounellis's static reliefs, which combine various disjunctive materials, project a powerful totemic presence in which organic materials charge the inert physicality of metal (see pls. 114–15; cat. nos. 77–78) and magically transform it into something less impenetrable and ominous, indeed, imparting a natural sensuousness.

Kounellis often depicts nature as an all-encompassing entropic force. His use of rotting wood fragments (artifacts if you will), often taken from torn-down or decaying buildings, suggests civilization's deconstruction to a natural state. Nature's entropic symbol, the spiral, echoes in the artist's use of toy trains that continually move along a spiral or circular track, turning back on their own paths as they move forward.

Many of Kounellis's most powerful installations involve the artist's fascination with fire. Kounellis has remarked, "My interest in this element is not only in fire as a problem but also in its references to medieval legends. Fire, in medieval legend, goes with punishment and purification."[8] Many of the artist's installations incorporate fire, often emitted from small kerosene burners. In other instances, the evidence of fire—soot or scorching—is all that remains. Such installations have the commanding presence of primitive altars, a place to worship a pure form of nature and spirit. The energy that burned Burri's surfaces is harnessed for its own properties. As if performing the magic ritual of a shaman, Kounellis has even been photographed with a flame-throwing gas jet in his mouth.[9]

Giuseppe Penone presents human forms growing out of trees, or plants cascading into anthropomorphic forms. In a clear illustration of Arte Povera's tendency to fuse culture and nature, he drives a metal hand into the trunk of a tree which, continuing to grow, eventually envelops and swallows the hand. He has written: "If the earth is mother... forming the earth is a sensuous act."[10] Penone's art, and that of his Arte Povera colleagues, presents itself as a forest of symbols evoking the primitive in an attempt to reconceive nature in the late twentieth century. This complex and powerful theme has by no means been lost on the next generation of Italians, though the means of the so-called Neo-Expressionists have changed significantly.

It is now almost a decade since the works of Sandro Chia, Francesco Clemente, Enzo Cucchi, and Mimmo Paladino emerged in New York. When these artists initially presented their works at the Gallery Sperone Westwater in Soho, their imagery was met with a sense of shock and bewilderment. The discussion was focused along nationalistic and stylistic lines. From one viewpoint, these paintings involved a symbolic reading too complex and culturally remote for Americans. From another, this was an art simply illustrating old myths. Most shocking, however, was the fact that these paintings were figurative, and thus regressive and nostalgic to those who had constructed a linear history of twentieth-century art based on the development of abstraction.

The work was further politicized by the Italian critic Achille Bonito Oliva, who explained the new imagery, christening the new art the "Transavanguardia," and pointing out its difference from past avant-gardes, especially the movement's belief in the freedom to form a "nomad creativity" between cultures and forms.[11] Oliva's texts involve an inspired but somewhat confusing attempt to drive a theoretical wedge between the aesthetics of the Arte Povera generation and that of his so-called Transavanguardia.

What changed was partly a matter of style and choice of materials. The new generation took on the challenge of building a body of work out of figurative painting, which (with a few key exceptions) had for decades seemed hopelessly conservative. In the hands of a new generation, however, a powerful thread of content in postwar Italian art was invigorated and brought into the painterly aesthetic of the 1980s. What has been ignored in focusing on the potential regression of a new style and approach is the essential continuity that exists between Arte Povera and the Transavanguardia. Like their elders, Chia, Clemente, Cucchi, and Paladino bring into their art the subversive drama of allegory, a perverse sense of the dignity of the ordinary world, and, above all, a concern for the elusive truth and authentic power of nature. In this sense, nature is not simply a pastoral jewel hopelessly lost to the postindustrial era, but a brute, primal force placed on equal footing with the so-called "civilized" mind. For these artists, the painter, in the end, is in the same existential predicament as other animals. The art of these painters is not simply figurative, it is an art about the body, its basic needs and fleshy instincts. These are artists who—as Clemente has put it—appreciate "those who have 'thought' with their bodies."[12] What Clemente spoke of is perhaps that "uncivilized" instinct shared by so-called primitives and animals.

Sandro Chia's art is a matrix of contradictions. He is given to baroque exaltation, a nervous elegance that can accommodate a variety of stylistic references. Chia plunders art-historical references and styles the way Merz has plundered disparate materials. A single painting or series of paintings may contain stylistic and iconographic references to Renaissance and Mannerist art, as well as to Impressionism, Fauvism, Futurism, Cubism, and German Expressionism. As Chia recently put it, "Style is the alter ego of ideas. We would go crazy with just the idea. In Italy, philosophers have always wrapped their ideas in poetic or comedic styles. It is a basic strategy of expression. Style allows us to dream on the idea, without choking."[13]

The stylish, jewellike hardness of Chia's surfaces nonetheless conveys an expressionistic assault on our senses and emotions, without which elegance is merely comforting. In a photograph by Gianfranco Gorgoni, we see Chia applying rich fistfuls of paint directly onto the canvas with his hands, as if the artist were working on the wall of a cave. The unity of his compositions, regardless of the inventory of styles he incorporates, comes from a sustained "passion of the moment," a frenzy of paint smears and cloudbursts of colors that are alternately cynical, comic, and indelicate: a kind of luminous and spectacular brutality. "Since the cave wall," Chia remarked recently, "art has been invented as a symbolic ritual, a ritual that replaces the real thing, the hunter scratching his image of desire on the cave wall."[14] Chia's stylistic eclecticism is not the content of his art, but a flexible means of expressing it. A central aspect of the content of Chia's art, like that of his colleagues, is an appreciation for the raw energy and passion of nature. In a letter written in 1983 to the then director of the Stedelijk Museum in Amsterdam, the artist couched his notion of art in the image of nature, writing that he found himself in his studio

> as if in the stomach of a whale. My paintings and my sculptures appear in this place like the undigested residues of a former repast and I recall the phrase with which Goethe opens his introduction to the magazine *Propylaen*: "The youth who begins to feel the attraction of nature and art believes that a serious effort alone will enable him to penetrate their inner sanctuary: but the man discovers after lengthy wanderings up and down that he is still in forecourt."...I could write about art only from the interior, from the cave, from the stomach of the whale. In this place, surrounded by my paintings and my sculptures, I am like a lion-tamer among his beasts.[15]

The hero/protagonist of Chia's paintings often takes the form of a lumbering, muscle-bound peasant who traffics in a nature of blunt realities. Chia does his best to convey the anxious, often brutish, and ill-mannered energies pent up in the human animal. Indeed, his iconography abounds with men whose physical appearance and rude actions make the distinction between "civilized" man and "primitive" animal seem subtle if not nonexistent.

Regardless of our ability to generate lofty thoughts and emotions, it is our biologies that anchor us at the animal level. In *Perpetual (E)motion* of 1978 (fig. 1), Chia accepted the fact that we cannot escape our bodily functions. The painting depicts a man fueling his dreams, guzzling a bottle of wine, only to urinate them away into his enclosed garden. Two sniffing dogs inhabit the same garden, oblivious to the man's active pun on himself. Speaking of the painting, Chia remarked, "The dogs add an element of

Figure 1. Sandro Chia, *Perpetual (E)motion*, 1978/79. Oil on
canvas, 59¾ x 37⅞ in. (152 x 96 cm). Collection
Susan and Lewis Manilow, Chicago.

chaos to balance the harmony of the image ... but it is a chaos we can or should relate to. We have the same presence in nature, the same basic needs: hunger, thirst, urination."[16]

In *Water Bearer* of 1981, a figure struggles to carry a fish equally his size. Speaking of the painting, Chia has remarked:

> The Fish is a symbol of death. Death is the main condition. It is the biggest thing we carry around with us. After all, we will be dead much longer than we will be alive. It's a very simple subject. Death is one of the reasons we can't forget nature. Death is a big part of nature. Until science delivers us into eternity, we still die — like dogs. In that sense, we are still in the cave age.[17]

In the painting *Leave the Artist Alone* of 1985, a lion perches on the lap of a dreaming artist, a scene Chia described as "a vision of a fierce beast protecting the artist, protecting the imagination."[18] In *Outdoor Scene* of 1984, a female figure — whom Chia referred to as "the female of creation" — is attacked by dogs as she transforms herself into a deer (Diana of the Hunt?). An interesting detail of the picture is that the tips of the deer's antlers are paintbrushes. Chia identifies with this mythological transformation, but as "an allegory of the artist. In nature or in art, when you have a metamorphosis, the rest of nature can turn against you. You are no longer the hunter but the prey."[19]

In a recent conversation, Chia spoke of the primitive and elemental relationship between nature and the self:

> The subject of art is always nature...but this sometimes bucolic image of mine is not plein air, not the outside world. It's something I conceive as nature. It's a compound of historical signals — quotations of paintings from history — to reinvent nature in my terms. It's very primitive to take earth and pigment and aspire to creation.... When we talk of nature, which nature are we talking about? Poussin's tree? There are so many trees. The primitive need to make a mark creates the tree, the tree we see in art. We are nature.[20]

At the same time, Chia has acknowledged this primal self as an elusive muse. One of his most remarkable pictures, *Melancholic Encampment* of 1982 (pl. 100; cat. no. 18), presents a dreamscape in which a tranquil if perhaps melancholic nature is pitted against the explosive energy of history. In the center of the picture an American Indian sleeps, his arm gently locked with the hind leg of a small sheep. It appears that he dreams of a chaotic journey into a future dominated by medieval tents, Modernist paintings, and ominous black machines. The nomadic Indian who lives close to nature and his animal companion become fragile remnants of a purer, uncluttered existence.

The development of Neo-Expressionist figurative painting did not emerge full-blown, as a conceptually predetermined gesture. Rather, it formed gradually, incubating its imagery, as it were, through drawing. Indeed, the medium of drawing — both delicate and notational — offered this new generation the most diplomatic transition from the Conceptual strategies of the 1970s to the object-oriented art of the 1980s. In the early 1970s, Mimmo Paladino devoted himself almost exclusively to drawing, introducing a range of subjects and symbols that would dominate his large-scale paintings, sculptures, and installations of the 1980s.

Paladino's works draw on diverse archaeological and stylistic sources. Inspired by folk art and African cave painting, as well as Egyptian, Etruscan, Greco-Roman, early Christian, and Romanesque art, his work presents a constellation of Christian and pagan symbols. Cruciform shapes and animal human hybrids are fused into surfaces of gold leaf, antiqued wood, or bronze. More austere and less sensuous than Chia's work, these paintings and sculptures are characterized by a refined and exquisite strangeness. Paladino's curious personages — suggestive variously of unwrapped mummies or carved icons — have an ethereal quality, as if they embodied the soul rather than the flesh of the depicted subject. These serene, otherworldly figures stare at the viewer, daring us to contemplate our mortality in nature's cycle of life and death. For Paladino, the human figure often exists as a floating emblem in a continually evolving landscape. As Henry Geldzahler has aptly described it, the human presence in Paladino's art is "ghostly—anti-anatomic. Man, Animals, Spirits, and the Dead coexist in a flattened nexus of painterly energy. Many of the strategies and devices of recent abstract art are used to create a choreography that smells of Death and Life, or rot and regeneration."[21]

A distinct theme surfacing in the work of this recent generation is the evocation of a primitive animism in which animals, mountains, and other natural elements project a strong, if enigmatic, spiritual presence. In the bronze relief *Allegory* of 1983 (pl. 117; cat. no. 131), Paladino has focused on the animal roots of man and on our origins in nature. Two figures intertwined around a central palette emerge from a tree or rock. A ram's head is embossed in the terrestrial lower section. As the figures ascend they become more human, elevated and held together by the palette, an emblem of creativity, style, and civilization. In the bronze *Besieged* of 1983, a human figure is caressed and protected by a group of four-legged, horned creatures, while in an untitled watercolor of 1984, human bodies and heads are buried in the bellies of dogs or horses; in some cases the animals appear to be giving birth to the human forms. In the serene bronze sculpture *Sound* of 1984, a head rests against the earth, a large tree growing from one side of its face. *The Lairs of Naples* of 1983 (pl. 118; cat. no. 132) offers a poignant summation of Paladino's attitude. A knotted tree limb is both snake and cryptic symbol, hovering above a puzzle of humanoid forms performing an allegory of our latent roots in nature. In the upper left corner of the picture, a figure caresses an embryonic animal, the human form echoing that of the animal; at the lower left, a flaming yellow tree grows from the head of another figure; and in yet another scene, at the upper right, a figure fits its head perfectly between the branches of a tree.

Paladino's art is perhaps not so much reflective of death as it is a meditation on the spiritual value of the common plane of energy humanity shares with nature, a place where both grow and die in a kind of intertwined orphic dream. In a recent letter the artist wrote about the role of nature in his work:

> I am interested in the contamination between nature and museum as a symbiosis of living metaphor. Nature is a flash, it is a meditative silence, where everything finds its own place. Animals wear wisdom; thoughts become actions inside men. Everyday the artist gets dangerously closer to the mystery.[22]

Enzo Cucchi is similarly driven by a passionate desire to regress to a primal state—as he put it, to an "earlier, much earlier" state of being.[23] In *Sacrificing Painting* of 1982, a primitive being silhouetted by a white aura emanating from his fist grasps a blood-red tree with his other hand, suggesting a prehistoric ritual or sacrifice to nature. Other Cucchi paintings depict lumbering, monkeylike creatures moving across stark primordial landscapes. Cucchi associates the strength and cunning required as a painter with the attributes of animals: "I'm a hawk—I'm like a tiger."[24]

In much of Cucchi's work, landscape and nature take on a monumental, at times apocalyptic, presence. In the early painting *Picture in the Dark by the Sea* of 1980, a delicate red line evokes a ship floating on a deep, black sea. Below the water a man swims in a passionate red pool. Such visionary landscapes in bright, animated color eventually developed into dark, eruptive images. A fiery untitled landscape of 1986 (pl. 113; cat. no. 39) depicts a primordial condition, reminiscent of the craggy and haunting abstractions of Clyfford Still. In this case, a bloody, rootlike configuration erupts in the center of the picture, giving birth to an immense sun or eyeball. Craggy flashes of light penetrate what might be the surface of the earth, which conceals a vast plane of skulls. The primordial character of such pictures is echoed in Cucchi's remark, "The pictures are like caves, like huge caves, full of fears, full of doubts and dark for all of us. All caves are full of fear, full of death, but out of this very death comes the possibility of inventing everything once again."[25]

Much has been said about the role of Cucchi's environment as a catalyst for his imagery. The artist has lived and worked in the port city of Ancona on the Adriatic Sea. The sea and the land in this area, known as the Marches, are the inspiration for many of Cucchi's paintings. His use of fire has been related to the local harvest celebrations of burning the fields to clear them for the next year.[26] While such a scene may indeed have been an initial inspiration, Cucchi's images carry a more ominous message.

Natural crisis and apocalypse thread through much of the artist's later work, presenting us with a visual word of warning. In the later paintings elegance is buried beneath aggressive earthen surfaces that resemble living chunks of the planet's surface. These immense formations often suggest ferocious movement, as though the earth's crust were heaving itself apart. Cucchi's turbulent and molten landscapes shake our belief in the benign and passive character of terrestrial matter. In one of Cucchi's most moving works, *A Painting of Precious Fires* of 1983 (pl. 112; cat. no. 38), the earth's pores spit geysers of fire into the air. This is a landscape of revenge, a landscape foreclosing on civilization's brief mortgage.

Cucchi's images are often grounded in reality. In *The Houses Are Going Downhill* of 1983, huge buildings slide into the foreground of the painting on a red-hot molten landscape. The year before Cucchi made the work, the area near the artist's studio experienced a traumatic earthquake and landslide (November 1982). Cucchi was struck by the event and its implications, remarking,

> I would have liked to have seen it. The animals must have heard the rumbling and they fled, but all the people could do was watch everything collapse. The landslide was caused primarily by the weight of excess building. But the disaster itself does not interest me; what does preoccupy me is how the earth's energy comes to the surface, how it becomes visible.[27]

Geldzahler described this landscape as

> the Earth as Goddess, mother of mankind; it is in her body that our bounty matures; the crops are planted, nurtured, cultivated, and harvested only with her intercession. The two extended wings (the buildings) double as the legs of the Goddess, the opening between them barely able to contain her blood-red essence.[28]

Cucchi's imagery is not solely a meditation on the apocalyptic capabilities of nature. Indeed, many of the artist's works suggest a longing for a unification with nature, for a reconciliation with the earth. In an undated drawing, a human head — the artist's emblematic, elongated self-portrait — gently caresses the earth, resting on the rolling topography. In other works petrified skulls are buried with charred tree fragments, a reminder that all living things finally rest under a blanket of earth, part of the same field of cosmic debris. Such images point to an ultimate truth: in every part of every living thing is the stuff that once was rock; certain minerals are common to both blood and rock. Indeed, Cucchi has compared his continued astonishment with the creative image to his amazement at the site of a mountain of earth:

> if anything there's the astonishment of that image. It's like looking at a mountain. A mountain's really boring because it is static and always the same, but it's also incredible because of what it contains, and that creates a state of astonishment in you. When you see this mountain, it could be a problem of realism — you ask yourself if you should describe it or if the inner problem is more important. I believe that the inner problem is what matters, because what you see has already gone, and it's not so important to describe it — but there's a lot of painting that does just that.[29]

Cucchi's imagery and his attitude toward the creative image reflect his quest for a primordial spirit akin to that of primitive art. For Cucchi, primitive art represents an "elevation of spirit. From the subterranean to the heights of revelation. It is not strange at all that I should like that type of art. It is pervaded with spirit."[30]

Of all the Italians, Francesco Clemente is perhaps the most elusive, jittery, and strangely provocative in his development. Encountering a Clemente exhibition is often a curiously anxious and liberating experience. His lexicon of images, or ideograms, as he has referred to them,[31] has revealed itself in cumulative bursts over the past decade, often inspired by the artist's itinerant behavior. Movement and dislocation are fundamental creative forces for Clemente and have become a way of life. Accompanied by his wife and two children, he has established an essentially nomadic existence by deliberately changing geographic and cultural perspective with an almost disciplined regularity. He maintains "home bases" on three continents: an apartment in Rome, a house in Madras, India, and a studio in New York. This peripatetic existence undoubtedly feeds Clemente's continuously changing imagery, which often focuses on nature as a means of pivoting between Eastern and Western cultures.

As it is for his colleagues, drawing is the seed of Clemente's imagery. Indeed, between 1970 and 1979, Clemente's graphic production consisted almost entirely of drawings. Spread out on the floor or neatly set in catalogued piles around Clemente's various studios, these drawings constitute an intense mental odyssey, exploring various pictographic signs, venting emotions, and puzzling over philosophical enigmas. For Clemente, drawing is equivalent to thinking, and both are centered upon the fluid experience of an elusive, primal self. In these hundreds, if not thousands, of early drawings, the artist carefully and deliberately coaxed forth the parameters and thematic sequences of his art. Three broad themes surface in these graphic explorations: a dramatically intimate, at times perverse, articulation of the human body and its organic-sexual impulses; an interest in identifying the human body with basic animal instincts and physical attributes; and an empathetic desire to integrate this animal/ primitive self with nature in a broad sense.

A large, untitled drawing of 1981 summarizes many of these themes. Male/female and animal/human forms perform a bizarre pictographic orgy in a graphic style suggestive of cave painting. Each

Figure 2. Francesco Clemente, *Self-Portrait with Bird*,
1980. Oil on canvas, 15¾ x 11¾ in. (40 x 30 cm).
Collection Anne and Ron Pizzutti.

protuberance and opening on the forms appears to suggest a primitive, psychological portal, an instinctual means of tapping the essence of being. The cuts of Fontana and the "bleeding wounds" of Burri find a unique sensual extension in the orifices in Clemente's imagery. Indeed, the body in all its primal magnificence and strange folds is the source of much of the artist's imagery. Clemente has said, "The source of an idea is in the body not in the idea."[52]

A significant turning point in Clemente's art occurred in 1979 with a series of powerful, full-size self-portraits on paper. Executed on a wall in his Rome studio, these anamorphic portrayals were developed as the artist's mind saw himself, without the use of a mirror. The result is a bizarre series of visionary self-critiques, in which the artist attempts to locate himself outside of culture in a larger, natural condition. *Self-Portrait: the First* of 1979 depicts a naked Clemente staring out apprehensively at the viewer, shrouded by groups of birds who crowd and snuggle his neck and face. The image begs a

comparison with Goya's *The Sleep of Reason Creates Monsters* of 1799, in which menacing black birds circle around a man sleeping at his desk. Clemente's birds—also symbols of thought and imagination—are less ominous. They gravitate to Clemente's body as if for warmth and companionship. The artist stands motionless, not sure whether they are the black birds that steal the soul—seen in one of Kounellis's surreal tableaux—or soaring spirits symbolic of angels.

Animals play a central role throughout Clemente's imagery. Seldom depicted as strictly good or evil, they represent a kind of pure or fundamental psyche that provides an analogue to the artist's unbridled exploration of the self. In the strange *Self-Portrait with Bird* of 1980 (fig. 2), Clemente is shown chest-to-

172

chest and mouth-to-beak with a large bird, suggesting that the animal is feeding the young artist. In an untitled painting of 1983, Clemente bows to greet a stag. Having no horns with which to flaunt his power, he uses a crucifix, the symbol of power in his world.

In later paintings, drawings, and frescoes, the artist virtually transforms himself into various animals. As in many of Chia's and Paladino's paintings, Clemente has abandoned himself to his animal side. One of the most powerful representations of this theme is an untitled painting of 1983 (pl. 104; cat. no. 22), in which we see Clemente's boyishly transcendent features give themselves over to canine ears and a snoutlike nose. Clemente ascends to the image of a wolf. In the pastel *Caduceus* of 1981, a human torso has grown a tail, which is interwoven with the tail of a rat. We are confronted with the coupling of one of the highest forms of nature and one of the lowest. The caduceus is familiar to most of us as a symbol of healing, usually depicted as snakes wrapped around a staff. In a hauntingly beautiful painting entitled *Unborn* of 1983, the artist is seen placidly asleep inside the body of a caged lion, presenting us with the flip side of the cliché that there exists a "beast" in man that should be contained. Indeed, it is inside this animal that the artist is most at peace.

In a recent series of pastels entitled *The Celtic Bestiary* of 1984 (pls. 120–27; cat no. 23), Clemente's free-associational imagery travels through a series of perplexing fantasies in which animals take center stage: the artist's head explodes into a constellation of primitive, insectlike forms; a fish sprouts a Clemente face; and in another image a small rodent rubs its back on Clemente's cheek. Such images hark back to a comment Clemente made a few years ago: "My self-portraits are not about how I look, but the way I see. It's a dynamic view that incorporates animals and nature, and many other things. I don't look at nature, but I try to have empathy with it. A tree, a rat, a bird—they are part of my imagination. Naturally I see them when I do a self-portrait."[33]

During one of Clemente's many stays in India, he created a series of miniatures (see fig. 3) by supervising a group of young boys trained in traditional miniature techniques who painted images developed by Clemente. These miniatures would seem to fall into the category of what in the Hindu religion are called the Nine Rasas. Roughly translated, *rasa* means sentiment or flavor; the nine are the erotic, comic, pathetic, furious, heroic, frightful, odious, wondrous, and quiescent. Clemente's series seems to touch on all of these; man, animal, and nature are juxtaposed in various ways. In the lower register of one of the pictures, a naked man is seated on a Persian rug. In the upper register, hierarchically more important, we see the same man naked in nature, though he has sprouted a tail. Clemente has remarked, "For me this is a key image. The civilized man against the animal. The animal has the advantage, the higher position.... Without the theater of logic, we should all be animals."[34]

In certain instances, Clemente has imagined a direct fusion with the earth and that which it nourishes. In the large, delicate, and spacious drawing *Self-Portrait as a Garden* of 1979, the artist saw himself not only within a garden but as the garden itself. Delicate, pencil-drawn foliage frames a meditative, "empty" space in the center of the drawing, the space Clemente presumably inhabits but in which he is not depicted. Indeed, this is one of the rare works in which Clemente's characteristic face does not play a part. Clemente has said that *Self-Portrait as a Garden* "was an attempt to draw the garden from the

garden's point of view.... In painting there can be no separation between nature and the painter."[35] Indeed, it is in this void that one finds the ultimate fusion between the self and nature.

In a telling portrait of the artist taken by the photographer Robert Mapplethorpe (fig. 4), Clemente quite literally presents himself as a tree. He stands in front of a 1985 painting of a huge tree that mysteriously produces fruits that glow like lanterns. Clemente mimics the stature of the tree as if he were its counterpart, if not offspring, as suggested by the painting's title, *Son*.

If we can think of Cucchi as evoking Clyfford Still, Clemente recalls Willem de Kooning. His facility, draftsmanship, and the libidinous quality of his imagery project a raw energy very much akin to de Kooning's figurative works and late landscapes. Indeed, as the sexual energy de Kooning imbued in the female form, particularly in his emphasis on the mouth, eventually exploded into rich, gluttonous landscapes, so Clemente's imagery might be thought of in post-Freudian, pastoral terms. In many ways, Clemente summarizes and intensifies the Arte Povera notion of the nomadic primitive, through an intense psychological identification with animals and nature. Even within Clemente's psychological trafficking between the sexes, there is a search for a fundamental, indivisible self. On the cover of the book *Francesco Clemente*—designed throughout by the artist—we see a male and female body intertwined and held by a ruby-red knot.[36] The knot, often used to symbolize Arte Povera, is a symbol of passion and androgyny—the psyche or human nature in perhaps its most complete and ancient form.

Postwar Italian art is paradigmatic of an age that opened with committed faith in the promises of scientific salvation and that is ending with the anticlimax of a worldwide bureaucracy and nuclear stalemate. In light of this, these artists articulate one of the most basic facts of human existence: we are human animals, part of the natural world, and yet have for most of our history been engaged in a struggle with nature.

One of the characteristics of twentieth-century art is its linking of "primitive" consciousness and the creative act. It is through this primitive consciousness, what John Graham referred to as the "source and storehouse of power and of all knowledge, past and future,"[37] that artistic notions of taste and style are imbued with communicative power. It is thought that in the end this primitive self is the key to a transcendent union with nature. Finding a portal to that self has been a primary subject of postwar Italian art.

1. Germano Celant, "From the Open Wound to the Resurrected Body, Lucio Fontana and Piero Manzoni," in *Italian Art in the 20th Century* (Munich, 1989), p. 296.

2. Ibid., p. 299.

3. Germano Celant, *Arte Povera* (New York, 1964), pp. 225-30.

4. Jackson Pollock once said to Lee Krasner and Hans Hofmann, "I am nature" (Michael Cannell, "An Interview with Lee Krasner," *Arts Magazine*, Sept. 1984, pp. 87–89).

5. The artist in conversation with the author, Berkeley, California, Jan. 15, 1980, on the occasion of his exhibition "Michelangelo Pistoletto: Matrix/Berkeley."

6. Susan Krane, in Albright-Knox Art Gallery, Buffalo, 1984, *Mario Merz: Paintings and Constructions*, p. 6.

7. In conversation with the author, Turin, Apr. 12, 1986, in response to a question about the meaning of the Albright-Knox painting *Tamburino*, which includes the image of a large chicken.

8. Kathan Brown, *Italians and American Italians* (Oakland, CA, 1981), n. pag.

9. Museum of Contemporary Art, Chicago, 1986, *Kounellis*, p. 78.

10. Caroline Tisdall, "Materia: The Context of Arte Povera," in *Italian Art* (note 1), p. 386.

11. Achille Bonito Oliva, *The Italian Trans-Avantgarde* (Milan, 1980), pp. 11, 18.

12. Giancarlo Politi, "Francesco Clemente," *Flash Art* 117 (Apr.–May 1984), p. 17.

13. In conversation with the author, New York, Apr. 12, 1989.

14. Ibid.

15. Letter from Sandro Chia to Edy de Wilde, Feb. 20, 1983, in Stedelijk Museum, Amsterdam, 1983, *Sandro Chia*, n. pag.

16. In conversation with the author, New York, Apr. 12, 1989.

17. Ibid.

18. Ibid.

19. Ibid.

20. Ibid.

21. Henry Geldzahler, in The Renaissance Society, The University of Chicago, 1984, *Contemporary Italian Masters*, p. 6.

22. Letter from the artist to the author, Apr. 11, 1989.

23. Lewis Kachur, "Enzo Cucchi," *Arts Magazine* 55, 8 (Apr. 1981), p. 13.

24. Giancarlo Politi and Helen Kontova, "An Interview with Enzo Cucchi," *Flash Art* 114 (Nov. 1983), p. 14.

25. The Fruitmarket Gallery, Edinburgh, 1987, *Enzo Cucchi: Testa*, n. pag.

26. Marja Bloem, "An Afternoon with E. C.," *Parkett* 1 (1984), p. 62.

27. Ibid.

28. Geldzahler (note 21), p. 8.

29. Politi and Kontova (note 24), p. 13.

30. Danny Berger, "Enzo Cucchi: An Interview," *Print Collector's Newsletter* 13, 4 (Sept.–Oct. 1982), p. 120.

31. Robin White, "Francesco Clemente," *View* 3, 6 (Nov. 1981), p. 26.

32. In conversation with the author, New York, May 11–12, 1984.

33. Ibid.

34. In conversation with the author, New York, May 11–12, 1984.

35. Ibid.

36. Michael Auping, *Francesco Clemente* (New York, 1985).

37. John Graham, "Primitive Art and Picasso," *Magazine of Art* 30 (Apr. 1937), p. 237.

Plate 100. *Malinconico Accampamento (Melancholic Encampment)*, 1982
      Oil on canvas
      114⅛ x 159 in. (290 x 404 cm)
      Cat. no. 18

Plate 101. *Untitled*, c. 1978
            Gouache, oil, and pencil on paper on canvas
            67 x 75 in. (170 x 190 cm)
            Cat. no. 19

Plate 102. *The Midnight Sun I*, 1982
Oil on canvas
79 x 98½ in. (170 x 250 cm)
Cat. no. 20

Plate 103. *Analogy*, 1983
Fresco on radiator part
34 x 17 x 3¼ in. (86 x 43 x 8 cm)
Cat. no. 21

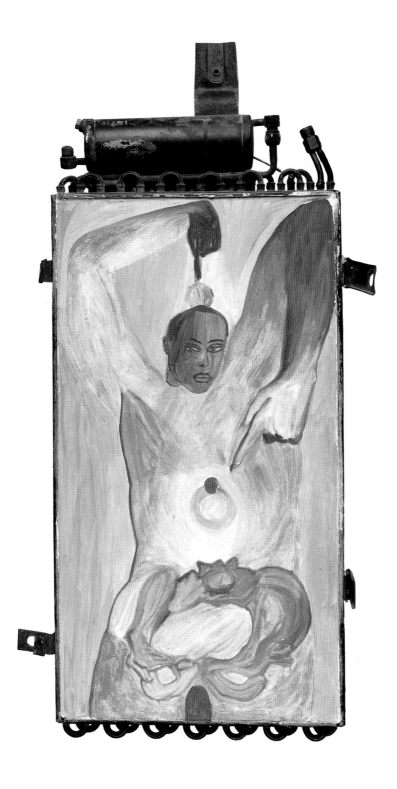

Plate 104. *Untitled*, 1983
Oil on canvas
78 x 93 in. (198 x 236 cm)
Cat. no. 22

Plate 105. *The Departure of the Argonaut*, 1985
Artist's book with text by Alberto Savinio
Forty-eight color lithographs, each 26 x 39 in. (66 x 99 cm)
Published by Petersburg Press, New York and London
Cat. no. 24

Plate 106. *Boat*, 1987
Oil on canvas
76 x 184 in. (193 x 467 cm)
Cat. no. 25

Plate 107. *The Vocali (A E I O U) A = Eat,* 1989
       Oil on linen
       47 x 55 in. (119 x 140 cm)
       Cat. no. 26

Plate 108. *The Vocali (A E I O U) E = Love*, 1989
    Oil on linen
    47 x 55 in. (119 x 140 cm)
    Cat. no. 27

FRANCESCO CLEMENTE

Plate 109. *The Vocali (A E I O U) I = Die*, 1989
Oil on linen
47 x 55 in. (119 x 140 cm)
Cat. no. 28

186

Plate 110. *The Vocali (A E I O U) O = Sleep*, 1989
Oil on linen
47 x 55 in. (119 x 140 cm)
Cat. no. 29

Plate 111. *The Vocali (A E I O U) U = Remember*, 1989
        Oil on linen
        47 x 55 in. (119 x 140 cm)
        Cat. no. 30

Plate 112. *Un quadro di fuochi preziosi (A Painting of Precious Fires)*, 1983
   Oil on canvas with neon
   117½ x 153½ in. (298 x 390 cm)
   Cat. no. 38

ENZO CUCCHI

Plate 113. *Untitled*, 1986
Oil, sheet metal, and iron on canvas
119 x 153½ in. (302 x 390 cm)
Cat. no. 39

190

Plate 114. *Untitled*, 1983
Wood and steel
66 x 95½ x 8 in. (167 x 243 x 20 cm)
Cat. no. 77

Plate 115. *Untitled*, 1988
    Steel, wood, coal, and burlap
    Two parts, overall 89 x 160 x 17 in. (226 x 406 x 43 cm)
    Cat. no. 78

Plate 116. *Igloo*, 1984–85
    Plate glass, steel, netting, neon, Plexiglas, and wax
    39¼ x 98¼ x 118¼ in. (100 x 250 x 300 cm)
    Cat. no. 98

Plate 117. *Allegoria (Allegory)*, 1983
Bronze with gold mosaic
77 x 30 x 4½ in. (196 x 76 x 11 cm)
Cat. no. 131

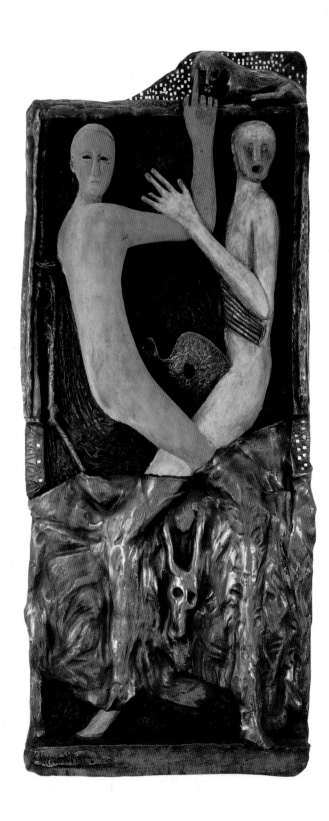

Plate 118. *Le Tane di Napoli (The Lairs of Naples)*, 1983
Oil on canvas and wood collage
107¼ x 83¼ in. (272 x 211 cm)
Cat. no. 132

Plate 119. *Untitled*, 1985
   Oil and metal on limestone
   47 x 20½ x 17¼ in. (119 x 52 x 44 cm)
   Cat. no. 133

Francesco Clemente's *Celtic Bestiary*

DOUGLAS W. DRUICK

The Celtic Bestiary (pls. 120–27; cat. no. 23) is one of many discrete cycles that Francesco Clemente has made in different media since the late 1970s.[1] These are a critical aspect of his production. The artist favors working in cycles because he likes the idea of "starting from the beginning and working my way through a technique or a process"; he views each medium as a "conventional frame" within which "to try out all its possibilities and even go beyond."[2] This idea of "working through" informs Clemente's expressed preference for calling such groups of works not cycles but rather "collections," an appellation that better reflects his avowed ambition that each collection "should be like the whole work of the artist." Despite this "obsession to create as complete a panorama as possible," Clemente has acknowledged that when working within the different frames of different techniques, he will necessarily create "collections of work that contradict each other"; the "different frame and different conventions" will naturally lead him to new ideas and "a new constellation of images." Clemente's contradiction indeed extends further. He has conceded that his attraction to the idea of a collection is rivaled by his interest in that of a fragment—"the idea that the work always refers to another work that can't be seen but that exists or will exist." His desire to make collections is counterbalanced by the wish that, once completed, the collection "would be scattered round the world and everyone would just see a fragment."[3]

Such fragmentation has not been the fate of *The Celtic Bestiary*, which remains intact in the Gerald S. Elliott Collection. Like all the artist's "collections," it is necessarily fragmentary insofar as it refers to earlier and later work. Nevertheless, when *The Celtic Bestiary* is considered in the context of the lengthy interviews given by Clemente both before and after its creation, this particular collection can be seen to offer a remarkably complete picture of the artist's ambitions and strategies.

In these interviews, Clemente has revealed the same apparently contradictory impulses reflected in his attitude towards his collections. Just as he wishes to create a whole picture and yet have it experienced only in fragments, so in discussing his art he has evidenced the similarly opposing desires to reveal and to conceal, to complete the picture of his art and to fragment it. On the one hand, Clemente has displayed a readiness to assist the interviewer—and his audience—in understanding his art. He has clearly addressed his view of the artist's role, his ideas regarding his use of title, medium, imagery, and formal devices, and his highly personal sense of place in both geographic and historic dimensions. On the other hand, Clemente believes of his art, "if I speak of it, it's like a prophet. It doesn't work."[4] This leads him to "want an obscurity to hang over the meaning of the work"—to view his "main job" as artist and interviewee as "really to forget," to fail to understand his own work.⁵ To do so protects what Clemente calls the "magic, that is, the instants in which the work says something that the painter didn't know, that the audience didn't expect to find." Perhaps his most succinct expression of concern for the safekeeping of the mystery of his art is his metaphor of the safe and the key: "I made a safe; I invented the safe, and I lost the key. And losing the key makes the work, gives the work this autonomy. It cannot be reduced. It cannot be brought back to its original elements. That makes it objectively poetical." In these two acts of inventing and forgetting, Clemente invokes the rational and the irrational; he acknowledges that "both Dionysus and Apollo are present when I work."⁶

This movement between seeming polarities, this oscillation between the rational and the irrational, is at the heart of Clemente's artistic enterprise; it is the key to understanding both the artist and his art. His nomadic personal life echoes his desire as artist to "move all the time," to "travel through mythology" and through cultures, to create works that "run through iconography" and in which "images...are moving."⁷ The artist's ultimate goal is to achieve an active balance between seeming opposites and to create works that are "crossing points for images." To achieve this he believes he must "invent a territory *in between*"—one that is "without enemies" insofar as it does not "belong to any known taste or device."⁸ In its many facets, *The Celtic Bestiary* represents this "in between" territory.

Clemente specially created this collection of eight pastels in response to an invitation from the Arts Council of Northern Ireland to exhibit in Belfast in 1984. *The Celtic Bestiary* was featured in the exhibition "Francesco Clemente in Belfast," which included examples of his work to date in a variety of media.⁹ Given these circumstances, one might assume the title of the collection—actually made in New York—simply acknowledges the ancient culture of the country for which it was made, were Clemente's complex strategies regarding titles not amply documented. He is keenly aware that "meanings are...the way the world wants to come to terms with the work" and that titles are seized upon as keys to unlock meaning. Since it is Clemente's position that "the work doesn't want to come to terms with the world," he devises titles that resist such use, that "smile to the critic and...all his nice notions." A notable case in point is the provocatively titled etching *Not St. Girolamo* of 1981. Responding to a question regarding the work's meaning, Clemente said, "I am not supposed to understand that drawing, given what I said [about the safe and the key]."¹⁰ His title echoes this resistance: "The title is *Not St. Girolamo*, so that's not St. Girolamo. So no interpretation—just the easiest title to give to a drawing where there is a lion and a man." Typically, Clemente retreated from this abrupt foreclosure and added: "It is St. Girolamo and it's not."¹¹ He later expanded on this qualification: "to say *Not St. Girolamo* is to point out that there is an opposite to that...the moment you give up all these notions [of using meaning to come to terms with the work]...one or the opposite is just the same." Thus Clemente conceded that the title does function as a key—not to unlock and fix the meaning of the work, but to suggest how to approach it on its terms. "In the case of...*Not St. Girolamo*, you don't try to focus; you are wandering. The images are results not of...focusing on a good idea, but of wandering from one idea to another without giving more weight to one or the other.... The title is part of this wandering from meaning to meaning and then from image to image."¹² Clemente's interest in working in cycles, or collections, is related to this idea of "wandering." A similar strategy of using titles

Douglas W. Druick

Figure 1. Celtic, escutcheon on hanging bowl from a ship burial at Miklebostad, Norway, variously dated c. 675 A.D. and ninth century A.D. Bronze with enamel and mille-fiori glasswork, h. approx. 3 in. (8 cm). Historisk Museum, Universitetet I Bergen, Norway.

to direct the viewer, to keep him "in between" and moving, informs *The Celtic Bestiary*, a collection whose title was critical to its genesis.

Clemente has stated that when working on a painting or a collection of works, "the title is always the last thing to come along," since he wishes to "condition" the work as little as possible. Yet he has also admitted that giving a title is "one of the steps one goes through in the making of a work," and that while this does not necessarily come at the beginning or end of the work, it occasionally corresponds with a project's starting point.[13] Evidence suggests this was the case with *The Celtic Bestiary*.

Despite the caution with which we must approach his titles, there is no doubt that Clemente was thinking of Celtic art when working on this collection. The clearest evidence of this is found in the eighth and final pastel in the collection. In *The Celtic Bestiary VIII* (pl. 127), the image of the artist's head surmounting a rectangular field of geometric design shows the influence of a much-reproduced,

199

Figure 2. Celtic, Ahenny north stone cross, c. 750 A.D.
    Ahenny, County Tipperary, Ireland.

Figure 2. Celtic, Ahenny north stone cross, c. 750 A.D.
    Ahenny, County Tipperary, Ireland.

ninth-century hanging bowl handle (fig. 1). The geometric pattern Clemente incorporated can also be related to the decorative designs found in Celtic stone work, like the eighth-century Ahenny north stone cross (fig. 2). Moreover, the device of symmetrical stylized beasts flanking the head recalls the decorations on the famous Gundestrup silver ritual cauldron (fig. 3), while the markings on the lizardlike creatures echo those found in Celtic enamel work, such as the celebrated purse from the ship burial at Sutton Hoo, England. However, while other works in the collection invoke Celtic visual sources, the more pervasive influence in *The Celtic Bestiary* is the Celtic mystical tradition itself.

The Celts regarded the human head as the seat of the soul and supreme source of spiritual power.[14] They also believed in both the sacred nature and the power of animals; they identified them with the ancestral spirit and their shamans used them in rituals of a psycho-sexual nature. There are correspondences between the mystical beliefs of the Celts and those of the Hindus—between Celtic Druidism and Hindu Brahmanism.[15] Given Clemente's long-standing interest in the mystical tradition of India, his attraction to that of the Celts is not surprising. Some of the broad themes evident in his prior

Figure 3. Celtic, ritual cauldron (Gundestrup cauldron)
from Gundestrup, Raevemosen, Aars, Denmark,
late second to early first century B.C. Silver,
h. 16½ in. (42 cm); dia. 26⅛ in. (69 cm).
Nationalmuseet, Copenhagen.

work anticipate those of *The Celtic Bestiary*: his interest in the human head and body, in exploring man's basic biologic and sexual impulses, in identifying man with his animal nature, and in seeking to restore man's primal integration with nature. While there is a correspondence between these interests and Indian mystical tradition, Clemente's expression of them in *The Celtic Bestiary* clearly draws on the mystic tradition of the Celts.

The thematic structure (as the title implies) is that of the bestiary, the medieval illustrated treatise on animals, their powers and human traits, that depended as heavily on fiction and folklore as on fact. The tradition of the bestiary can be traced back to the second century. The form achieved full development only in the twelfth century, and thereafter enjoyed great popularity for two hundred years. But while the temporal distance separating the present from both Celtic culture and the tradition of the bestiary would seem to lend plausibility to the concept of a Celtic bestiary, it is in fact oxymoronic: the two traditions did not overlap and while Celtic illuminated manuscripts are filled with animals, they include no bestiaries. Thus Clemente's *Celtic Bestiary* can be seen to fall "in between"—and to bridge — these two historically exclusive traditions. Influenced by each but fixed by neither, it creates a new territory.

This act of bridging different realities is, in fact, central to Clemente's experience of making art: "When I'm inside the work … it really seems that it's something that flows. I feel like I'm a messenger between two worlds."[16] As such, he sees himself as performing a shamanistic function akin to that of the Celtic Druids, who believed that the physical, spiritual, and imaginative worlds interpenetrated each other, and who sought access to the otherworld through ritualistically induced trances.[17] Clemente's imagery in *The Celtic Bestiary* underscores this shamanistic identification.

Several of the images in this collection conjoin man and animal in ways that allude to shamanistic belief and imply Clemente's role as artist-shaman. Since the Celts believed animals possess transcendental powers enabling them to communicate with the otherworld, the shamans sought to identify with them and thus to tap their latent powers. Friendship with animals, knowledge of their language, and transformation into an animal nature were signs that the shaman had reestablished the paradisal state lost at the dawn of time. In rituals involving animals, the shaman entered a trance in which past and present, psychic and physical realities merged; he could bridge the gulf separating man and animal, visit the spirit realm, and there negotiate on behalf of his fellows with its largely animal inhabitants.[18] In *The Celtic Bestiary I* (pl. 120), Clemente suggested this identification between shaman and animal, as well as between himself and shaman. Physically linking the image of his own head with the rodent that appears to have emerged from his mouth, the artist implies the symbolic identification between his spiritual power and that of the animal whose ability to burrow gave it, in Celtic belief, special access to the center of the world and its spiritual energy. Another ferreting creature appears in *The Celtic Bestiary III* (pl. 122), positioned on a background with scratch patterns that recall Celtic pictographs on stone and near eight circular, stonelike forms each bearing three markings. Not only did the number three have magical and religious connotations for the Celts, but the disposition of the three marks here gives each circular form the appearance of a disembodied head, as mute as the beady-eyed creature.[19] It is the shaman who must tap their latent magic.

A still closer identification between man and animal nature, between Clemente and shaman, is found in *The Celtic Bestiary VI* (pl. 125): the image of Clemente partially metamorphosed into a fish recalls the shape-shifting by man into his animal transformation that was featured in both Celtic tales and ritual. This particular metamorphosis is significant since the fish was another creature the Celts regarded as naturally equipped to communicate with the powers at the earth's center. In this composition the egglike shape evident in the background of *The Celtic Bestiary I* takes on more definite form, encompassing the changeling and suggesting the moment of conception. For Clemente, this would symbolize the dawning of that prenatal intelligence we begin to lose at birth — that superior "intelligence as an experience of integrity and unity"[20] which life erodes and which the shaman seeks to rediscover. A similar egglike form appears again in *The Celtic Bestiary II* (pl. 121), where the rabbit surmounting the copulating couple ensures its symbolic association with fertility; but here it seems to hover in an ocher void like a foreign moon whose cycles govern — and so unite — both man and beast, as they were sexually and symbolically reunited in Celtic rituals.[21]

The conception of the shaman's spirit flight to the otherworld involves, in many cultures, the shedding of the flesh. The reduction to the state of a skeleton becomes the symbol of the stripping away of illusion and deliverance from the human condition, of transcendence and mystical rebirth.[22] The presence of the skeletal stick figure standing in the background of *The Celtic Bestiary I* seems to function as a symbol of this state and thus reinforces the reading of the conjunction of man and animal as an image of transcendence. Similarly *The Celtic Bestiary IV* (pl. 123) lends itself to being read in terms of the shamanistic shedding of the flesh. Clemente has depicted his bloated, transparent body as transfixed by an amorphous skeletal form related to both the skeleton in *The Celtic Bestiary I* and the loops it appears to hold; while the body seems to fall, the skeletal form ascends. The allusion to the process of transcendence is underscored by the image of the presiding bird, the animal the Celts regarded as the manifestation of the soul as it leaves the body.

While these compositions lend themselves to the above readings, Clemente has associated individual images in such a way as to resist the imposition of a strictly sequential, narrative exposition. Rather, he has fulfilled his wish to create an "all-poetical" visual language analogous to that found in the poetry of Ezra Pound and in Chinese ideographs. Clemente wants each composition to function ideographically as a "field of relations that makes reference to another field of relations without resorting to direct allusion." In this field, "each element cannot be reduced" and is intended not to be "seen by itself but only in a chain of meaning" that is "ever shifting" as it invites different associations. Unexpected juxtapositions and fragmentation of forms are the devices he employs to make pictorial space into "force fields like those diagrams in the crossword section of the paper where you have to connect the dots."[23]

Despite their fluidity, the images in *The Celtic Bestiary* invite poetic association with Celtic mysteries. In so doing, they draw on the artist's use of the body to symbolize "the place between the external world and the inner world," the skin the point of contact between "the space inside and the space outside." Clemente has considered this concept of "a landscape of the world and...an inner landscape" of the imagination to be "one of the most dominant elements" of his work which—like *The Celtic Bestiary*—involves self-portraiture. His avowed interest in the relative "weights these two spaces have" relates to his belief that "the artist's job is to bring back the consciousness that...rational things...and facts and events, are not any more necessary than imaginary things...just more substantial." Part of the shamanistic role Clemente has assumed in *The Celtic Bestiary* is to stimulate the awareness that despite differences in substance or weight, the imaginary world and the rational world are "real to the same degree."[24] He not only has depicted himself as bridging the gap between animal and human nature, but also as bringing together the external and inner worlds. In *The Celtic Bestiary VII* (pl. 126), both worlds merge with the eradication of the boundary separating the crown of the artist's head and the surrounding field. The artist's ability thus to elide the "space inside and the space outside" is also evoked in *The Celtic Bestiary VIII*. Here the rectangular field of patterning simultaneously suggests an x-ray image of the artist's insides—the literal inner space of the body's functionings that Clemente has often represented—and alludes to the mystic center that is symbolized by the similarly patterned geometric field in the Celtic prototype (fig. 1). Moreover, the artist steps through an aperture whose form suggests the holed stones that in ancient rites of initiation and rebirth symbolized the birth passage and were positioned at the entrance to burial chambers.[25] Straddling this entrance, Clemente is the messenger between the two worlds who, with a foot in each, brings them into equilibrium.

The concept of the artist as likewise establishing a balance between the different parts of his work is central to Clemente's thinking. He views all the elements that come to bear on the making of a work of art as having different weights: from the artist's style — "the weight of what you are" — to the relative "lightness" of the civilization in which the artist works and upon which he draws; from the weight that the title exerts by conditioning the creation and reading of a work to that of the mythological and iconographical traditions that inform the imagery.[26] For Clemente, success involves maintaining "the economy of the work" by keeping the "relative value" of the component elements in a state of equilibrium. For this, the artist's choice of medium is also critical. Clemente prescribes: "the heavier the image, the lighter the medium, or the heavier the medium, the lighter the image."[27] Thus Clemente's choice of pastel for *The Celtic Bestiary* is part of his overall strategy to keep "in between" and "moving."

Clemente views the many different media in which he works as having "their given weight within a tradition." Here notions of the relative position a medium occupies within an accepted hierarchical structure and the associations with past example have given each medium its valence. In the face of this tradition, Clemente strives to assert his own territorial claims. He has stated that "there is no hierarchy in [my] work," thereby actively opposing the notion that "you are supposed to make a major statement about your ideas in your big paintings, and you are supposed to take your leisure in your small drawings."[28] For a number of years at the beginning of his career, Clemente contradicted this dictum by concentrating on drawing to the exclusion of painting. Moreover, by choosing to work in pastel long before involving himself with oil paints, he flaunted accepted notions of the relative importance of the different color media.[29]

The attractions pastel holds for Clemente are several. Chief, perhaps, is the special place pastel occupies between drawing and color media insofar as it enables an artist simultaneously to draw and color his image. Moreover, Clemente has spoken of the advantageous portability of pastel and of the fact that it enables him to work with "quickness . . . that means . . . not to get caught by the visual logic which is always conventional logic."[30] By contrast, Clemente experiences oil painting as a "slow process" that "can't be rushed." While he sees that fresco and watercolor are, like pastel, "very, very fast," they demand "lengthy preparation." Because of the physical requirements of the media as well as the fact that they do not readily permit reworking and so disallow mistakes, fresco and watercolor "can't be done on the spur of the moment" and yet they must be "done quickly."[31]

The physically liberating aspects of pastel are enhanced by Clemente's view of the medium as being "lighter, more discreet and open" than oil painting, since it is less encumbered by the weight of past example. Oil painting, for Clemente, is inextricably linked with Italy's "terrifying past" as a power both culturally — its "unique deposit of marvelous paintings" — and commercially — "oil paintings are the paintings of banks." Since "to believe you belong to [this past] is a delusion . . . [and to] ignore it is ingenuous," Clemente sees oil painting as a territory with "enemies." Due to the oppressive weight of this past and its associations, Clemente has confessed, "I had to be far enough away from Italy, as I am in New York, to paint in oils."[32] While for Clemente the burden of historical association weighs less

Figure 4. Odilon Redon, *The Signal Light* (*Le Fanal*),
c. 1895/1900. Pastel, 20 x 14⅛ in. (51 x 36 cm). The
Art Institute of Chicago, gift of Mrs. Rue W. Shaw
and Theodora W. Brown in memory of Anne R.
Winterbotham, 1973.513.

heavily on fresco, it is not unencumbered. He regards fresco as "born from a feeling of communality"
and thus, unlike painting, "exactly at the opposite pole from any sort of hierarchy." Nevertheless, fresco
does have significant associations with Italy's artistic past: with the Pompeian wall paintings to be
found near Clemente's native Naples, and with the Renaissance, the great age of mural painting.[33]

Although pastel is not without its own historical associations and connotations, these have served
Clemente's strategy to "invent a territory *in between*." A relative latecomer to the roster of traditional
media, pastel flourished in the eighteenth century. As a result of the example of proponents such as
Rosalba Carriera and Maurice Quentin de La Tour, pastel became synonymous with a flattering type of
portraiture characterized by grace, delicacy, and soft melting color. In the nineteenth century, this
reputation became stigmatic; pastel came to be considered a fragile medium for fragile talents,
unsuited both constitutionally and aesthetically for producing major, lasting works of art. But it was in
these pejorative associations that, in the 1870s, Edgar Degas recognized the medium's desirable
potential for invention and artistic freedom.[34] Degas capitalized on pastel's association with feminine
beauty and evanescence to lend added pathos to his depictions of the fictive, illusory beauty of the
performer's world on stage. Using the wide range of vivid colors spawned by the new chemical

pigments, Degas successfully captured the strangely unreal spectacle of the commonplace transformed by the intense, distorting lights of the stage. In the ensuing pastel revival, Odilon Redon seized upon the almost hallucinatory intensity that can be achieved using pastel's vivid colors and rich, matte surfaces to depict the visionary inner world of the imagination (see fig. 4).

The work in pastel by these two artists exemplifies Clemente's notions of the "space inside and the space outside," as well as what he referred to as "the two lineages of light" in art: the "secular light" of the "outside" world, and the "light that comes from within." Clemente has revived this tradition of pastel in works such as *The Celtic Bestiary*, which reflect his idea that "the rational picture of the world is also an imagination." His tendency to manipulate pictorial space — to exaggerate perspective and employ quirky points of view — and his use of visual synecdoche can be traced back to Degas. Clearly Clemente's attempt to create a nonnarrative, "all-poetical [visual] language" through the devices of fragmentation and unexpected juxtaposition links him to Redon's pastel production, as do his interest in the mystical and his special fondness for the image of the disembodied head. Nonetheless, the tradition Clemente thus carries forth is not onerous. Few in this century have followed the lead of Degas and Redon; indeed, the primacy Clemente has given to pastel in works like *The Celtic Bestiary* is rivaled only by the careers of these illustrious predecessors. But Clemente has distinguished — and distanced — himself from their practice through his conscious intention to give his work a "political valence." How Clemente incorporates this "absolutely necessary element for an artist" is particularly evident in *The Celtic Bestiary*.[35]

In responding to the invitation to prepare a work for exhibition in Belfast, Clemente could not but be influenced by his abiding dismay that "the whole world is filled with ethnic wars" and his concern that "what that means…no one tries to find out." In conceiving a work for the city that had become synonymous with such conflict, Clemente was guided by his art-political position that his "technique of fragmentation…is a political stand." He has outlined his position:

> All parties are working toward destruction of the earth, the destruction of animal life, the destruction of the diversity of cultures, the destruction of the diversity of sexes, destruction of all diversities. So someone who wants to be political in this direction has to be a dilettante. He can't belong to any group, because all groups are working in the same direction.… All techniques we have been taught, psychoanalytical techniques and so on, are all about making all these pieces into one thing that is under control, which you can hold tight to throughout your life. Maybe one can try the opposite, and just let it go to pieces. So the model of fragmentation might be a strategy for survival, for freedom.[36]

The dislocation of form, the dilettante's borrowing from different artistic and cultural traditions, the shamanistic breaking down of boundaries between realms of experience — all serve Clemente's strategy of fragmentation in *The Celtic Bestiary*. Even in the title of the collection, the artist has sought to get "in between" the overly determined "ethnic" positions that have ensured the continuation of the Irish conflict. For not only is the title a contradiction in traditions, even the term Celtic resists a tidy cultural designation. Defined linguistically, this term includes not only the people of Ireland but also those of the Scottish Hebrides and Highlands, the Isle of Man, Wales, Cornwall, and Brittany. Defined ethnographically, it refers to a people first found in Southwest Germany and Eastern France and who only subsequently spread throughout Europe and to the British Isles. Rather than the celebration of cultural identity the title may initially seem to promise, *The Celtic Bestiary* for Belfast thus becomes, on scrutiny, a subversive model for liberation from destructive nationalism.

The author wishes to thank Jeanne Wyshak, Research Assistant, Department of Prints and Drawings, The Art Institute of Chicago, for her work in the preparation of this text.

1. Clemente's first cycle in pastel was produced in 1979; in oil paints in 1980; in fresco in 1981.

2. Robin White, "Interview with Francesco Clemente," *View* (Oakland, CA) 3, 6 (1981), p. 10; Giancarlo Politi, "Francesco Clemente," *Flash Art* 117 (Apr.–May 1984), p. 14. The quotations by the artist used throughout this text derive from these interviews as well as from Rainer Crone and Georgia Marsh, *An Interview with Francesco Clemente* (New York, 1987). Because of the number of the artist's quotations incorporated into this article and the fact that his views on any subject have often been spliced together from different sources, the footnotes do not follow each citation. When they appear, they refer to the preceding quotations and are listed in the order in which they appear in the text.

3. White (note 2), pp. 10, 17; Politi (note 2), p. 14.

4. White (note 2), p. 19.

5. Politi (note 2), p. 13; Crone and Marsh (note 2), p. 54.

6. Politi (note 2), p. 20; Crone and Marsh (note 2), pp. 42–43; Politi (note 2), p. 16.

7. White (note 2), pp. 9, 7; Politi (note 2), p. 14; White (note 2), p. 23.

8. Crone and Marsh (note 2), pp. 26, 60.

9. Arts Council of Northern Ireland, Belfast, 1984, *Francesco Clemente in Belfast.*

10. Politi (note 2), p 44.

11. White (note 2), p. 25.

12. Crone and Marsh (note 2), pp. 42–44.

13. Politi (note 2), pp. 14, 20; Crone and Marsh (note 2), p. 42; Politi (note 2), p. 20.

14. The Celts were head hunters and their decorative use of real or man-made heads reflects the protective powers they believed resided in the head. See Anne Ross, *Pagan Celtic Britain: Studies in Iconography and Tradition* (London and New York, 1967), p. 124.

15. Ward Rutherford, *Celtic Mythology: The Nature and Influence of Celtic Myth— From Druidism to Arthurian Legend* (Northhamptonshire, England, 1987), pp. 97–98.

16. Politi (note 2), p. 16.

17. John Sharkey, *Celtic Mysteries: The Ancient Religion* (London, 1979), p. 12.

18. Mircea Eliade, *Shamanism: Archaic Techniques of Ecstasy* (Princeton, NJ, 1964), p. 63; Rutherford (note 15), p. 100.

19. Ross (note 14), p. 73.

20. Crone and Marsh (note 2), pp. 37–38.

21. Sharkey (note 17), p. 13.

22. Eliade (note 18), pp. 59, 62–63.

23. Politi (note 2), p. 14; Crone and Marsh (note 2), p. 42; Politi (note 2), p. 16.

24. Crone and Marsh (note 2), pp. 46–47, 61.

25. Sharkey (note 17), fig. 21.

26. Crone and Marsh (note 2), p. 26; Politi (note 2), p. 26; Crone and Marsh (note 2), p. 39; Politi (note 2), pp. 13–14.

27. Crone and Marsh (note 2), p. 42.

28. Ibid., p. 44.

29. Clemente first began to work in pastels in 1973 and in oils in 1980.

30. Crone and Marsh (note 2), p. 48; White (note 2), pp. 26–27.

31. Politi (note 2), pp. 15, 18. For Clemente's discussion of the positive aspects of oil, see ibid., p. 20.

32. Crone and Marsh (note 2), pp. 26, 48, 26, 49.

33. Ibid., pp. 56, 49.

34. Douglas Druick and Peter Zegers, "Scientific Realism: 1873–1881," in The Metropolitan Museum of Art, New York, and The National Gallery of Canada, Ottawa, 1988, *Degas*, pp. 200 ff.

35. Crone and Marsh (note 2), pp. 46, 56, 62, 55.

36. Ibid., pp. 35, 60.

Plates 120–27. *The Celtic Bestiary*, 1984
Pastel on paper
Eight works, each 26 x 19 in. (66 x 48 cm)
Cat. no. 23

Plate 120.

Plate 121.

Plate 122.

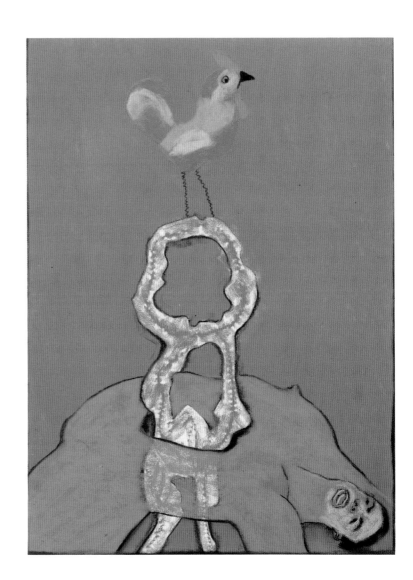

Plate 123.

The Celtic Bestiary, 1984

Plate 124.

Plate 125.

Plate 126.

Plate 127.

The Object on Trial: Contemporary British Sculpture

LYNNE COOKE

In 1972 Anne Seymour organized the exhibition "The New Art" at the Hayward Gallery, London. In her introduction to the catalogue, she described her intention to present work that "recently extended the historical continuum of art a little further. Land Art, Conceptual Art, Art Povera [sic], Process Art are some of the labels which have been allotted to parts of it....[It is] basically work which does not necessarily presuppose the traditional categories of painting and sculpture."[1] The raison d'être for the exhibition lay in the limited exposure much of this work had had at home, though part of an international manifestation and already widely known through exhibitions abroad. Seymour argued, "there has certainly been no real acceptance in this country of the fact that art may never be the same again since the artists, British and foreign, who showed in these exhibitions appeared on the scene." Because the roster included artists working with film, text, the earth's surface, and their own bodies, as well as with found objects, it seemed reasonable to suppose that new categories of art-making had indeed been established.

"Starlit Waters" was the title of the exhibition that, some fifteen years later, marked the inauguration of the Tate Gallery Liverpool.[2] Subtitled "British Sculpture, An International Art 1968–1988," it placed the focus of recent British achievement securely in the realm of that art form. By including Art & Language, Michael Craig-Martin, Barry Flanagan, Hamish Fulton, Richard Long, and Bruce McLean among the older generation of artists,[3] it seemed, at least by implication, to reverse the previous claims made for their early work when it was shown in "The New Art": now it was considered to be part of sculpture's history. The new categories that Seymour had seen heralding a situation in which "art would never be the same again" appeared to have been swept aside: sculpture had been firmly reinstated in a premium position. Works that once had been thought to be beyond the traditional categories of painting and sculpture were, with hindsight, supposed to lie clearly within them.

The designation of sculpture given to the work of all those participants of "The New Art" subsequently included in "Starlit Waters" was not a casual or incidental act. It cannot be accounted for simply in terms of a shift in terminology, as a matter of semantics. Nor is it a question of historical reinterpretation of the kind that occurred, for example, with Marcel Duchamp's *Bottle Rack*, which began as the vehicle of a Dadaist gesture and later became a revered icon in the history of modern sculpture. This situation was more complicated. Whereas Duchamp was not attempting to change the boundaries of sculpture qua sculpture and hence his work was not meant to be seen in those terms, a number of these British artists have always considered themselves to be sculptors. They therefore have been concerned more with stretching the boundaries of that art form than with working outside them;

Long and Flanagan are notable in this respect. By contrast, others, such as Art & Language, clearly wished to quit the whole debate in favor of what they deemed more urgent and substantive issues; and yet others, such as Michael Craig-Martin and Bruce McLean, have focused on making works that on occasion enter the debate about sculpture without, however, taking a fixed position on whether some form of Modernist sculptural practice is still viable. Hence, while it is possible to see all the works included in "Starlit Waters" as pertinent to a history of British sculpture in this period, this does not imply that all the makers considered themselves sculptors or even that their works were indeed sculptures. It is significant, however, that those who did define themselves in these terms, most notably Long and Flanagan, have proved to be the most influential for the next group of sculptors to emerge, the group comprising the later section of "Starlit Waters": Tony Cragg, Richard Deacon, Anish Kapoor, Bill Woodrow, et al.

In the past three decades, the issue of what Modernist sculpture is or might be seems to have been debated, analyzed, and fought over in Britain in a plethora of ways and with an intensity that find no exact parallels elsewhere. Thus, though Seymour quite properly saw the new work that emerged in the late 1960s — Land art, Performance art, Conceptual art, Body art, etc. (many terms were proposed for the miscellany of new types of work then flowering simultaneously throughout Western Europe and the United States) — as going beyond the traditional categories of painting and sculpture, some of its key British exponents paradoxically insisted on situating themselves within those very categories. In a much quoted letter of 1963, Barry Flanagan, for example, then still a student at London's St. Martin's School of Art, wrote to Anthony Caro, the doyen of abstract formalist sculpture as well as the most influential teacher in that school: "Is it the only useful thing a sculptor can do, being a three-dimensional thinker and therefore one hopes a responsible thinker, to assert himself twice as hard in a negative way....I might claim to be a sculptor and do everything else but sculpture. This is my dilemma."[4] In 1967, while he, too, was a student there, Bruce McLean made "Floataway Sculptures" from bits of chipboard and linoleum thrown into a river, and "Splash Sculptures" from stones hitting the water's surface. Also in the same year two other students, Gilbert Proesch and George Passmore, joined forces in a collaborative venture. Billing themselves as "The Living Sculptors," they proceeded to make "Nerve Sculpture," "Interview Sculpture," "Magazine Sculpture," "Postal Sculpture," etc. More-over, although virtually all their subsequent work has adhered to the plane of the wall, and generally to a rectilinear pictorial format, Gilbert and George have strenuously clung to this label.

Part of the reason for this preoccupation with issues relating to sculpture as such must lie in the situation that prevailed at St. Martin's School of Art where many of the future participants of "The New Art" were enrolled in the late 1960s: in addition to Flanagan, Long, Gilbert and George, and McLean, John Hilliard and David Dye also studied there. In general, these students reacted fiercely, and often provocatively, to what they perceived to be the rigid and narrow aesthetic of their elders, an aesthetic that was, in effect, a straightforward transmission of the formalist theories of the American critic Clement Greenberg. Greenberg and several of his disciples, most notably Michael Fried, had eagerly embraced the work of the British artist Anthony Caro and that of some of his confrères as the acme of Modernist sculpture, finding in it a three-dimensional counterpart to the color-field painting of the Americans Kenneth Noland, Morris Louis, and Jules Olitski which they were then championing. Caro, and to some extent others of the New Generation sculptors such as William Tucker and Tim Scott, proceeded to base their teaching on this aesthetic. Yet, as Charles Harrison has argued, a spirit of avant-gardism alone cannot account for this obstinate attachment to the category of sculpture on the part of a number of burgeoning artists: their attachment bespoke a strategy with far-reaching ramifications.[5] In their hands the term sculpture no longer designated a category of three-dimensional artistic objects but was used "to claim a sort of aesthetic privilege for certain types of enterprise and activity as against others....[and to emphasize] that how the artist means his work to be regarded should be accepted as defining what that work categorically is."[6]

Significantly, the majority of younger artists working in three-dimensions who emerged a decade later, on the cusp of the 1980s, have also adopted this appellation, though not without some initial hesitation.[7] Many of them, too, were at one time students at St. Martin's, or, alternatively, at London's Royal College of Art where the battle over the definition and parameters of sculpture continued into the 1970s.[8] Whereas many of the leading younger artists abroad who currently work in three-dimensions, particularly in West Germany and the United States, prefer to term themselves "object-makers" rather than "sculptors," this is rarely the case in Britain. While there are certainly also avowed sculptors among the younger generation in North America and West Germany, it is telling that the most incisive three-dimensional work is currently conceived by (self-styled) object-makers—Robert Gober, Stephan Huber, Jon Kessler, Harald Klingelhöller, Jeff Koons, Thomas Schütte, and others.[9] The opposite is the case in Britain. Among object-makers who wish to be thought of as "artists" rather than as "sculptors," the more interesting tend either to belong to the older generation, as do Craig-Martin and McLean, or to take on questions germane to sculpture from a position on its margins, as does Julian Opie. It was, therefore, neither an unprecedented nor even a particularly contentious position for the organizers of "Starlit Waters" to adopt when they championed sculpture as a major achievement in British art over the past quarter century. Issues central to sculpture have preoccupied the art scene in Britain with a vigor and resonance rarely found elsewhere.

A number of diverse and not always related factors have contributed to this vitality. Some of these causes were operative by 1972, others emerged only later. Many artists working in three-dimensions in the United States in the late 1960s sought to break free of both orthodox categories—painting and sculpture; like Donald Judd, in moving from oil on canvas into three-dimensional art, they tended to try to separate their work rigorously from all sculpture of the past. Judd's seminal essay of 1965, "Specific Objects," put the case forcefully.[10] By contrast, though Modernist sculpture in Britain had evolved largely in relation to external stimuli, English artists tended to place themselves in a national lineage even while attempting to redefine the terms of reference. Hence, while in the 1930s Henry Moore was closely bound up with ideas and theories developed by the Surrealists and Constructivists on the Continent, he still saw himself as a kind of successor to Jacob Epstein, then the leading vanguard sculptor in England. (Epstein in turn championed the younger man from the onset of his career.) Similarly Anthony Caro, who as a young artist worked as a studio assistant to Moore and later acknowledged his help, nonetheless saw himself as reinvigorating a sculptural tradition that had grown moribund in his predecessor's hands; he felt bound to challenge rather than simply to ignore the terms in which the older man construed his art. Relationships of this type have served to reinforce the widespread tendency to view British sculpture in terms of a succession of different generations. Yet this point of view is far from being exclusively the product of artists' actions and theoretical disputes; larger social forces have also contributed. For example, an ardent supporter of Moore's work, the British Council fanned his reputation abroad with numerous shows. Exhibitions devoted to more recent British sculpture followed. In the early 1980s this packaging became even more pronounced with the promotion of the New British Sculpture (Cragg, Deacon, Kapoor, Woodrow, et al.) as a national counterpart to the groups of Italians and Germans who were then surfacing on the international stage: the Transavanguardia, the Neue Wilden, etc.[11]

Yet, even during the 1970s, the rupture that Seymour had pinpointed and that was genuinely part of a larger phenomenon, perhaps signifying a cultural caesura (which itself grew out of wider socio-political changes initiated in the late 1960s), was gradually smoothed over through the staging of shows such as "Henry Moore to Gilbert and George" (Palais des Beaux-Arts, Brussels, 1973) which postulated a continuous though not necessarily seamless British sculptural tradition. Shows such as this should not be dismissed as simply exercises in cultural politics, for similar redefinitions and repositionings were taking place locally; indeed they might be said to have gained center stage by the mid-1970s. In 1975 the Arts Council of Great Britain invited William Tucker, sculptor, critic, and teacher at St. Martin's when Long et al. were students there, to curate an international sculpture show at the Hayward Gallery, the very venue that Seymour's exhibition had occupied just three years earlier. Titled "The Condition of Sculpture," Tucker's show was clearly devised as a riposte to the challenge posited by the novel modes, and more particularly by "the extended field of sculpture," featured in Seymour's show.[12] As Tucker conceived it, both meanings implicit in the title—the health and the essence of this art—were under review. While he defined sculpture broadly as self-sufficient, freestanding, fixed plastic entities subject to gravity and revealed by light, in practice he chose his examples much more narrowly: most of the work belonged to an abstract formalist idiom, a kind of international, post-Cubist, constructed sculpture. Conspicuously absent were those sculptors—Long, Flanagan, Fulton—who had appeared in Seymour's show, and who, some twelve years later, would reappear in "Starlit Waters." If Tucker's show looked then, as it still does, like a rearguard action, it nonetheless intensified the vigor of the debate. By the end of the decade, however, the issue seemed to have been resolved. The British representatives at the Venice Biennales of 1976, 1980, and 1982 were not only sculptors, but were all makers of self-contained, three-dimensional entities, subject to gravity and revealed by light. They were Richard Long, Tim Head, Nicholas Pope, and Barry Flanagan.[13] Although only Pope was included in Tucker's show, the other three, too, showed work in Venice that could be classed as sculpture, according to Tucker's definition. For example, Long exhibited a single, monumental piece, *Stone Sculpture*, and Flanagan (who had made an installation for "The New Art" show in 1972) presented carved stone sculptures and bronze hares—that is, only works executed after 1973. A significant reorientation had occurred in their art.

Seymour had divided the participants in her show into two broad categories, categories that she defined by attitude rather than in relation to the materials and media that the artists deployed:

> One might perhaps say that there seem to be two poles of principle within the criteria which
> motivate them. There is the one which is most obviously recognised in the Art-Language

group, which has deliberately, by dint of philosophy and commonsense, expanded its work beyond the aestheticism of so-called "modernist" art. Its systems and weapons are logic, mathematics, information theory, philosophy, history, cybernetics — almost anything with a solid basis of thought is grist to its mill.

On the opposite side of the coin you have an approach, as exemplified by the work of Long and Fulton, which repudiates not only aesthetic discussion of art, but emphasises that it is necessary to work according to no preconceived philosophies, as far as possible from the great art history machine. Long's concern is with things at their rawest, their simplest, their most pure.[14]

Generally speaking, those whose approach was theoretical, epistemological, and analytical, who investigated the premises of art itself or questions pertaining to representation, the commodification of the artwork, and the framing discourses of institutions, found fighting over the categories of sculpture and nonsculpture irrelevant or marginal, to the point where they seceded from such debates altogether. Preoccupied with such wider issues, Art & Language, Burgin, and Hilliard all left the field. By contrast, those who sought a direct, unmediated, "authentic" experience of the world at large and who wanted to avoid theoretical issues tended to regard themselves as sculptors. Shunning theory, they sought, albeit naively, to free themselves from cultural presuppositions, an ideal exemplified in Long's assertion, "My art is in the nature of things."[15] Much of their activity at this time was therefore sculpture by fiat, by the assertion of the artist's will.

At other moments, however, they seemed to adopt quite different tactics and operated comfortably within the orthodox parameters of Modernist sculpture. Long's indoor sculptures made of stones (see pl. 140; cat. no. 88), for example, are autonomous objects that clearly belong to a particular artistic category and are to be situated in a gallery or museum for aesthetic contemplation. Their subject matter, materials, and techniques are not always traditional, but they do not otherwise strain those familiar boundaries of sculpture established by the mid-1960s. While Long continued to make outdoor pieces, these too were recovered for the gallery, mostly via photographs, which in the majority of cases became unique works in their own right and hence were elevated above the status of mere documentation; far more than catalysts, mere vehicles for engendering conceptual experiences, these images were treated as valuable entities.

By the mid-1970s the (self-styled) sculptors who had been featured in Seymour's show were devoting a significant amount of their practice to the production of unique, autonomous objects. Although, in contrast to predecessors like Caro, Long drew extensively on nature for the context and the content of his art, like them he could be said to be working within the gallery/museum structure and within the paradigms of Modernist sculpture. In consequence Long and others around him, including Flanagan, Fulton, Nash, Pope, and Tremlett, functioned very differently from their American peers, such as Walter De Maria, Richard Serra, and Robert Smithson, for whom sculpture became merely one of a set of possibilities within an "expanded field" of three-dimensional art activity. Long and his circle were equally removed from Conceptualists such as Michael Asher, Dan Graham, and Lawrence Weiner, who dealt with actual places and/or physical matter but who did so without resorting to the making of concrete entities. In short, these British artists were quite right to insist on being called sculptors and to contest the issue of sculpture with forbears like Caro and Tucker, for from the early 1970s onwards, the best, that is, the most significant and substantial, of their works lay securely within well-defined Modernist parameters.

For the younger generation who graduated in the mid-1970s, both the close-knit character of the British art world and the importance of the art school system as a training ground meant that most of them matured within the intellectual context sketched above and were subject to its debates. The courses in which they were enrolled offered important forums for such inquiry, with teachers such as Peter Kardia stressing a clear-headed, analytic understanding of the artist's role as object-maker and a responsibility for his or her art and actions that went beyond that of self-expression, being based on more than personal will or whim. Such courses encouraged working with a wide variety of materials that were at hand, cheap, available in quantity, and that lent themselves to a process-based activity. And while there was considerable openness as to the type of work produced, some kind of object-making or installation work was required of students involved in sculpture courses. The art that Cragg, Deacon, Kapoor, and Woodrow executed as students falls roughly into these categories, though several also experimented briefly with ephemeral modes (known now only through documentation), such as performance and time-based activities. Of their British predecessors, it was Long and Flanagan who were arguably of most relevance to them; and of the older artists' works, it was their object-based gallery sculptures that were most pertinent. Yet, as a result of being exposed to the theoretical debates of the previous decade, Cragg, Deacon, and Woodrow, in particular, developed a degree of self-consciousness and critical self-awareness that led them to a greater involvement with the physical means by which content was to be conveyed in a sculpture, and to the conviction that a work should gain its identity as sculpture by objective, materialist criteria rather than subjective nomination. Moreover, they felt that their work had to be self-evidently engaged with issues that were considered socially relevant and overtly contemporary.[16] Cragg summarized this crystallizing of their aesthetic when he stated: "for me, in the mid-seventies, the crucial question became one of finding a content, and, from that came the idea that this might evolve through a more formal approach to the work."[17]

But it was not until 1978 with *New Stones: Newton's Tones* (fig. 1) that Cragg can be said to have made the work that signaled a crucial turning point. The title of this piece is telling: *Newton's Tones* invokes the color spectrum of white light which provided Cragg with an "objective" mode of ordering his components; perhaps also, albeit indirectly, it refers ironically to Tucker's definition of sculpture as objects revealed by light and subject to gravity. In contrast to Long's organic material culled from remote sites, Cragg's "stones," made from plastic discards collected in the streets surrounding the gallery, are insistently contemporary, insistently urban. The world of untouched pure nature has been replaced by a metropolitan one, one which to some observers carried additional allusions to the state of Britain whose cities were then considered to be suffering severe decline, as well as proving the sites for race riots and the rapidly escalating invasion of punk, a street culture of disaffected working-class youth.

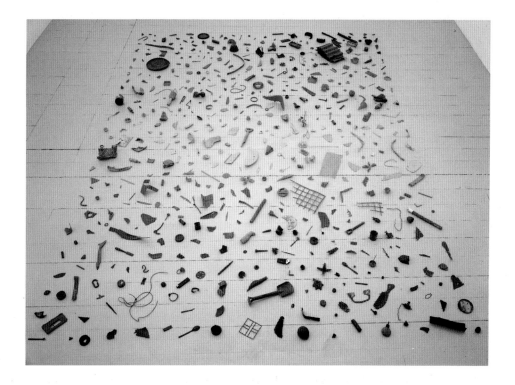

If Long's works provide the most obvious point of departure and of critique for Cragg's sculpture, Carl Andre's were also relevant. When not composed of contiguous forms laid out systematically, Andre's works are ordered by repetition and permutation, thereby subordinating the individual elements to a larger holistic shape (or image). Similar "rational," objective modes formed the basis of much of Cragg's early work, which was also assertively "materialist" in its stance. The art of the American Minimalist had become the subject of considerable controversy in 1976 when the Tate Gallery exhibited *Equivalent VIII*, which it had recently purchased. Soon after the drama over the "bricks affair," as it came to be known in the popular press, Andre had a retrospective at the Whitechapel Gallery in London.[18] He accompanied this exhibition with a number of clear statements of his position and aesthetic; among the most pertinent of these were his adherence to the category of sculpture in favor of other conceptual modes and forms, and his belief in the importance of thinking in concrete, literal terms.[19] Andre stressed his conviction that sculpture takes its place in an ongoing tradition, in a living continuum, and that for him it gains its content from its materials and process, establishing through them its relationship to contemporary society.

By the mid-1970s Joseph Beuys's work had also begun to make an impact in Britain.[20] Beuys's large ambitions for sculpture were not lost on many of his audience. For some, like Kapoor, for whom the idealistic basis of Beuys's thinking was more pertinent than the rational analytic premises of Andre's stance, it was the shamanistic aspects of the German artist's vision, his aspirations for a healing, spiritual art, that were to prove essential. For others, like Cragg, it was the fact that Beuys dealt with his specific, fractured cultural tradition, together with more general contemporary social ills, in powerful images that spoke viscerally, not abstractly or didactically. Together, the issues raised by Andre and Beuys, though not always the terms in which they addressed them, became increasingly crucial for younger sculptors in Britain during the late 1970s. In different ways each can be said to have offered models for an engaged and critical art, one that was not caught in the hermeticism and self-referentiality of Caro's sculpture, nor was lost in a nature pantheism as was Long's, but rather was concerned with apprehending the contemporary world through an engagement with the literal, material objecthood of the sculpture and with the way it interacts with its site—its social and its physical site. Faced, on the one hand, with solipsism and/or escapism, and, on the other, with wildly exaggerated claims for the role of art as an agent of social change, these younger sculptors rejected equally a reductivist view of art and an instrumentalist one. Each recognized necessary limits separating the artwork from and yet linking it to society and culture. For them art operates in and is determined by its status as art; it must acknowledge the conditions of its own existence, and of its making and character, as a preliminary to effecting a larger statement.

Over the past decade Cragg's work has attested to a voracious appetite for materials, processes, and ways of working that has few equals among object-makers of the 1980s. Although fascinated with the products of the manufactured world, Cragg no more confines himself to it than he feels inhibited from drawing at times on the conventional processes of sculpture—carving and casting—or even on the natural matter preferred by Long and his disciples. But materials are never ends in themselves for him; they are always put in the service of sculpture which he conceives of as "thinking models": objects that serve as catalysts to provoke the viewer into questioning, criticizing, and expanding his or her knowledge of the contemporary world and the means, values, and beliefs that determine it.[21] Hence visualizing rather than imagining lies at the heart of his approach: "I talk about visualisation in my work, in the sense that a telescope makes the moon and the galaxies beyond it visual to us, as a microscope does with cellular structures or even an electron microscope does with molecular structures."[22] As evidenced in *St. George and the Dragon* and in *Membrane* (pls. 131–32; cat. nos. 34–35), content is constructed not only by way of metaphor, metonymy, and condensed elliptical con-figurations, but through physical confrontation with the piece. For Cragg, scale, form, texture, and materials are all essential devices for imputing meaning, much of which centers around the problems of unraveling certain constraining or clichéd cultural myths, not least the false but ubiquitous dichotomy between nature and culture that informs so much current thinking. Cragg insists that much of what remains of nature today has been irreversibly altered and mediated by man; moreover, the larger part of ordinary daily experience is determined by elements that are part of the manu-factured environment, rather than an organic one.

Like Cragg, Bill Woodrow has sought to open the frame of reference in his art to current concerns, especially those symptomatic of contemporary urban existence; for him, too, daily life is as much framed and constructed by the media and information technology as it is by concrete experiences. And much of his raw material is likewise scavenged from his immediate context, from skips, from the streets, or from repositories for second-hand matter—used-car lots, junk stores, scrap yards, etc. As seen in *On the Other Hand* (pl. 141; cat. no. 174), he creates images by cutting into the skins of such objects. The new entities he fashions generally have a close relationship to their parent form, and a reciprocal set of interconnections between various kinds and levels of reality, dependence, and indebtedness ensues. Woodrow's mode is personal but not private; his works are obviously fashioned by the hand of the artist, but at a level of skill that recalls home improvements; and if they draw on his own experiences, these are the types of experience to which most of his audience have direct access. In this way he sets up a one-to-one engagement with the spectator, an involvement often enhanced by his dry wit. Yet Woodrow's mode of address remains elliptical, poetic rather than didactic or illustrational. Interpretation remains to some extent open-ended, for though much communal or shared experience is banal or undeniably ordinary, it is nonetheless modulated by the individual who invests it with a private pertinence and an individualized relevance. *On the Other Hand* is typical of Woodrow's art in its distillation of the familiar into actual, yet paradoxically imaginary, images that function as compelling, abbreviated propositions; it is typical too in that these visual propositions incorporate a moral dimension without becoming simplistic.

Both Richard Deacon and Anish Kapoor also choose to work within the framework offered by the gallery/museum situation, partly because for them, as for most of their generation, there are no legitimate "alternative" sites, no positions outside this structure and system. Around 1980 Kapoor's Indian heritage, reawakened after a visit there in 1979, began to dovetail with certain interests he had developed as a student, first in the work of Beuys and later in that of other artists, like Yves Klein. These artists sought a spiritual dimension for their art and considered the physical as the vehicle through which the immaterial might be attained, investing certain selected materials with quasi-talismanic properties. In Kapoor's work powdered pigment of an intense, high-keyed hue imbues the forms with a radiance and luminosity that lift them above the ordinary and diurnal. This impression is reinforced by the delicate surfaces which cannot be touched without blemishing, that is, without being violated, as well as by the imagery, for his shapes are reminiscent of generative entities, of seeds, and of sexual organs. As seen in *Hole and Vessel* of 1984 (pl. 138; cat. no. 68), Kapoor's art presupposes the sanctified sites of the art gallery (or its surrogates) where it may be contemplated by the solitary viewer. In his use of what is widely regarded as a universalizing vocabulary, one that purportedly stands outside the specifics of time and place, he has affinities with Long whose choice of archetypal imagery, such as circles, lines, and crosses, and of organic matter for his interior sculptures — witness *Fire Rock Circle* of 1987 (pl. 140; cat. no. 88) — also invokes notions of the primal and universal.

Deacon's works, too, are self-contained, autonomous sculptures that presuppose a museum context. However, such a context is not for him a private place for introspective communion. In contrast to the essentially contemplative, transcendental experiences elicited by the use of pure form and timeless imagery in the art of Kapoor and Long, Deacon posits an intersubjective contemporary world, a world in which subjective and objective reality are not rigorously separable, a world that is structured by language. The colloquialisms in his titles together with their tone of "direct speech" reinforce this. Being of necessity a shared phenomenon, language is not only the agent by which all experience is given form and character, but the arena in which all forms of communication take place. If language not only shapes experience but gives structure to the world as mankind knows it, then apprehension of any form, irrespective of whether it is abstract or representational, must involve the mediating actions of language. Deacon's works are generally made by hand, by processes that are straightforwardly revealed and require little above basic workshop skills; he likens these physical means to the activities of language forming. And since making, for him, operates analogously to language (as a way of shaping our world), the processes and materials, together with the allusions and references that they convey, are as crucial to the construction of meaning as are the associations embedded in the forms of his sculpture. As found in *Falling on Deaf Ears No. 2* of 1984–85 and *These Are the Facts* of 1987–88 (pls. 135, 137; cat. nos. 40, 42), Deacon seeks to make the act of active, physical confrontation with one of his sculptures analogous to the basic experiences involved in apprehending, construing, and perceiving the world at large.

The period around 1968–72 witnessed substantial protests against what were perceived to be the untenably rigid and narrow preoccupations governing much contemporary Modernist art. Since its hermeticism was closely linked to a strict maintenance of the orthodox categories of painting and sculpture, these time-honored art forms themselves came into disrepute. Yet in the rush for relevance and pertinence many artists lost sight of the framing discourses within which any construction of meaning must take place. Much of the self-consciously radical work of that era failed because it never managed to establish an objective and cogent set of alternative terms within which it might operate as art. Too often, the results were equivalent to gestures and interventions: topical, transitory, ephemeral, and devoid of any sustaining conceptual structure. The rigor of thinking and the critical self-awareness that Modernist theory had at its best provided was rarely replaced by anything equally cogent and coherent. Nonetheless, alternative conceptual models gradually were forged, largely by recourse to different cultural discourses, and these models have, in turn, spawned various types of Postmodernist practice, seen, for example, in the work of John Hilliard and Victor Burgin. However, for certain young artists maturing in the mid-1970s in London, the city's unique conjunction of artistic context, legacy, and debate suggested something quite different, namely that the Modernist aesthetic might not have been in fact fully played out and that a form of late Modernist sculpture was still viable.

---

1. Anne Seymour, "Introduction," in Arts Council of Great Britain, London, 1972, *The New Art*, p. 5. Fifteen artists were included: Keith Arnatt, Art-Language [sic], Victor Burgin, Michael Craig-Martin, David Dye, Barry Flanagan, Hamish Fulton, Gilbert and George, John Hilliard, Richard Long, Keith Milow, Gerald Newman, John Stezaker, and David Tremlett.

2. "Starlit Waters: British Sculpture, An International Art 1968–1988" was selected by Lewis Biggs and Richard Francis. The artists included in the show were Art & Language, Tony Cragg, Michael Craig-Martin, Richard Deacon, Barry Flanagan, Hamish Fulton, Antony Gormley, Ian Hamilton Finlay, John Hilliard, Shirazeh Houshiary, Anish Kapoor, John Latham, Richard Long, Bruce McLean, William Tucker, Richard Wentworth, Alison Wilding, and Bill Woodrow.

3. Bruce McLean had declined to participate in "The New Art" in 1972 on the grounds that he no longer considered himself an artist. Gilbert and George agreed to take part in "Starlit Waters," but later withdrew on technical grounds.

4. Dated June 7, 1963, published in *Silâns* 6 (Jan. 1965), n. pag.

5. Charles Harrison, "Sculpture's Recent Past," in Museum of Contemporary Art, Chicago, and San Francisco Museum of Modern Art, 1987, *A Quiet Revolution: British Sculpture Since 1965*, p. 27.

6. Ibid.

7. Deacon, for example, for a time insisted upon being called a fabricator.

8. In 1974, for example, the Royal College staged an exhibition titled "Sculpture Now: Dissolution or Redefinition," which contained work by, among others, Flanagan and Long.

9. In an interview in the catalogue accompanying a joint exhibition of these four British sculptors with four German object-makers (Isa Genzken, Harald Klingelhöller, Reiner Ruthenbeck, and Thomas Schütte), Kaspar König argued that there was a "Nontradition" of German sculpture and that young artists like Schütte were more

influenced by the work of Dan Graham and Michael Asher, as well as Vladimir Tatlin and Alexander Rodchenko, than by sculptors per se. See "An Ongoing Conversation: Alanna Heiss Interviews Kaspar König," in P.S. 1, The Institute for Art and Urban Resources, Long Island, New York, 1987, *Juxtapositions*.

10. Donald Judd, "Specific Objects," in Judd, *Complete Writings 1959–1975* (Halifax and New York, 1975), pp. 181–89 (orig. published in *Arts Yearbook 8*, 1965).

11. Market forces and the demise of so-called alternative venues must also be taken into account, together with the fact that these four sculptors and several others closely associated with them, including Edward Allington, Shirazeh Houshiary, and Richard Wentworth, all have the same London dealer, Nicholas Logsdail at the Lisson Gallery.

12. This term is taken from Rosalind Krauss's influential essay "Sculpture in the Expanded Field," first published in *October* 8 (Spring 1979), reprinted in Krauss, *The Originality of the Avant-Garde and Other Modernist Myths* (Cambridge, MA, and London, 1986), pp. 275–90.

13. Head had been educated at St. Martin's with Long et al. Pope was among the youngest of the forty-one sculptors in Tucker's show.

14. Seymour (note 1), p. 6.

15. Richard Long, in The Solomon R. Guggenheim Museum, New York, 1986, *Richard Long*, text by R. H. Fuchs, p. 9.

16. There is a considerable difference in the approach of Kapoor, who in many ways is most closely connected with Long in his meditative attitudes as well as his methods. Cragg, by contrast, styles himself a "materialist," a position that Woodrow and Deacon could also be said to manifest. The materialist position of Carl Andre, and of Minimalist artists in general, entails a stress on real space and actual time in contradistinction to Caro's concern with optical, rather than literal, reality and with presentness in his sculpture. Given his preoccupation with pure form and timeless matter, Long's indoor sculptures are in many respects closer to Caro's work than to Andre's (exception should be made for certain of the early interior pieces which, like Andre's, tried consciously to adapt to the space in which they were shown by, in effect, using the floor as a landscape). Some of Cragg's early floor pieces, including *New Stones: Newton's Tones*, might be said to be concerned with the tension between opticality and literalness: his later works, like Andre's, are engaged with mass and with the actualities of the space and site, though without becoming site-specific. Debates centered on issues of opticality versus literalness, and presentness versus location in actual time and space, had raged since Michael Fried published his much discussed essay "Art and Objecthood" in *Artforum* 5, 10 (Summer 1967), in which he attacked the Minimalists, while supporting Caro and his disciples. Cragg, Deacon, and Woodrow came down firmly on the side of the Minimalists, as indeed Flanagan did (at least early in his career).

17. Lynne Cooke, "Tony Cragg Interviewed by Lynne Cooke," in Arts Council of Great Britain, London, 1987, *Tony Cragg*, p. 24.

18. For the best account of this, see Richard Morphet, "Carl Andre's Bricks," *The Burlington Magazine* 118, 884 (Nov. 1976), pp. 762–67.

19. See, in particular, his interviews with Peter Fuller, first published in *Artmonthly* 16 (May 1978), pp. 5–11, and *Artmonthly* 17 (June 1978), pp. 5–11.

20. Although Beuys had been included in "When Attitudes Become Form," a seminal show held in 1968 at the Institute of Contemporary Arts, London, in which the new international avant-garde was introduced into Britain, his influence really began to be felt only after 1974, as a consequence of two exhibitions. The suite of 266 drawings "The Secret Block for a Secret Person in Ireland" was shown at the Museum of Modern Art in Oxford in 1974, then in Edinburgh and London later that year. Some months after, Beuys participated in "Art into Society—Society into Art" at the Institute of Contemporary Arts in London. He presented a teaching performance in the form of dialogues and actions that took place in an environment that he constructed.

21. Cooke (note 17), p. 36.

22. Demosthenes Davvetas, "Tony Cragg: An Interview by Demosthenes Davvetas," *Art & Design* 4, 9–10 (Nov. 1988), p. 80.

Plate 128. *Red Bottle*, 1982
Plastic objects
84 x 24 in. (213 x 61 cm)
Cat. no. 31

Plate 129. *Drawn Objects: "Waiting,"* 1983
    Mixed media and crayon
    86½ x 26 x 28 in. (220 x 66 x 71 cm)
    Cat. no. 32

Plate 130. *Shed*, 1984
  Stone, particle board, and wood
  39 x 33 x 13½ in. (99 x 84 x 34 cm)
  Cat. no. 33

Plate 131. *St. George and the Dragon*, 1985
Metal, plastic, and wood
71 x 102 x 40 in. (180 x 259 x 102 cm)
Cat. no. 34

Plate 132. *Membrane*, 1986
  Wood, metal, and plaster
  44½ x 46 x 32 in. (113 x 117 x 81 cm)
  Cat. no. 35

Plate 133. *Spill*, 1987
Bronze
39 x 79 x 39 in. (100 x 200 x 100 cm)
Cat. no. 36

Plate 134. *Loco*, 1988
Wood
63 x 94½ x 86⅝ in. (160 x 240 x 220 cm)
Cat. no. 37

Plate 135. *Falling on Deaf Ears No. 2*, 1984–85
Galvanized steel and canvas
48 x 48 x 48 in. (122 x 122 x 122 cm)
Cat. no. 40

Plate 136. *Art for Other People No. 21*, 1986
Plastic and stainless steel
12 x 24 x 6 in. (30 x 60 x 15 cm)
Cat. no. 41

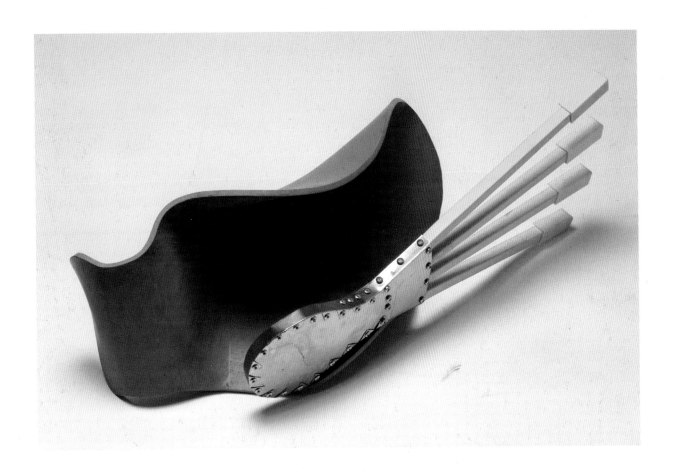

Plate 137. *These Are the Facts*, 1987–88
Masonite, mild steel, carpet, and phosphor bronze
78 x 76 x 52 in. (198 x 193 x 132 cm)
Cat. no. 42

Plate 138. *Hole and Vessel*, 1984
   Polystyrene, cement, earth, acrylic medium, and pigment
   37½ x 64 x 43 in. (95 x 162 x 109 cm)
   Cat. no. 68

Plate 139. *Watermarks*, 1979
      Photographs, pencil, and graphite on matboard
      Two panels, each 34⅞ x 48½ in. (89 x 123 cm)
      Cat. no. 87

Plate 140. *Fire Rock Circle*, 1987
Sixty fire rock stones
Dia. 110 in. (280 cm)
Cat. no. 88

Plate 141. *On the Other Hand*, 1987
Roto-dryer with acrylic and spray enamel
72 x 39 x 12 in. (183 x 99 x 30 cm)
Cat. no. 174

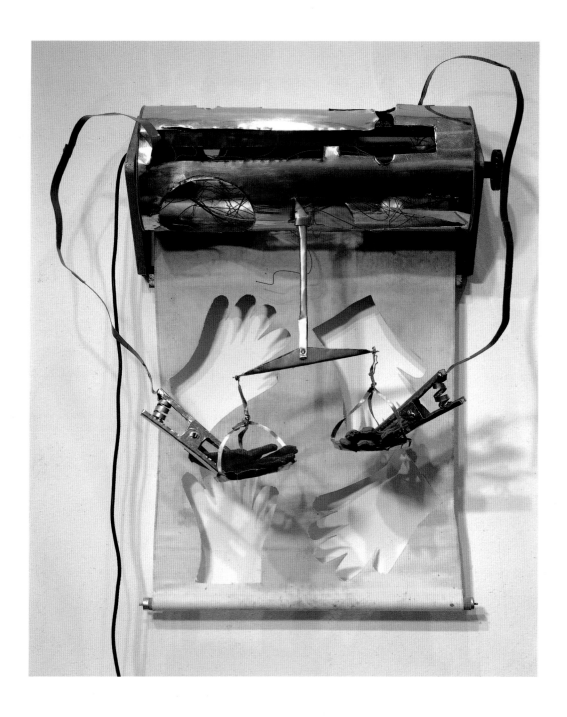

Redefining Conceptualism

JUDITH RUSSI KIRSHNER

Although Richard Prince constructs his artwork from photographs, he is also an author of fiction and essays, and in recent exhibitions showed paintings of jokes written across the surface of the canvas. These paintings provocatively represent a historical intersection—of Minimalism, with its blank, uninflected canvases; of Conceptual art, with text as the subject of painting; and of Pop, with its dead-pan appropriation of mass culture into the realm of high art. At this intersection, we can also orient the work of other Neo-Conceptualists in the Gerald S. Elliott Collection. In the sense that Prince, Vito Acconci, Jenny Holzer, and Sherrie Levine have all been, despite their obvious diversity, invigorated by theories of Structuralism, Poststructuralism, and feminism, their art has been categorized broadly as Postmodern.

Considering their works, we become, like the artists themselves, readers as well as viewers. Their use of language has emerged from the rigorous, de-aestheticized investigations of 1970s Conceptual art, but now, renovated and self-conscious, it incorporates the spectacular effects of 1980s signage. Emphasizing the pervasive impact of language on social and cultural relations, on objects and events, this work demonstrates an understanding of the arbitrary and artificial nature of the sign. Focusing on signifiers rather than what is signified or represented, it acknowledges the idea of a subject no longer intact but decentered, without subject or referent. This art can be incarnated in the traditional media of painting and sculpture, often relying, to a greater or lesser degree, on combinations of image and text and, by extension, on questions of authorship, authority, and subjectivity. Shifting in and out of discourses of creation and production, Conceptual art has moved out of the isolated studio to be informed by larger political, economic, and social contexts.

Among these new Conceptualists, Sherrie Levine has fabricated a career with techniques of confiscation and a reconstitution of the past that relies on existing representations. Her first works to win attention, rephotographed images by artists such as Edward Weston and Walker Evans, provided a kind of allegorical model in reverse—a process of depletion or unraveling that constitutes a parallel narrative to the subject matter that is being constructed—for a group of photo-based artists associated with the "Pictures" exhibition curated by Douglas Crimp at Artists Space in New York in 1977. Their work was given critical reinforcement by Crimp's influential essay "The Photographic Activity of Postmodernism," published in *October* several years later.[1] Disillusioned with the possibility of expression or neo-expression, this group of artists denied the power of authenticity in an age of mechanical and electronic reproduction, and rejected the heroic gesture and posture of expressionistic display.

Facilitating their editing out of the rhetoric of originality was the Postmodernist practitioners' reliance on French literary theory. A merger of Marxism and psychoanalysis, this discourse on the problems of representation lurked in the background of straightforward, mute, or cryptic translations and appropriations from recognizable imagery that included, for example, advertisements in Prince, master works in Levine, and truisms in the work of Holzer. Although borrowing from the bank of Modernism, they also rejected the very system whose authority was repeatedly rehearsed in the autonomous masterpiece. Authority bequeathed to the artist was exchanged, revalued, and re-presented in a subversion of the entire economy of the Modernist system, an institutional economy or cartel that included museums, galleries, and private collections. Parenthetically, the stubborn resistance to one authority was predictably and eventually consumed by the dominance of another—the media— spewing out the advertisements illustrating daily life that provided the core of Andy Warhol's philosophy and the reproductions that Levine copied in her watercolors. The journal *Reallife* eponymously pointed out that only signification and the media were real; its editor, Thomas Lawson, had produced a cogent literary statement of a last-exit position for artists which recognized the impossibility of anything but re-presentation, especially in painting.[2] If originality and authorship were up for grabs, so too were individual authors and subjects—who proliferated, for example, in Cindy Sherman's impersonations of a self multiplied and eternally other—as well as their institutionalization in museum collections, which Crimp elegiacally called "the museum's ruins."[3]

If Levine's photographic works read as fragments of the visual representation of cultural history, her delicate watercolors, acts of a copyist associated with obedient women's work, undermine the perceptual and ethical bases of her viewers' expectations and reactions. A tiny watercolor, handmade from a reproduction of an Arthur Dove painting or a Matisse, chosen according to desire, is far more disturbing than the photographs, whose authenticity and originality have already been eroded by their technological production. Levine's recent check and stripe paintings function as synecdoche; bits of generic abstraction, they are reminders rather than imposters of the basic units of formalism. Despite their handmade process, they are as dependent on theories of language and representation as her photographs. In this collection, a stripe painting on a chair seat and a knothole painting (see pls. 159–60; cat. nos. 80–81) call out, according to the artist, the uneasy death of Modernism. Perhaps in response to Neo-Geo rediscoveries, Levine has finally crossed her own negative path of anti-origin and gone beyond, or at least around, the deconstructions and melancholy associated with Walter Benjamin's philosophy. Her paintings function as literal fragments of something else—plywood, Gene Davis canvases, or George Herriman cartoons. In the panels devoted to Herriman's Krazy Kat and Ignatz, an absurd kind of love between species destined to be enemies is mediated by our knowledge that the author of the cartoon was himself a member of an oppressed minority.[4] The narrative of unrequited love is played out again and again; the potential for repetition is as endless as in the ongoing stripes, in which Modernism itself seems the object of desire, never achieved.

The knothole paintings, whose precious lacunae are filled or painted with copper, gold, and white, are dictated by a Duchampian code as well as the givens of a manufactured pattern on plywood. Denials of a surface that is simultaneously privileged and protected under glass, these works are defined by what is missing, the knots—"not painting." The pun is extended so that positive and negative become interchangeable, as they always are in the checked and striped patterns or more recently in combinations of the two on lead, held in a kind of perceptual, optical stand-off or stalemate. The pleasure of choice is checked by palette decisions that are strategic, based on what goes with what in a formalist scheme. This visual equivalence equals aesthetic equivocation, and is intensified and rendered mute to the point of becoming decorative when the works are shown in a series. The striped paintings on wooden seats, hollowed out to face the viewer head on, are less subtle readymades, in which the impress of a body is transferred to the wall to bear the index of the artist's gesture. In the lead panels, additional alchemical associations produce a kind of transformation in reverse in which this seductive material, itself a staple of meaning in current work by European artists Anselm Kiefer, Jannis Kounellis, and Gunther Förg, is infected with the contagion of decoration. Additionally, there is the game implied by these patterned boards; one thinks of Duchamp's later activity. The conceptual elegance of chess and backgammon moves connotes and confers a kind of social status on these already status-conscious artistic forms of cultural exchange, objects of desire.

Occasionally Levine's ease at interchanging authors shows her desire for masquerade, another well-used strategy of political minorities, particularly women. Attached to reproductions, masterpieces, and the ruthless rationale of geometry, a neat intellectualized attempt to ward off the anxiety of expression and influence produces in Levine's work an economy of insistent repetition. Levine reaches for an alternative mode of painting production which is less problem solving and more about resisting the authority of painting by recontextualizing it in a relational process of communication and connection.[5] Sherman, Holzer, and Mary Kelly are more overtly and self-consciously feminist in their work than Levine, whose art derives its authority from quiet, modestly scaled but insistent attempts to shift and assume power apart from the Modernist inheritance. The scale and means of Levine's work have been consistently and strategically at variance with what I believe is the breadth of her ambition and intention.

What is striking about the work of Levine and Prince, whose earliest rephotographs are coincident, is how similar their means and their subjects might be and yet how utterly different, because of gender among other things, their strategies and theoretical positions are. The differences exist, I think, because Levine recites, in an open-ended and ironic manner, every buzzword of Postmodern discourse and still offers veiled hints at subjectivity. Not as direct as Prince's sometimes perverse challenge, Levine's is a feminine one of acting "nice" while acting like someone whose authority is unquestioned and whose canonic mastery she uses as a camouflage—but not quite. Apparent in her work is the desire of a learned woman to manipulate rules and invert them against the game. She is conversant with feminist, and specifically Lacanian, theories;[6] Prince's appropriations of found imagery, on the other hand, are paradoxically best explained by his own words. Framed by many interviews, the artist's discourse is his signature, his voice still authoritative:

> First let me say, rephotography was always a technique to make the image again and to make it look as natural looking as it did when it first appeared. It never had the trailer of an ideology. It never attempted to produce a copy…a resemblance, yes, but never a copy. It's not a mechanical technique. It's a technological one. It's also a physical activity that locates the

author behind the camera, not in front of it, not beside and not away from it. There's a whole lot of authorship going on.... Second, as far as the criticality is concerned, the picture that I take, that I steal...happens to be an image that appears in the advertising section of a magazine. I've always had the ability to misread these images...disassociate them from their original intentions. I happen to like these images and see them in much the same way I see moving pictures in a movie.[7]

Prince has used the convention of the interview as an opportunity for another layer of information as uninflected and deadpan as the visual work. In his first published book, *Why I Go to the Movies Alone* (1983), he created an affectless dialogue that seems as noncommittal as if simulated life were as believable as the reality of his de-originated photoworks. Prince's fictional characters, as Brian Wallis noted,

> demonstrate...an inclination to conform to or disappear into the security of this closed system. The real world is presented in contrast as bland and lacking in pleasure. So pleasure for its own sake provides a goal, while alienation from the real world—withdrawal, lack of emotion, inability to socialize—finds its expression not in anxiety but in the pure mindless pleasures of solitude: the inward-focused release of drugs, television, drinking, and movies.[8]

Pleasures can take on a nightmarish quality, however, against Prince's orange and red backgrounds depicting a postnuclear, sunburnt screen across which figures are branded and locked in excited embraces (pl. 161; cat. no. 135). Their ecstasy reads ambivalently as violent or sexual, hyped up from the fantasies of vacation brochures. The dislocation process by which Prince crops and then enlarges images, superimposes screens, then reshoots the scene in color against appropriated sunsets, transforms eternally desirable false paradises into potential horror stories.

Available and recognizable from advertising, Prince's rephotographed figures, whether Marlboro cowboys or Santa Claus, are purposefully elusive in terms of meaning and never relate, except as "gangs," a concept also borrowed from advertising for arranging works in series. Like Levine, Prince depends on repetition of similarities to underscore difference. The gangs tend to be classified according to gender and have included entertainers, biker models, male or female models. In *Super-Heavy Santa* (pl. 162; cat. no. 136), Prince grouped images of Santa with details from Superman comics and photos of rock stars. A casting call for male roles, the piece also comments on how clothes make the man—how mild-mannered Clark Kent becomes larger than life, or how a fat man in a red suit becomes a paternal and beneficent figure.

Prince's art, honed down to cultural one-liners, culminates a Modernist chronology of the outsider, the alienated artist as melancholic clown or masquerader. Levine's photographs of Egon Schiele's self-portraits, titled *Self-Portraits of Sherrie Levine after Egon Schiele* (1984), explore another's narcissism, but her choice of a tortured, victimized, and brooding Expressionist suggests a sense of longing, desire rather than identification or projection. The work both rehearses and deconstructs that mythification of genius. Closer to the tradition of artist as jokester or sad fool is *Pressure* of 1982–83 by Robert Longo, a painting in which a young man in white-face bears on his shoulders the heavy burden of Modernism. Here Modernism is symbolized by a three-dimensional relief of International Style architecture;

Longo's painting became the emblem for The Museum of Modern Art's reopening exhibition in 1984. But Prince is more of the stand-up comic, constantly traveling, looking for an audience to give him authority, applause, or simply reaction; he is a dandy on the late-night circuit of the twentieth century. In his work, lack of expression has replaced the white-face mask or make-up of an earlier Pierrot. According to Prince, "there was a time when the famous were revered. Now fame is associated with clowns and fools. Gifted people will choose to step out of the public eye because it might be more of an advantage—or more manipulative—to know when to step in and step out again."9

His jokes are conventional, predictable, independent of any single author; their assumptions, about communication, how we relate to each other with gifts of humor, led to another situation where jokes carry the wrong punch lines or no punch line at all. In some of the cartoon paintings, there is a gender reversal; the image of a wife surprising her husband in the arms of another woman is captioned with a narrative of a husband who discovers his wife with her lover. In the painting of 1988, where only the text disturbs the canvas, the salesman is invited to sleep not with the farmer's daughter but with the farmer's son, and the punch line reads "I'm in the wrong joke." Also interesting is what these paintings say about our aesthetic expectations and how they are constructed. Reading one of Prince's jokes compares to reading a painting, waiting for the punch line, waiting to get it. Like colors on a palette, the jokes change in succession. The artist, who works with about fifteen jokes in his routine, believes that these are jokes on himself,10 on the presumed death of the author. According to Prince, the punch lines are often added by someone else; if one can no longer believe in the power of communication, one can still enjoy the pirated pleasures of transgression. Prince is his own first viewer and his own worst viewer, a locker-room audience or the guy who tells the off-color joke. There is a perverse economy where jokes are traded not in a real exchange but are one-sided, a narration of what is most exhausted about our own culture. One feels as though one could never really get it, or it is just too obvious to be anything but that which it is. "There's nothing to interpret," Prince has insisted, "nothing to appreciate. There's nothing to speculate about. I wanted to point to it and say what it was. It's a joke."11 One can dissect the text, see how the comedy is set up, realize that the punch line never comes or, if it does, seems sick. These strategically selected jokes are like last gasps, fulfilling expectations of convention but not signification; there is little mirth, release is never experienced, only a sense of incompleteness and a feeling that there should be another joke in the routine. Finding novelty in what is as old as the hills, Prince finds jokes painfully rich in everything but humor. His texts do not necessarily match his images, and in earlier jokes, the texts simply float on monochromatic grounds but provoke our attention; in the face of a joke, we see its structure, see it coming, but are too self-conscious to laugh at painting, at art, or at how much it has cost us to arrive at a place where we are laughing at ourselves.

For Jenny Holzer, authorship and authority commingle in spectacular high-tech delivery systems. "High-technologies," she has remarked, "do seem to be the media of authority, especially in the eighties. If you're considered radical, you're either shot or ignored, so I think I can be trickier and possibly more effective if the message seems to come from on high, rather than from beneath."12 Since her first printed handbills, pasted on city walls in the streets, Holzer's art by definition has been public. Her *Truisms* of 1987–89 (see pl. 157; cat. no. 56), alphabetically organized one-liners, such as "Abuse of power comes as no surprise," "Fathers often use too much force," and "Money creates taste," have appeared on T-shirts, on the Spectacolor board in Times Square, and on museum walls. Seizing the potential of the printed format utilized by Dan Graham, Joseph Kosuth, and Sol LeWitt, Holzer has covered a variety of surfaces with vernacular statements constructed with craft, economic precision, and literary invention. Although her declarations tend to be critical, to express outrage, she speaks in an almost slangy voice, in language that flashes quickly past individuals accustomed to reacting, or not reacting, to constant, instantaneous messages from the media. Holzer is attracted to electronic signs and high-technology media because of their capacity to deliver quantities of information efficiently. She has attempted with her Truisms "to speak about important things, in places where people can see them and...are going to get it."[13]

After the *Essays* of 1979–82 (see pl. 55; cat. no. 54), restricted to posters, Holzer switched to a more institutional, neutral tone, recalling safety warnings and public service notices in a voice she labels "upper anonymous."[14] Upper anonymous could also signify the autonomous realms of the inheritance of Modernism, issued from above. Authoritative and familiar, it elicits the ambivalence one feels toward an overly vigilant bigger brother whose presence is felt and absorbed, like it or not. It is the voice of someone invisible, ever-present, protective; it is warning, surveillance, admonition, or threat, and is informed by an insight from Michel Foucault that even the powers that protect and advise do so only to inhibit and repress.

In her *Living Series* of 1980–82 (see pl. 154; cat. no. 53), observations about everyday occurrences were inscribed on bronze plaques and in L.E.D. (light electronic diode) signs, and include phrases such as "There's the sensation of a lot of flesh when every single hair stands up. This happens when you're cold and naked, aroused or simply terrified." "Simply terrified" is an oxymoron that underscores Holzer's rhetorical gift at bringing extremes together in only a few words, presenting a narrative of physical fear, evoking an image of a body and feeling one's own body — all in relief on a bronze plaque usually reserved for commemorative functions. But when this *Living Series* seemed too tolerant, Holzer assumed a voice closer to her own in the more urgent *Survival Series* (1983–85), in which messages have become blatantly political: "People smell two deaths: regular and nuclear," or "Savor kindness because cruelty is always possible later," and "Men don't protect you anymore." Another phrase from this series is "What a shock when they tell you that it won't hurt and you almost turn inside out when they begin." The upper anonymous is the "they," referring to nonspecific authorities.

The clichés, lessons, and predictions Holzer conveys often depend on their context, as well as their materials, to supplement their readings; emblazoned on the marquee of a casino in Las Vegas, for instance, her imperative "Protect me from what I want" becomes a spectacular code of desire signaling sexuality and capitalism. First shown in 1986, *Under a Rock* (see pl. 156; cat. no. 55) was a very ambitious project extending her discursive syntax but incorporating objects as support. With texts engraved on granite benches arranged in front of L.E.D. signs, Holzer introduced narratives referring more specifically to war in tropical countries, to violence, atrocities, and political oppression. In 1989 she assembled her most ambitious environment, *Laments*; it included thirteen stone caskets with inscriptions orchestrated with the messages of the L.E.D. signs.

Holzer's installations are powerful, monumental, and authoritative; they inspire hushed and meditative attitudes usually evoked by chapels or war memorials. In spite of the high drama and apocalyptic aura, Holzer escapes the tone of righteous moralization by assuming a narrative syntax of everyday speech that balances between the anecdotal and the reportorial. Although her work often depends on issues of gender, that of the narrator as well as the reader, the more recent texts, especially *Under a Rock*, deal with abuses of power not limited to gender or culture.

When there is a critical message in Vito Acconci's structures, it is stated plainly and concisely, betraying the artist's early activity as a writer and usually articulated in language previously recorded and inscribed on the piece. Like Holzer and Prince, Acconci uses language that is direct and commonplace. (Prince's observation "I like to think of normality as the next special effect" is relevant here.[15]) Politically sensitive, these artists all avoid didacticism; they manipulate strategies grafted from the media to transmit their messages to as large an audiences as possible. In Acconci's architectural inventions, such as *Making Shelter* (*House of Used Parts*) (pl. 143; cat. no. 2), the vernacular materials and forthright presentation are independent of theoretical foundations and spontaneously evoke the perils of contemporary entrapment, the ways in which cultural, linguistic, and architectural conventions, for example, can determine or limit behavior. Acconci might be preaching to the converted, but there is the sense of an artist forcing the question of his own ideological containment.

A poet before he became an artist, Acconci has described his earliest text pieces as excursions onto a white page. He has commented that in the early *Following Piece* (1969), the relationship between the artist following the unsuspecting subject was not unlike the relationship between the writer and reader, a contract that if successful engages both parties. This relationship differs from that found in performance, which Acconci sees as too inherently theatrical. (Indeed, Acconci characterized his role in live pieces as that of a stand-up comedian.) Since the late 1960s, this artist, whose early stylistic allegiance was with Minimalism, has produced a complex group of works that have moved literally from the page to the gallery, the museum, the street, and finally the park. Minimalism was not exclusively an intellectual mode of artistic production, defined by economic form and industrial materials, but could also be productively illogical. It was LeWitt, identified primarily with Minimalism, who stated in 1969 that "conceptual artists are mystics rather than rationalists. They leap to conclusions that logic cannot reach."[16] But that leap almost always demands a comparable leap from the viewer, and Acconci is perhaps one of the most demanding artists in that he requires our participation to animate and inhabit the instruments he conceives. In *Stretch* of 1969 (pl. 142; cat. no. 1), for instance, directions for actions were given in combination with photographs of these basic moves. By 1973, in a piece titled *Command Performance*, Acconci made it clear that the spotlight literally had shifted to the audience, whose position was marked by a spotlit stool; the audience was required to activate the moving parts of Acconci's structures. These conglomerate structures were often assembled from building supplies and furniture; like words in syntax, their literal and figurative arrangement produced meaning for viewers and were modeled after his drawings which in turn included sound or text. Recently his public sculpture has taken on aspects of public access and public address, already incipient in *Peoplemobile*, which traveled through Europe in the summer of 1979.

Always inscribed or impressed in Acconci's sculptural pieces is a negative space that calls out the presence and expectation of a human figure. In his assemblages, empty chairs are surrogates that provide traces or negatives of bodies reanimated and rendered positive when individuals engage in the work. In many of his pieces, Acconci is author and subject and often situates a body, if not his own, in the gaps he leaves there, the cut-outs in *Houses Up the Wall* and *People's Wall*, both from 1985, or the seats in *Making Shelter*. This shift in his work, really an invitation to a reader's response, opened it to more meanings and more space for social interaction. Because we read Acconci's desire to move us, house us, seat us, and even touch us as genuine, we are moved by the urgency of that desire to respond. Following the example of this artist's journey from private encounter to public occasions, our artistic excursions edge away from narcissistic investigations to public demonstrations.

What is indelible about Acconci's art, whether objects or text and photos, is its overt psychological edge, its direct insights into subjectivity. The critical response to his work has often been a reaction to the artist's autobiography and to the confessional aspect of his early work. His subjectivity was made available as content in projects that documented his own search for self in personal disclosure and psychological revelation. Even when Acconci stopped performing his own actions, he used his signature voice as a surrogate presence. There is still a touch of the sad clown or stand-up comic in Acconci's position as a continual outsider; his persistence as a kind of underground conscience relentlessly reminding us that art must go outside of the museum and even off the page to engage social and political areas of life merits admiration.

For many sculptors working in the 1980s, commissions for public projects have provided new avenues of expression and demand. Acconci has increasingly devoted himself to such ambitious projects, so ideas of shelter and seating have become central to his concerns about site-specific accommodation and a more expansive redefinition of monuments and memory. *House of Cars* (1983/87) is a monument to failed attempts at housing the homeless and to the relics of automobile society. Built of abandoned vehicles, this form of nomadic living becomes radically decontextualized and apostrophized as art. A master of bricolage, Acconci draws common building materials from the vernacular: usually inexpensive, generally available in large quantities, often discarded as inappropriate for aesthetic transformation. By reinvesting cast-off artifacts of American culture with aesthetic value, Acconci straddles sculptural issues of placement and displacement, of centering and decentering. He has produced houses from daydreams and nightmares, such as *Bad Dream House* of 1987, and constructed them in ways in which we usually construct meaning. The origins of these large-scale, user-friendly conglomerates are in Acconci's early conceptual, text, and photo works where the linkages between conceptualization and creativity were established through directions for actions. Now his work is the instrument of our actions, suggesting that we perform his texts.

Because Acconci has always preferred his work to be seen as sculpture as opposed to performance, it seems that his allegiance to the Minimalist object is still a major strand in his art. His most recent work resides in the spaces he constructs between his authorship and his resistance to authority. His settings are obviously derived from and modeled after architecture. But the politics of architectural styles, the artistic nuances of Minimalism and Modernism are less important to him than the more immediate reactions we bring to enclosure and confinement, whether political, social, or psychological. His inspiration is a narrative of self-exploration, of interrogation at its most painful and deeply probing level, and yet his work is consistently legible to a large public.

One of the hermeneutic projects taken up by Postmodernist thinkers has been the replacement of the primary expressive character of the author with the pleasure of the text and the reader's pleasure. Appropriation, allegory, and parody function instrumentally inside and outside the museum in visual and literary representations so that the authority of the author and the artist has been eroded and subverted. Using language as a readymade, contemporary artists alternately frame common cartoons in the context of high art and apply the signs of Modernism to unexpected surfaces to test how art is more or less meaningful, more or less legible than cartoons. It might be that the proliferation of meanings, reproductions, and even simulations has unsettled the firm position of reference and resemblance, as well as the cultural construction of a single author. Certainly artists since Duchamp have continually questioned the secure position of Modernist authority. Elaborating on why there has been a shift in the role of the author, Foucault, in "What Is an Author?," suggested that the author has played the role of the regulator of the fictive:

> The author is not an indefinite source of significations which fill a work; the author does not precede the works, he is a certain functional principle by which in our culture, one limits, excludes, and chooses; in short, by which one impedes the free circulation, the free manipulation, the free composition, decomposition, and recomposition of fiction. In fact, if we are accustomed to presenting the author as a genius, as a perpetual surging of invention, it is because in reality, we make him function in exactly the opposite fashion . . . the author is therefore the ideological figure by which one marks the manner in which we fear the proliferation of meaning."[17]

Taking advantage of decomposition and recomposition, artists have resisted the restrictions of Modernist authority, the category of genius, in order to extend their own and their audience's manipulation of meaning. Richard Prince's statement becomes a succinct acknowledgment of this condition: "I think the audience has always been the author of an artist's work. What's different now is that the artist can become the author of someone else's work."[18] The security and economy of his Modernist authority continues to be a central and contested issue for artists motivated by ideas as well as forms, artists whose persistent inquiries allow for the unimpeded circulation of meaning.

---

1. Douglas Crimp, "The Photographic Activity of Postmodernism," *October* 15 (Winter 1980), pp. 91–101. The history of early 1980s art hinges, to a great degree, on the theoretical assertions disseminated through this journal, politically allied with photobased art rather than the Neo-Expressionism then dominating the international art world.

2. Thomas Lawson, "Last Exit: Painting," *Artforum* 20, 2 (Oct. 1981), pp. 40–47. Reprinted in Brian Wallis, ed., *Art after Modernism: Rethinking Representation* (New York, 1984), pp. 153–65.

3. Douglas Crimp, "On the Museum's Ruins," in Hal Foster, ed., *The Anti-Aesthetic: Essays on Postmodern Culture* (Port Townsend, WA, 1983), pp. 43–56 (orig. published in *October* 13 [Summer 1980].

4. Ronald Jones, "Even Picasso: Sherrie Levine," *Artscribe International* 72 (Nov.–Dec. 1988), p. 51.

5. Kathleen B. Jones, "On Authority: Or, Why Women Are Not Entitled to Speak," in Irene Diamond and Lee Quinby, *Feminism*

and Foucault: Reflections on Resistance (Boston, 1988), pp. 122–26.

6. Jacques Lacan (1901–1981) was an influential psychoanalyst whose seminars in Paris were devoted to deconstructing the relationship between psychoanalysis and language. Lacan's reappraisals of Freudian thought have had a major impact on American literary theory, feminism, and art criticism. See Jacques Lacan, *The Four Fundamental Concepts of Psycho-Analysis* (New York, 1981), and Juliet Mitchell and Jacqueline Rose, *Feminine Sexuality: Jacques Lacan and the Ecole Freudienne*, trans. Jacqueline Rose (New York, 1985).

7. Peter Halley "Richard Prince Interviewed by Peter Halley," *ZG* 10 (May 1984), p. 5.

8. Brian Wallis, "Mindless Pleasure: Richard Prince's Fictions," *Parkett* 6 (1985), pp. 61–62.

9. Stuart Morgan, "Tell Me Everything," *Artscribe International* 73 (Jan.–Feb. 1989), p. 49.

10. Ibid.

11. Elizabeth Sussman and David Ross, "Interview with Richard Prince," in Institute of Contemporary Art, Boston, and Museum of Fine Arts, Boston, 1988, *American Art of the Late 80s*, p.164.

12. Bruce Ferguson, "Wordsmith: An Interview with Jenny Holzer by Bruce Ferguson," in Des Moines Art Center, Iowa, 1986, *Jenny Holzer: Signs*, p. 75. This interview was abridged and reprinted under the same title in *Art in America* 74, 12 (Dec. 1986), pp. 108–15, 153.

13. Ibid., p. 74.

14. Ibid., p. 70.

15. Daniela Salvioni, "On Richard Prince," *Flash Art* 142 (Oct. 1988), pp. 88–89.

16. Sol LeWitt, "Sentences on Conceptual Art," *Art Language* 1 (May 1969), pp. 11–13, reprinted in The Museum of Modern Art, New York, 1978, *Sol LeWitt*, and in Ellen H. Johnson, ed., *American Artists on Art from 1940 to 1980* (New York, 1982), pp. 125–27.

17. Michel Foucault, "What Is an Author?," in Josué V. Harari, *Textual Strategies: Perspectives in Post-Structuralist Criticism* (Ithaca, NY, 1979), p. 159.

18. Jeffrey Rian, "Social Science Fiction: An Interview with Richard Prince," *Art in America* 75, 3 (Mar. 1987), p. 90.

Plate 142. *Stretch*, 1969
    Black-and-white photographs and text panels on foamcore
    Nine parts, overall 54 x 54 in. (137 x 137 cm)
    Cat. no. 1

Plate 143. *Making Shelter (House of Used Parts)*, 1985
    Aluminum ladders, doors, windows, wood, canvas, and vinyl seat cushions
    108 x 72 x 72 in. (274 x 183 x 183 cm)
    Cat. no. 2

Plate 144. *Armadillo*, 1977–85
　　Black-and-white photographs
　　Three parts, overall dimensions variable; each 26½ x 33 in. (67 x 84 cm)
　　Cat. no. 8

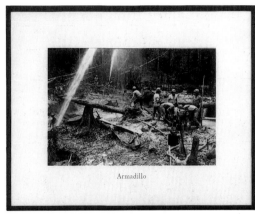

Armadillo

Plate 145. *Ana-Uaik (7 Venezuelan Rivers)*, 1985 (left)
    Wall painting
    39 x 47 in. (99 x 119 cm)
    Cat. no. 9

Plate 146. *Cooling Towers*, 1983
    Black-and-white photographs
    Twelve parts, each 20 x 16 in. (51 x 41 cm)
    Cat. no. 10

Plate 147. *Corbeau et renard*, 1968
Paint on photographic linen
30¾ x 50¾ in. (78 x 129 cm)
Cat. no. 15

Plate 148. *Chaise avec briques et pelle*, 1969–71–73
  Chair, spade, wood, metal, bricks, and paper
  Chair 34⅝ x 17 x 14¼ in. (88 x 43 x 36 cm); spade 45 x 7 in. (115 x 20 cm)
  Cat. no. 16

Plate 149. *La Soupe de Daguerre*, 1975
Color photographs on board
21 x 20½ in. (53 x 52 cm)
Cat. no. 17

Plate 150. *E.U.R. Palazzo della Civiltà*, 1983–88
Black-and-white photograph
71 x 47 in. (180 x 120 cm)
Cat. no. 47

Plate 151. *Untitled*, 1987
Acrylic on lead on wood
100⅜ x 82⅝ in. (255 x 210 cm)
Cat. no. 48

Plate 152. *Untitled*, 1988
Bronze
35½ x 23⅝ x 2 in. (90 x 60 x 5 cm)
Cat. no. 49

Plate 153. *Bedroom Dining Room Model House*, 1967
Color photographs
29 x 39 x 2 in. (74 x 99 x 5 cm)
Cat. no. 50

Plate 154. *Untitled* from the *Living Series*, 1981
Bronze
7½ x 10 in. (19 x 25 cm)
Cat. no. 53

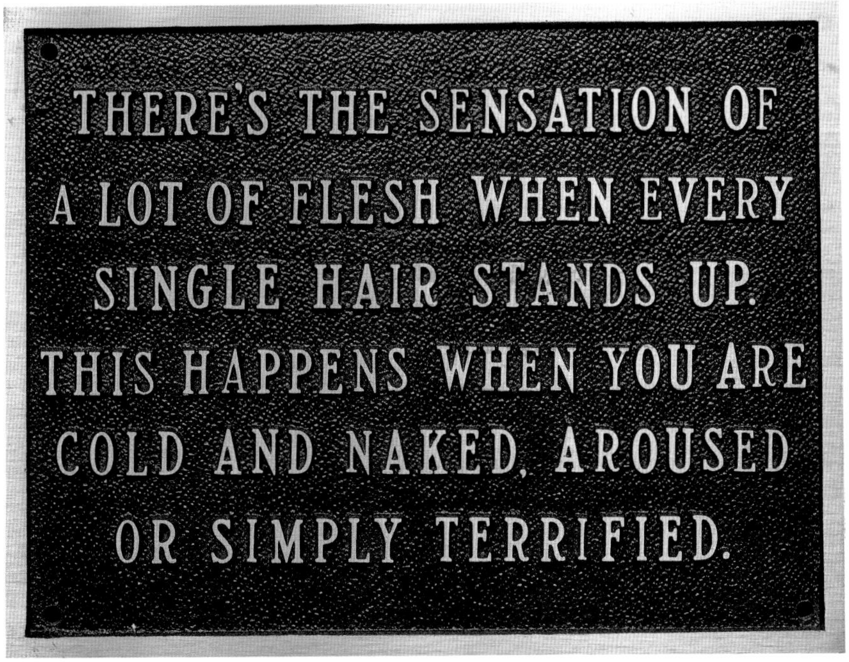

THERE'S THE SENSATION OF A LOT OF FLESH WHEN EVERY SINGLE HAIR STANDS UP. THIS HAPPENS WHEN YOU ARE COLD AND NAKED, AROUSED OR SIMPLY TERRIFIED.

Plate 155. *Essays*, 1982 (detail)
Offset posters
Twenty-nine parts, each 17 x 17 in. (43 x 43 cm)
Cat. no. 54

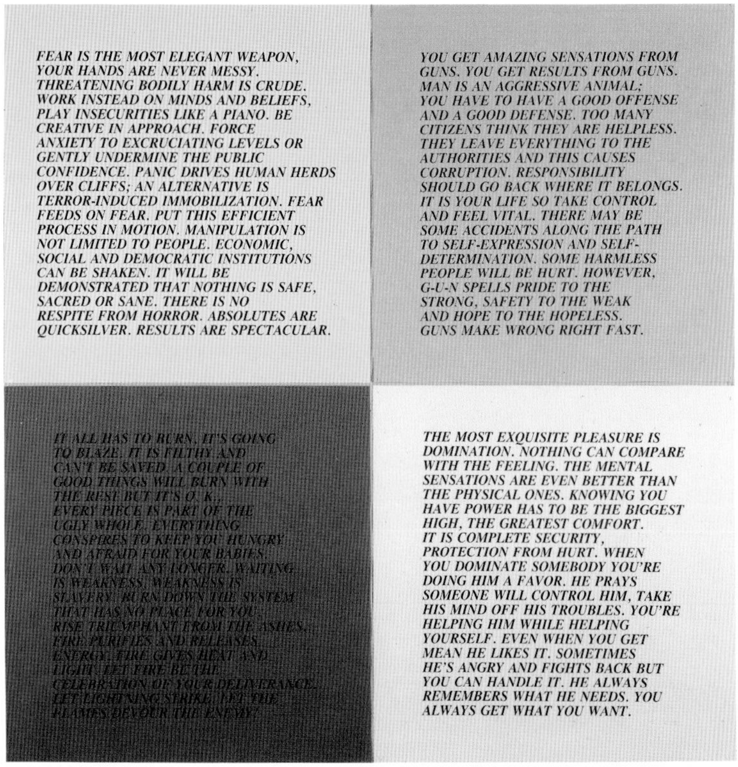

FEAR IS THE MOST ELEGANT WEAPON, YOUR HANDS ARE NEVER MESSY. THREATENING BODILY HARM IS CRUDE. WORK INSTEAD ON MINDS AND BELIEFS, PLAY INSECURITIES LIKE A PIANO. BE CREATIVE IN APPROACH. FORCE ANXIETY TO EXCRUCIATING LEVELS OR GENTLY UNDERMINE THE PUBLIC CONFIDENCE. PANIC DRIVES HUMAN HERDS OVER CLIFFS; AN ALTERNATIVE IS TERROR-INDUCED IMMOBILIZATION. FEAR FEEDS ON FEAR. PUT THIS EFFICIENT PROCESS IN MOTION. MANIPULATION IS NOT LIMITED TO PEOPLE. ECONOMIC, SOCIAL AND DEMOCRATIC INSTITUTIONS CAN BE SHAKEN. IT WILL BE DEMONSTRATED THAT NOTHING IS SAFE, SACRED OR SANE. THERE IS NO RESPITE FROM HORROR. ABSOLUTES ARE QUICKSILVER. RESULTS ARE SPECTACULAR.

YOU GET AMAZING SENSATIONS FROM GUNS. YOU GET RESULTS FROM GUNS. MAN IS AN AGGRESSIVE ANIMAL; YOU HAVE TO HAVE A GOOD OFFENSE AND A GOOD DEFENSE. TOO MANY CITIZENS THINK THEY ARE HELPLESS. THEY LEAVE EVERYTHING TO THE AUTHORITIES AND THIS CAUSES CORRUPTION. RESPONSIBILITY SHOULD GO BACK WHERE IT BELONGS. IT IS YOUR LIFE SO TAKE CONTROL AND FEEL VITAL. THERE MAY BE SOME ACCIDENTS ALONG THE PATH TO SELF-EXPRESSION AND SELF-DETERMINATION. SOME HARMLESS PEOPLE WILL BE HURT. HOWEVER, G-U-N SPELLS PRIDE TO THE STRONG, SAFETY TO THE WEAK AND HOPE TO THE HOPELESS. GUNS MAKE WRONG RIGHT FAST.

CHANGE IS THE BASIS OF ALL HISTORY, THE PROOF OF VIGOR. THE OLD IS SOILED AND DISGUSTING BY NATURE. STALE FOOD IS REPELLENT, MONOGAMOUS LOVE BREEDS CONTEMPT, SENILITY CRIPPLES THE GOVERNMENT THAT IS TOO POWERFUL TOO LONG. UPHEAVAL IS DESIRABLE BECAUSE FRESH, UNTAINTED GROUPS SEIZE OPPORTUNITY. VIOLENT OVERTHROW IS APPROPRIATE WHEN THE SITUATION IS INTOLERABLE. SLOW MODIFICATION CAN BE EFFECTIVE; MEN CHANGE BEFORE THEY NOTICE AND RESIST. THE DECADENT AND THE POWERFUL CHAMPION CONTINUITY. "NOTHING ESSENTIAL CHANGES." THAT IS A MYTH. IT WILL BE REFUTED. THE NECESSARY BIRTH CONVULSIONS WILL BE TRIGGERED. ACTION WILL BRING THE EVIDENCE TO YOUR DOORSTEP.

SNAKES ARE EVIL INCARNATE. THEY ARE A MANIFESTATION OF THE DARK SIDE OF NATURE. THEY LIE TWINED IN DAMP PLACES, THEIR BODIES COLD TO THE TOUCH. THE FORM OF THE SNAKE IS DREADFUL; THE TONGUE AND WORM-BODY INSPIRE LOATHING. THE SERPENT IS SLY, HE ABIDES WHERE YOU KNOW NOT. HE COMES CRAWLING TO BITE AND POISON. HE HAS MULTIPLIED SO HE INFESTS THE FACE OF THE EARTH. HE IS NOT CONTENT TO EXIST, HE MUST CORRUPT THAT WHICH IS PURE. THE APPEARANCE OF THE SERPENT SIGNIFIES ALL IS LOST. HE IS A SYMBOL OF OUR FAILURE AND OUR FATE.

IT ALL HAS TO BURN, IT'S GOING TO BLAZE. IT IS FILTHY AND CAN'T BE SAVED. A COUPLE OF GOOD THINGS WILL BURN WITH THE REST BUT IT'S O.K. EVERY PIECE IS PART OF THE UGLY WHOLE. EVERYTHING CONSPIRES TO KEEP YOU HUNGRY AND AFRAID FOR YOUR BABIES. DON'T WAIT ANY LONGER. WAITING IS WEAKNESS, WEAKNESS IS SLAVERY. BURN DOWN THE SYSTEM THAT HAS NO PLACE FOR YOU. RISE TRIUMPHANT FROM THE ASHES. FIRE PURIFIES AND RELEASES ENERGY. FIRE GIVES HEAT AND LIGHT. LET FIRE BE THE CELEBRATION OF YOUR DELIVERANCE. LET LIGHTNING STRIKE, LET THE FLAMES DEVOUR THE ENEMY.

THE MOST EXQUISITE PLEASURE IS DOMINATION. NOTHING CAN COMPARE WITH THE FEELING. THE MENTAL SENSATIONS ARE EVEN BETTER THAN THE PHYSICAL ONES. KNOWING YOU HAVE POWER HAS TO BE THE BIGGEST HIGH, THE GREATEST COMFORT. IT IS COMPLETE SECURITY, PROTECTION FROM HURT. WHEN YOU DOMINATE SOMEBODY YOU'RE DOING HIM A FAVOR. HE PRAYS SOMEONE WILL CONTROL HIM, TAKE HIS MIND OFF HIS TROUBLES. YOU'RE HELPING HIM WHILE HELPING YOURSELF. EVEN WHEN YOU GET MEAN HE LIKES IT. SOMETIMES HE'S ANGRY AND FIGHTS BACK BUT YOU CAN HANDLE IT. HE ALWAYS REMEMBERS WHAT HE NEEDS. YOU ALWAYS GET WHAT YOU WANT.

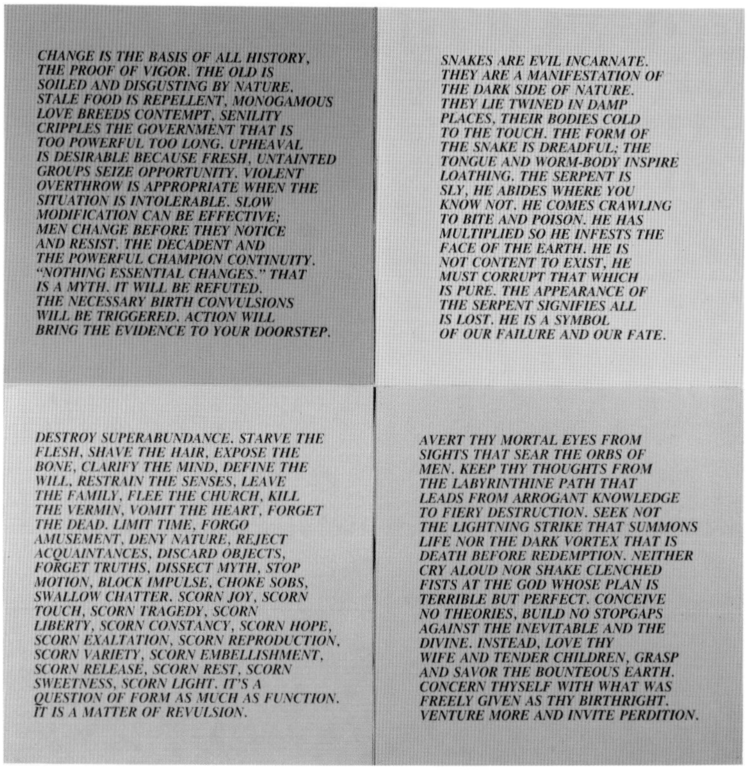

DESTROY SUPERABUNDANCE. STARVE THE FLESH, SHAVE THE HAIR, EXPOSE THE BONE, CLARIFY THE MIND, DEFINE THE WILL, RESTRAIN THE SENSES, LEAVE THE FAMILY, FLEE THE CHURCH, KILL THE VERMIN, VOMIT THE HEART, FORGET THE DEAD. LIMIT TIME, FORGO AMUSEMENT, DENY NATURE, REJECT ACQUAINTANCES, DISCARD OBJECTS, FORGET TRUTHS, DISSECT MYTH, STOP MOTION, BLOCK IMPULSE, CHOKE SOBS, SWALLOW CHATTER. SCORN JOY, SCORN TOUCH, SCORN TRAGEDY, SCORN LIBERTY, SCORN CONSTANCY, SCORN HOPE, SCORN EXALTATION, SCORN REPRODUCTION, SCORN VARIETY, SCORN EMBELLISHMENT, SCORN RELEASE, SCORN REST, SCORN SWEETNESS, SCORN LIGHT. IT'S A QUESTION OF FORM AS MUCH AS FUNCTION. IT IS A MATTER OF REVULSION.

AVERT THY MORTAL EYES FROM SIGHTS THAT SEAR THE ORBS OF MEN. KEEP THY THOUGHTS FROM THE LABYRINTHINE PATH THAT LEADS FROM ARROGANT KNOWLEDGE TO FIERY DESTRUCTION. SEEK NOT THE LIGHTNING STRIKE THAT SUMMONS LIFE NOR THE DARK VORTEX THAT IS DEATH BEFORE REDEMPTION. NEITHER CRY ALOUD NOR SHAKE CLENCHED FISTS AT THE GOD WHOSE PLAN IS TERRIBLE BUT PERFECT. CONCEIVE NO THEORIES, BUILD NO STOPGAPS AGAINST THE INEVITABLE AND THE DIVINE. INSTEAD, LOVE THY WIFE AND TENDER CHILDREN, GRASP AND SAVOR THE BOUNTEOUS EARTH. CONCERN THYSELF WITH WHAT WAS FREELY GIVEN AS THY BIRTHRIGHT. VENTURE MORE AND INVITE PERDITION.

Plate 156. *Selections from Under a Rock*, 1986 (detail)
Electronic L.E.D. sign and red and green diodes
10 x 112½ x 4½ in. (25 x 286 x 11 cm)
Cat. no. 55

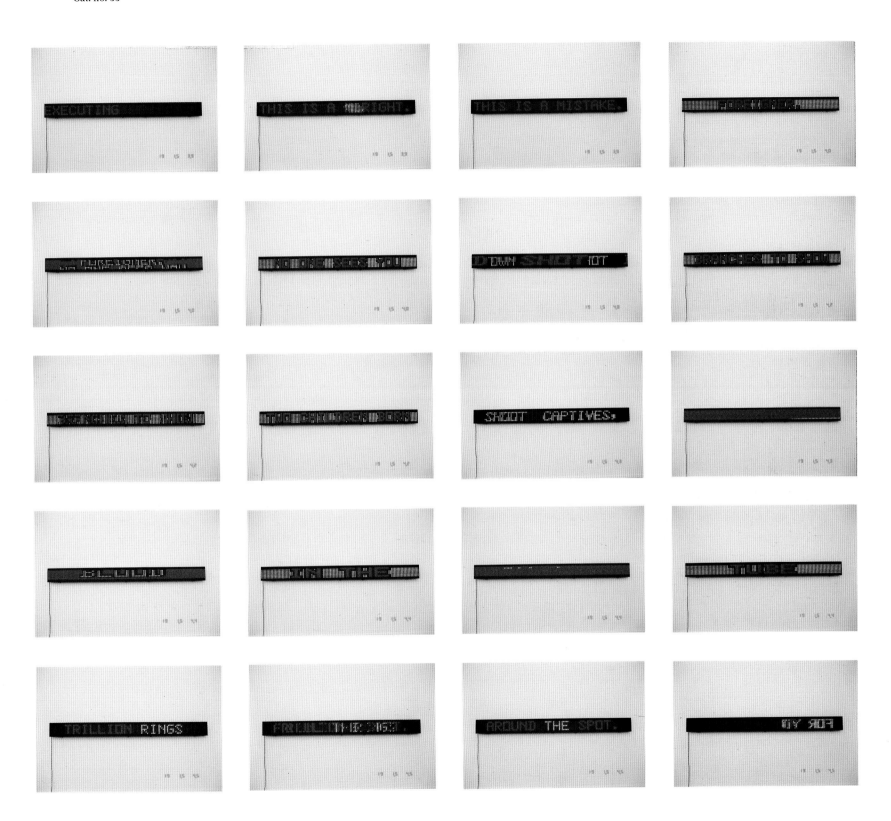

Plate 157. *Untitled (Selections from Truisms)*, 1987
Danby royal marble
17 x 54 x 25 in. (43 x 137 x 64 cm)
Cat. no. 56

Plate 158. *Between Reagan and Bush*, 1989
        Cibachrome print, painted wall, and text
        24 x 20 in. (61 x 51 cm)
        Cat. no. 79

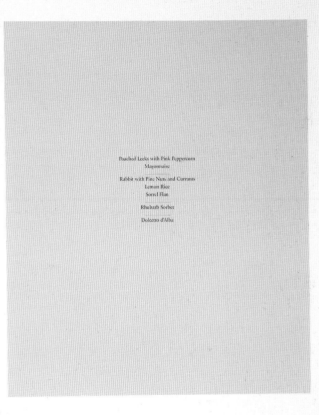

Poached Leeks with Pink Peppercorn
Mayonnaise

Rabbit with Pine Nuts and Currants
Lemon Rice
Sorrel Flan

Rhubarb Sorbet

Dolcetto d'Alba

Plate 159. *Untitled (Chair Seat: No. 10)*, 1986
Casein on wood
18¼ x 18⅛ in. (47 x 46 cm)
Cat. no. 80

SHERRIE LEVINE

Plate 160. *Untitled (Copper Knots: No. 1)*, 1988
Metallic paint and wood
45¼ x 36 in. (115 x 92 cm)
Cat. no. 81

Plate 161. *Untitled (Sunset)*, 1981
Ektacolor print
30 x 45 in. (76 x 114 cm)
Cat. no. 135

Plate 162. *Super-Heavy Santa*, 1986
Ektacolor print
86 x 48 in. (218 x 122 cm)
Cat. no. 136

Plate 163. *New York*, 1989
  Oil on color photograph
  4¼ x 5¾ in. (11 x 15 cm)
  Cat. no. 137

Plate 164. *Sils Maria*, 1989
Oil on color photograph
4¼ x 5¾ in. (11 x 15 cm)
Cat. no. 138

Plate 165. *Sils Maria*, 1989
Oil on color photograph
4¼ x 5¾ in. (11 x 15 cm)
Cat. no. 139

Plate 166. *Portrait*, 1988
Cibachrome print
83 x 65 in. (211 x 165 cm)
Cat. no. 143

Plate 167. *Portrait*, 1988
Cibachrome print
83 x 65 in. (211 x 165 cm)
Cat. no. 144

Plate 168. *The Shimada Family, Yamaguchi 1986*, 1988
          Color photograph
          26½ x 33½ in. (67 x 85 cm)
          Cat. no. 168

Plate 169. *Via Giovanni a Mare, Rome*, 1988
          Black-and-white photograph
          With frame 26½ x 33¾ in. (67 x 86 cm)
          Cat. no. 169

Plate 170. *Via Medina, Naples*, 1988
Black-and-white photograph
With frame 26½ x 33¾ in. (67 x 86 cm)
Cat. no. 170

Plate 171. *Via Sanità, Naples*, 1988
Black-and-white photograph
With frame 26½ x 33¾ in. (67 x 86 cm)
Cat. no. 171

Plate 172. *Pleading*, 1989
Steel, Plexiglas, and Cibachrome print
54 x 73½ x 9¼ in. (137 x 187 x 24 cm)
Cat. no. 172

Plate 173. *From Major to Minor, From Small to Large*, 1974–86
Wall painting
Dimensions variable
Cat. no. 173

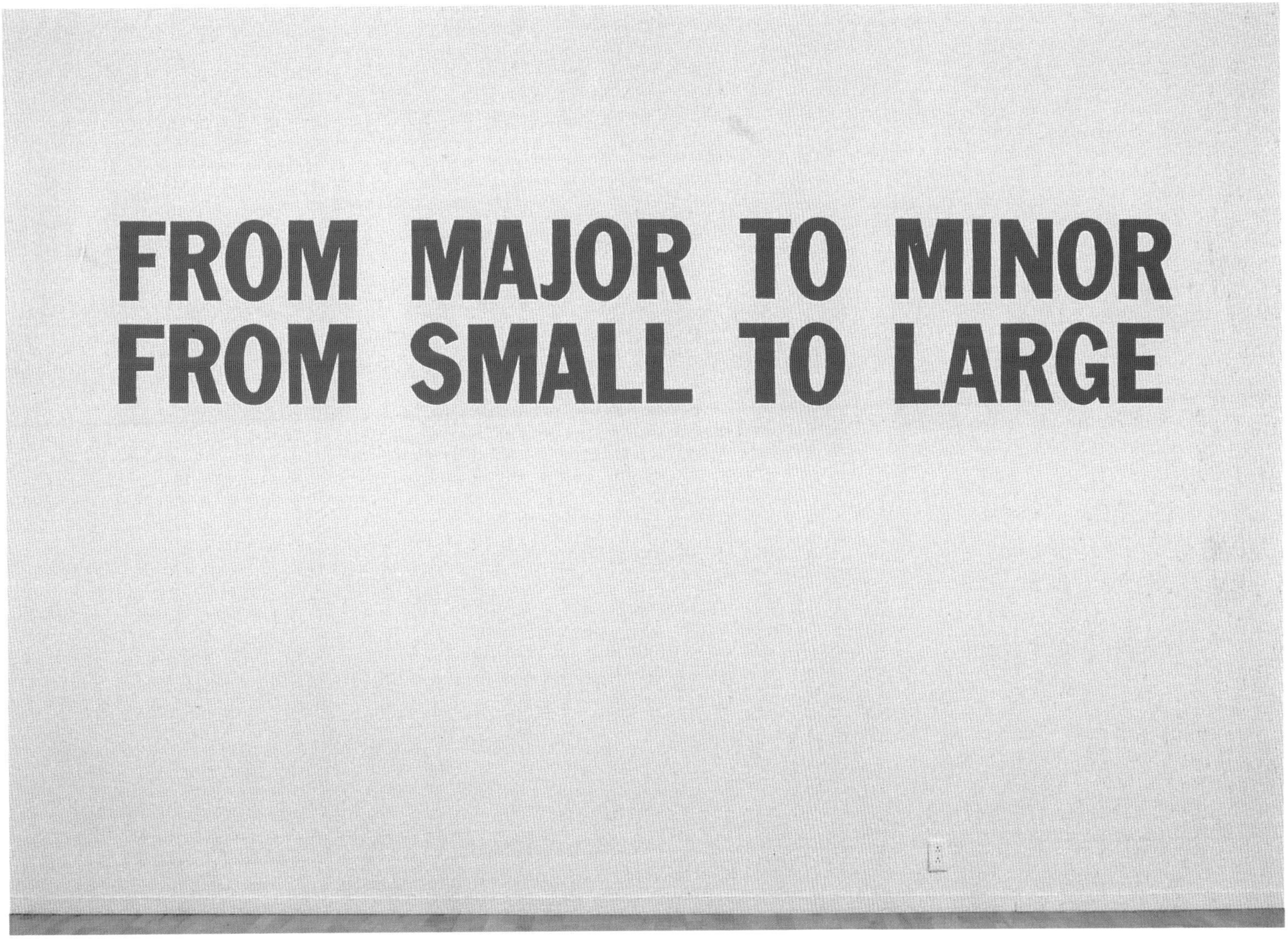

Art and Commodities

I. MICHAEL DANOFF

No matter how exalted the circumstances of its creation, once brought into being most art today commences its journey through the world in the marketplace. Artists generally hand over their latest efforts to commercial galleries; curators and collectors then vie with one another to be first through these portals of commerce in a competition reflecting the heated-up consumer society of the 1980s.

Some artists surrender to the pressures of this system, turning out—not creating—objects for a marketplace wherein, at the upper price reaches, supply is often insufficient to meet demand. But certain artists find issues of consumerism and its circumstances at the deepest core of their concerns. Ashley Bickerton, Peter Halley, Jeff Koons, and Haim Steinbach create art rooted in their consciousness of a culture caught up in manufactured commodities and their consumption. They are both fascinated by and concerned with a society obsessed with these commodities and thus vulnerable to their marketing.

To realize such a vision is risky because the artists who do so are also, like everyone else, consumers. They are somewhat in the position of being players in a cast who also must critique the production. Bickerton thinks it can be done: "We're now able to step back and merge, in fact to *implode* a variety of different strategies and epistemologies into the total art object that is capable of speaking of its own predicament as well as in general."[1]

The works these artists make are largely fabricated rather than handmade by the artist and are created from materials associated with mass-production rather than the fine arts. Some works contain components that are appropriated from the world of existing manufactured objects. These works evoke a society that is urban, highly industrialized, captivated by technology, and addicted to the media as a primary means of "interfacing." Being situated in the New York art world/market center heightens this consciousness. In expressing this vision, these artists are linked with many others whose work exhibits social and political concerns in a vocabulary emphasizing fabrication, technology, appropriation, and photography.

Unlike the other artists named above, Peter Halley works exclusively in the realm of paintings, which he executes himself. His works demonstrate a preoccupation with the geometric, which he sees as expressive of the urban, technological, communications-ridden environment in which consumerism prospers; his palette has the intensity of color television with the contrast turned high.

Figure 1. Peter Halley, *White Cell with Conduit*, 1987. Day-Glo acrylic, acrylic, and Roll-a-Tex on canvas, 80¼ x 140 in. (204 x 356 cm). The Oliver-Hoffmann Collection, Chicago.

Modern cities are geometrically laid out in grids, and manufactured objects—such as the buildings that Halley represents in fundamental units he calls "cells"[2]—tend to be geometrically regular, perhaps because it is easier to manufacture them that way. Halley also deploys the image and theme of the "conduit," symbolizing the way in which we link up through, for example, streets, pipes, tunnels, wiring; in *White Cell with Conduit* of 1987 (fig. 1), a conduit system is presented beneath an implied white cell.

Some of Halley's paintings look like renderings of exploded computer chips. These components became particularly prominent in communications technology in the 1980s, a decade in which the United States and many other nations became hyperactive in electronics communication (as demonstrated by the proliferation of personal computers and as reflected in the ongoing popularity of films such as the *Star Wars* trilogy, *Short Circuit*, *Robocop*, and so forth).

In addressing issues of consumerism, these four artists were expressing a phenomenon of extraordinary intensity in the late 1970s and in the 1980s, as witnessed by such T-shirt philosophy as: "When the going gets tough, the tough go shopping"; "The difference between men and boys is the price of their toys"; "He who dies with the most toys wins"; "Born to shop"; and "I shop, therefore I am." Many writers have addressed the role of consumerism in modern culture, and their words provide a helpful context for demonstrating the profundity of the issues that compel Bickerton, Halley, Koons, and Steinbach. The historian T. J. Jackson Lears has delineated how consumerism has a history reaching back to the last century:

Around the turn of the century a fundamental cultural transformation occurred within the educated strata of Western capitalist nations. In the United States as elsewhere the bourgeois ethos had enjoined perpetual work, compulsive saving, civic responsibility and a rigid morality of self-denial. By the early 20th century that outlook had begun to give way to a new set of values sanctioning periodic leisure, compulsive spending, apolitical passivity, and an apparently permissive (but subtly coercive) morality of individual fulfillment.[3]

Lears theorized that manufactured objects came to play a vital role in the lives of Americans toward the end of the last century. This was a response to two factors. First, individuals became distanced from traditional contact with the physical world as society ceased being primarily agrarian. And second, there was diminishing peace of mind as traditional spiritual values waned. Possessing manufactured things was a less satisfying and obsessive attempt to compensate for these losses. Appropriation, by which manufactured objects are incorporated into works of art, has a notable history in art of this century and has blossomed in the 1980s because it reflects the attraction to manufactured things.[4]

Vulnerability to consuming manufactured objects has been capitalized upon by the advertising industry. In 1957 Vance Packard published his widely read *The Hidden Persuaders*, revised and released again in 1980. Packard took the position of exposing how many advertising firms plotted to have their way with a largely unknowing public: "many of us are being influenced and manipulated, far more than we realize, in the patterns of our daily lives."[5] Packard attributed this to the change in the economy from issues of production to those of consumption: "In the early fifties, with overproduction threatening on many fronts, a fundamental shift occurred in the preoccupation of people in executive suites. Production now became a relatively secondary concern. Executive planners changed from being maker-minded to marketing-minded"; Packard went on to quote an executive as saying: "Consumerism is king!"[6]

In *The Lonely Crowd*, sociologist David Riesman wrote of a "sort of revolution...a shift from an age of production to an age of consumption."[7] He found this to be a world-wide phenomenon but most evident in the United States because of the extent of its "capitalism, industrialism and urbanization."[8] He observed that the character of the middle class was becoming "other-directed," which is "a tendency to be sensitized to the expectations and preferences of others."[9] Moreover, "the other-directed person's tremendous outpouring of energy is channeled into the ever-expanding frontiers of consumption."[10] For this new majority, "training in consumer taste...tends to replace [training in] etiquette."[11]

Bickerton, Koons, and Steinbach all reflect in their own ways consumer obsession in the 1980s. Steinbach has said his art has to do with "one's taking pleasure in objects and commodities...a stronger sense of being complicit with the production of desire, what we traditionally call beautiful seductive objects."[12] He is seduced by the pleasure of shopping—"I spend a lot of time shopping"[13]—and by the beauty of manufactured objects and their ample, repetitious presentation in stores (see fig. 2). Commenting on a sculpture of his that includes a progressively smaller stack of flaming orange enamel pots, he recalled how he was walking down the street, saw them in a store, and said to himself, "Wow! Look at that!" He specified he was attracted to them not because they made a statement about consumerism but because he found them visually appealing.[14]

Figure 2. Haim Steinbach, *ultra red #1*, 1986. Formica shelf, six digital clocks, seventeen enameled pots, and four lava lamps, 59 x 107 x 19 in. (150 x 272 x 48 cm). Edition: 1/2. The Oliver-Hoffmann Collection, Chicago.

Thus, Steinbach enjoys consumerism while being wary of it. He is sincerely affected by the beauty of these objects, which he presents on an altarlike mantel (see pl. 181; cat. no. 167). But at the same time he questions being compelled by such materialism. However much the shelves are physically beautiful, they are shelves for presentation and thus a vehicle for marketing. Steinbach has stated that the anxiety of late capitalistic culture is in us.[15] There is an obsessive thrill-seeking to consumerism, which is self-perpetuating because it is never completely fulfilling.

Jeff Koons knows that manufactured objects can compel us, as demonstrated in a series titled *The New* begun in 1980 (see pl. 177; cat. no. 72), consisting of factory-fresh vacuum cleaners enclosed in Plexiglas and illuminated by visible fluorescent bulbs (the latter recalling Dan Flavin's sculptures). These works demonstrate an obsession with the "brand new" and celebrate that pristine condition through the careful way in which the objects are displayed in custom-fabricated cases with intense, self-contained lighting.[16]

Once a consumer object is showcased, it must be advertised. Koons has addressed commodity promotion through paintings taken quite literally from advertising (for example, *I Could Go for Something Gordon's*, pl. 174; cat. no. 74). In these works he means to take a moral stance on advertising. In the paintings dealing with advertisements for alcoholic beverages, he believes the images to be degrading

Plate 174. Jeff Koons, *I Could Go for Something Gordon's*, 1986.
Oil inks on canvas, 45 x 86½ in. (114 x 220 cm).
Cat. no. 74

and opportunistic. One in particular — *Hennessy, The Civilized Way to Lay Down the Law* of 1986 — he finds sexist. In a series based on advertisements for sporting goods, he wanted to point up the discrepancy between the fantasy being created and the harsh realities that prevent the vast majority from reaching that fantasy.

Koons's group of stainless-steel sculptures are derived mostly from well-known public figures or types, done up in souvenir format, which the artist casts in stainless steel and places on a pedestal (for example, *Louis XIV*, pl. 179; cat. no. 75). The layering of references — the original subject, the souvenir statue of the subject, and Koons's sculpture — focus attention on the variety of sociological meanings that referents can have and how those meanings are conveyed. The choice of material has meaning too: stainless steel is associated with twentieth-century commodities and is closer to everyday urban reality than silver, bronze, or other precious metals associated with the fine arts.

In series after series of startling visual diversity, Koons has built his work on appropriated objects, whether vacuum cleaners, basketballs (see pl. 178; cat. no. 73), kitsch statues, or such media images as those of Michael Jackson or the Pink Panther (see pl. 180; cat. no. 76). These are all objects of appeal to the unsophisticated art consumer. Through the ways in which he appropriates, presents, and fabricates commercial merchandise, he imbues it with moods, feelings, and issues that transcend its original limited associations, thus elevating his sources into resonant works of art.

Ashley Bickerton fabricates boxlike sculptures that recall the basic shape of some of Donald Judd's objects. But he adds a mélange of materials, ornamentation, and words intended to evoke a diverse array of meanings beyond what is encountered in Judd's "specific objects." He sees his art as being not only about aesthetics, but also about art history, the art market, and the personality of the artist. "I wanted to address... what that object is, how it operates, how one contemplates exactly what it is one is dealing with in all of its facets."[17] Elsewhere he has stated:

> the art object has now been placed in a discursive relationship with the larger scenario of the political and social reality of which it is a part. In a self-conscious and ongoing dialogue with the social, political and intellectual climate of the time and place it will operate in, and with the entire process of its absorption.[18]

To emphasize the fact that art makes its way through the marketplace, he has sometimes included the current market value and cleaning and handling instructions as part of the work.

Bickerton's objects are also intended to be personally expressive. Of a work that alludes to van Gogh (*Tormented Self-Portrait [Susie at Arles] No. 2* of 1988, pl. 176; cat. no. 12), he said: "My piece says as much about myself as a self-portrait of van Gogh's did about him."[19] Bickerton does this "By seeing myself through the products I used."[20] The work makes explicit reference to Sprint, Marlboro cigarettes, Integral Yoga, and Wholefood for the Whole Person. In his "word" paintings, he has included "the most fundamental utterances of the mind/body unit: the guttural grunts of sex, defecation, terror and glee, or in a weightier sense, birth and death."[21]

While aspects of consumerism form the vocabulary and much of the theme of these four artists, it would be a mistake to assume consumerism is their exclusive subject. Like Bickerton, each of these artists is involved in personal expression.

The expressive aspects of Haim Steinbach's art are achieved through the traditional components of image, color, and composition. The objects he presents constitute a vocabulary of feelings which he builds into images. Prosthetic devices (see, for example, *Code of Silence* of 1987) simply call forth gloomier associations than do lava lamps (see *Ultra Life No. 2* of 1988). The objects he selects do not remain mute, but become images rich in association. A recent closet piece with rows of rifles (*Untitled [guns, hats]* of 1987) is disturbing in a way that a series of cooking pots is not. Composition — juxtaposition, that is — also impacts; associations are thus generated in the most traditional of ways. The color of the objects also counts, not only in what is selected but in the "shelves" that Steinbach builds for them and which link his sculptures to the genre of still life.

Color also is an important expressive vehicle for Koons. The orange basketballs and dark brown bronze of the flotation works are autumnal and melancholy. Many of the sculptures from *The New* are done in brighter, more cheerful colors. There is a tremendous amount of expressive value focusing on the single issue of containment, with its implications ranging from incubator to coffin. The early inflatables, the vacuum cleaners and the cases surrounding them, the tanks in the flotation works, the life vests and inflatable boat, all these reflect aspects of containment. Furthermore, what is contained is air with its overtones of life-sustaining breath (the inflatables, the basketballs, the vacuum cleaners). This gives the objects an anthropomorphic quality that further sets the stage for expressive associations.

Halley also is involved with expressive concerns. A canvas in which light and air have been forced out by blackness is frighteningly nihilistic, one interpretation that the artist finds comfortable.[22] Halley uses color to suggest feelings on a very basic level: bright is hopeful and dark is dour. Color also expresses his feelings about the forces that regularize and control our lives. For Halley, as for any artist, some works will be more successful aesthetic achievements than others. Whatever the images transmit about culture, the individual works also offer an integration of aesthetic components as traditional as color, composition, texture, and line.

A discussion of the antecedents for the work of these four artists underscores the existence of their social and political leanings. At the time these artists emerged, Figurative Expressionism enjoyed the highest profile in contemporary art. These four artists, however, preferred to make an art in which the overt revelation of sensibility was not primary and that was more about sociological issues and their impact on the individual. Their work has a strong affinity with Pop and Minimal art from two decades past. The reason for this affinity is not simply that both generations often preferred the geometric. Rather, the geometric and industrial emphases expressed a profound interest in issues of productivity and consumerism, the first generation leaning more toward the former and the second toward the latter.

The works of Pop and Minimal artists are steeped in images reflective of industrial production and America's post–World War II prosperity, during which time these artists matured. The materials of Minimal artists such as Judd, Flavin, and others recall manufactured goods — stainless steel, fluorescent light fixtures, Formica, etc. The repeated image in many works by Andy Warhol and the repeated unit found in Judd's work are suggestive of product uniformity and the assembly line. Pop artists also made use of manufactured materials or at least worked toward that look, as exemplified by Warhol's silkscreen technique and Roy Lichtenstein's use of Ben Day dots. The fact that so many images in Pop art are media-based reflects upon issues of consumerism, since the primary tool of consumerism, advertising, is prominent in American media. Bickerton, Halley, Koons, and Steinbach focus more on issues of consumerism than of production, reflecting the shift in cultural attitudes noted by Reisman and Packard.

There are artists who emerged just prior to the four considered here who share with them similar interests in methodology and issues. Robert Longo's important work commenced at the end of the 1970s. His *Men in the Cities* drawings (see pl. 78; cat. no. 89) and *Corporate Wars* of 1982 relief demonstrate his concern with social and consumer issues. "I think an artist has a real obligation to catch his time," the artist said.[23] *Corporate Wars* is Longo's response to his first-hand observations of daily trading activities on the floors of Wall Street. Also, his approach to many of the large works involved fabrication rather than the touch of the artist's hand (see pl. 79; cat. no. 90) and assistants helped him produce *Men in the Cities*.

R. M. Fischer was one of the first artists of a younger generation to resurrect aspects of Pop and Minimal art by addressing issues of production and consumption. In the late 1970s he openly acknowledged admiration for Warhol.[24] By 1978 he was making objects that are simultaneously sculptures and functional lamps, a major step into appropriation. Insofar as the objects are functional, they exemplify appropriation from "the real world" to a degree beyond Warhol's Brillo boxes.

Fischer said his goal was to create an art that allowed for sociological references without abandoning the object. A clue to the nature of those references is in his stated belief that art must be more democratic than ever before because of the increasingly pervasive influence of the media, television and movies in particular. Consumer desire thereby becomes widely distributed and approaches uniformity; thus, sociological references pertain to the media and the influence of advertising upon consumers. Fischer acknowledged his interest in the media and promotion most openly in 1979 when, with Elliott Wertheim, he founded Ronell Productions, whose purpose was to promote his work through advertising techniques.

Bickerton, Halley, Koons, and Steinbach are forcing viewers to examine aspects of one of the most problematic issues of the 1980s: consumerism. Moreover, despite its differences, their work have an affinity with that of Pop and Minimal artists. Nevertheless, although Pop and Minimalism have been widely accepted, this new art has frequently met with cynicism, transmitted more often in conversation than in print. The term "Neo-Geo" (meaning art of the 1980s that emphasizes geometry and appropriation and quickly entered the marketplace), so often used in reference to their work, not only focuses on a formal similarity (geometry) rather than the more profound issues of content, but its rhyming suggests a cuteness that is demeaning and deprecatory, establishing a tone that does not encourage serious consideration. Moreover, the "neo" prefix has a copycat implication.

This cynicism about "Neo-Geo" is based on the assumption that art so labeled is solely a shallow marketing creation rather than the expression of the artist's unique vision and voice about consumerism. It is as though viewers understood aspects of the content but could not allow for the possibility of its being embodied in authentic or serious works of art.

The work has been criticized for having gained attention too quickly, as though the artists were too young for such success and had not paid adequate dues. Referring to the work of Bickerton, Halley, Koons, and Meyer Vaisman, one critic wrote: "I have never seen so much hype and hoopla directed at four artists whose résumés, aside from student exhibitions, barely reach back to 1984."[25] Certainly these artists were caught up in a wave of exposure in the mid-1980s, during which time critics, curators, collectors, and dealers all were awaiting the arrival of the next direction following Figurative Expressionism. But while the exposure as a group was rather sudden and intense, Koons had his first show of *The New* in 1980, and Halley's cells and conduits and Steinbach's shelf sculptures were underway in the early years of this decade. Furthermore, there is precedent for contemporary artists who garnered attention early on: Frank Stella readily comes to mind. Nevertheless, it is a fact that today many artists have had gallery exposure by the time they complete graduate training, a situation not exclusive to New York. But how quickly or slowly an artist is accepted remains extrinsic to the merit of the art produced—a distinction some critics have difficulty making.

It was often heard art-world talk that the prices obtained by Bickerton, Halley, Koons, and Steinbach, especially once they were represented by the prestigious and well-established Sonnabend Gallery, were too great for so new a movement and were inconsistent with artistic merit. Reflecting the feelings of many in the art world, Kay Larson wrote: "Nothing about the Neoists is unique except their lust for money."[26] The fact that these artists were dealing with issues of consumerism unintentionally reinforced the sense that what they were creating was more sizzle than steak.

Underlying all these misgivings is the assumption that this work is a mindless expression of crass capitalism. The artists are seen to manifest no social and political consciousness in the content of their art or their role in its making, which once again has played into the hands of those who wanted to see this art as overpriced art-market junk food. But the consumer-oriented works of these four artists link up with a kind of secret sharer that has occupied the art world in the 1980s. That "other" is self-conscious socially and politically oriented art, in particular a postexpressionistic kind emphasizing fabrication, appropriation, and photography, as seen in the work of Gretchen Bender, Hans Haacke, Alfredo Jaar, and others.

By virtue of their attitudes toward consumer society, the four artists discussed in this essay are as political or social in their work as the artists more often touted for such leanings. While Haacke is generally more explicitly social and political than Bickerton, Halley, Koons, or Steinbach, others, such as Alfredo Jaar in his works about the impoverished and downtrodden, and Ronald Jones in his art about rooms associated with political atrocities, are just as implicit. The main difference is that those who have been seen as social and political artists were never marketed as a movement and perhaps were seen more as polemicists than as artists creating aesthetic objects.

Bickerton, Halley, Koons, and Steinbach link up not only with social and political postexpressionists working in three dimensions but also with those working with photography, such as Sarah Charlesworth, Barbara Kruger, and Richard Prince. The latter are connected with consumerism because they appropriate from that world; but, instead of appropriating objects, they appropriate images from advertising, the vehicle through which the identity of consumer objects is created.

In the early 1970s Barbara Kruger was immersed in an eleven-year career as designer and photo editor at Condé Nast (whose publications include *Mademoiselle* and *Vogue*). By 1978 she had turned to photography and texts: "I'm interested in words and pictures and their effect on culture."[27] Her visual technique is highly seductive because she combines words with appropriated images and gives them the look of contemporary commercial advertising design.

Prince and Charlesworth also have been concerned with advertising. As early as 1977 Prince was engaged in "re-photography" with images from television and magazines as his most frequent sources. Charlesworth's images also are derived from advertisements.

One cannot write about these artists wrestling with issues of commodities without dealing with the media, because attitudes toward commodities are shaped—often controlled—by advertising which works through the media. The upscale pots that caught Steinbach's eye are not simply cooking utensils but "the good life." Many consumers make of commodities something metaphysical by conferring on them a hyperreality. The media-projected world can seem more real than the material world. In *The Minimal Self*, the historian Christopher Lasch wrote:

> Commodity production and consumerism alter perceptions not just of the self but of the world outside the self. They create a world of mirrors, insubstantial images, illusions increasingly indistinguishable from reality.... The consumer lives surrounded not so much by things as by fantasies. He lives in a world that has no objective or independent existence and seems to exist only to gratify or thwart his desires.[28]

This finding of metaphysical qualities in commodities is connected to the growth of consumer culture since the end of the last century. The metaphysical perception of highly promoted commodities is tied to the sense of unreality that has developed in this century. Lears used the terms "weightless" and "unreal" to describe our relation to commodities.[29] He wrote that since the late nineteenth century, "a dread of unreality, a yearning to experience intense 'real life' in all its forms" is characteristic of urban existence.[30] That unreality has to do with feelings of distance from direct contact with the physical world characteristic of the agrarian society which no longer exists. Lears further wrote: "Consumers acquire commodities not only through purchasing them but through a kind of all-purposive knowingness, a thoroughgoing acquaintance with commodities' actual and imagined attributes."[31] What he described is the metaphysical quality of commodities, their hyperreality.

Unwelcome though it may be, Bickerton, Halley, Koons, and Steinbach suggest that in this intensely consumer-oriented society, attitudes toward promoted commodities are similar to attitudes toward art. Manufactured commodities are given a metaphysical cast by promoters who intend to manipulate the consumer's response in a particular way; Prince says that certain media images are so intense for him that he wonders what the images are imagining.[32] Artists likewise have the audience look at objects that are created to shape response in a particular way.[33] The distinction between works of art and nonart commodities is blurred. Works of art have a kinship with the images surrounding media-promoted objects. Experiencing the inanimate, "imagined attributes" of objects that consumers crave to consume is close kin to experiencing the metaphysical aspects of the inanimate art object.

It is not that art and advertising are identical. The artist generally puts the viewer in touch with a worldview that is rich and complex. The advertiser usually puts the consumer in touch with a metaphysical aura less complex or profound. But one cannot deny that many individuals are susceptible to developing an attachment to commodities—or, more precisely, their advertised image—that is profoundly meaningful to them and troubling to those who see art as more exalted than advertising or nonart commodities.

Such are the kinds of questions raised by Bickerton, Halley, Koons, and Steinbach. They may be of the yuppie generation; they may genuinely delight in manufactured objects and advertisements for commodities; and they may well enjoy the material profits from their creative labors. But those possibilities or even realities are unrelated to the quality of the works of art they make, which should be evaluated as are any works of art—by the extent to which each particular one is visually remarkable and effectively evocative of the artist's worldview.

1. Peter Nagy, moderator, "From Criticism to Complicity," *Flash Art* 129 (Summer 1986), p. 46.

2. Halley's ideas on cells and conduits are presented in "On Line," reprinted in *Peter Halley: Collected Essays, 1981–87* (Zurich, 1988), pp. 152–59.

3. T. J. Jackson Lears, "From Salvation to Self-Realization: Advertising and the Therapeutic Roots of the Consumer Culture, 1880–1930," in Richard Wrightman Fox and T. J. Jackson Lears, eds., *The Culture of Consumption* (New York, 1983), p. 3.

4. For a discussion of the relation of appropriation in this century to the history of consumerism, see Museum of Contemporary Art, Chicago, 1988, *Jeff Koons*, exh. cat. by I. Michael Danoff, p. 16.

5. Vance Packard, *The Hidden Persuaders* (New York, 1980), p. 1.

6. Ibid., p. 18.

7. David Riesman with Nathan Glazer and Reuel Denney, *The Lonely Crowd* (New York, 1961 [first published 1950]), p. 6.

8. Ibid., p. 20.

9. Ibid., p. 8.

10. Ibid., p. 78.

11. Ibid., p. 74.

12. Nagy (note 1), p. 46.

13. Ibid., p. 47.

14. Haim Steinbach in conversation with the author, c. 1986.

15. Nagy (note 1), p. 49.

16. That preserving the aura of newness is important to Koons is indicated by the fact that he has wondered whether Steinbach sculptures may eventually have a diminished impact since there is no encasement to protect the objects appropriated. Newness per se, however, is less of an issue for Steinbach than for Koons (Koons in conversation with the author, June 1986).

17. Shaun Caley, "Ashley Bickerton, a Revealing Exposé of the Application of Art," *Flash Art International* 143 (Nov. 1988), p. 79.

18. Nagy (note 1), p. 46.

19. Caley (note 17), p. 80.

20. Ibid.

21. Ashley Bickerton and Aimee Rankin, "Fluid Mechanics: A Conversation between Ashley Bickerton and Aimee Rankin," *Arts* 62, 4 (Dec. 1987), p. 82.

22. Peter Halley in conversation with the author, c. 1986.

23. Akron Art Museum, Akron, Ohio, 1984, *Robert Longo: Drawings and Reliefs*, exh. cat. by I. Michael Danoff, p. 5.

24. See Nina Felschin, "R. M. Fischer: An Interview," in *R. M. Fischer* (Cincinnati, 1981).

25. Kay Larson, "Masters of Hype," *New York* 19, 44 (Nov. 10, 1986), p. 100.

26. Ibid., p. 103.

27. Barbara Kruger, in Jamie Gambrell, "What is Political Art…Now," *Village Voice* 42 (Oct. 15, 1985), p. 73.

28. Christopher Lasch, *The Minimal Self* (New York, 1984), p. 30.

29. Fox and Lears (note 3), p. xiii.

30. Ibid., p. 6.

31. Ibid., p. xv.

32. David Robbins, "Richard Prince: An Interview," *Aperture* 100 (Fall 1985), p. 7.

33. I realize this viewpoint is unfashionable in light of Roland Barthes's celebrated position that meaning is the result of interaction between reader and text rather than the reader's passively consuming the author's preconceived intention (see "The Death of the Author," in *Image, Music, Text*, trans. Stephen Heath [New York, 1977]). However, preconceived intention always is present to a notable extent, even if the artist/author's intent is to allow the viewer/reader to bring many personal associations to the encounter with the work of art. A recent and strong alternative to the position of Barthes is found in Richard Wollheim, *Painting as an Art* (Princeton, NJ, 1987)

Plate 175. *God*, 1986
Acrylic, aluminum paint, and resin on wood with aluminum
48 x 96 x 11 in. (122 x 244 x 28 cm)
Cat. no. 11

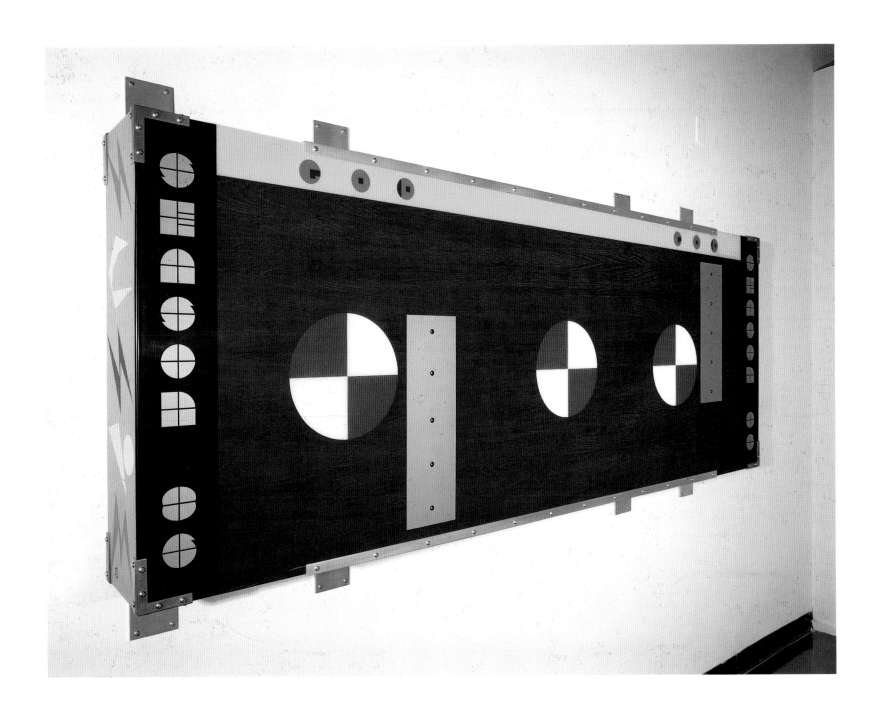

Plate 176. *Tormented Self-Portrait (Susie at Arles) No. 2,* 1988
Mixed-media construction with leather padding
90 x 69 x 18 in. (229 x 175 x 46 cm)
Cat. no. 12

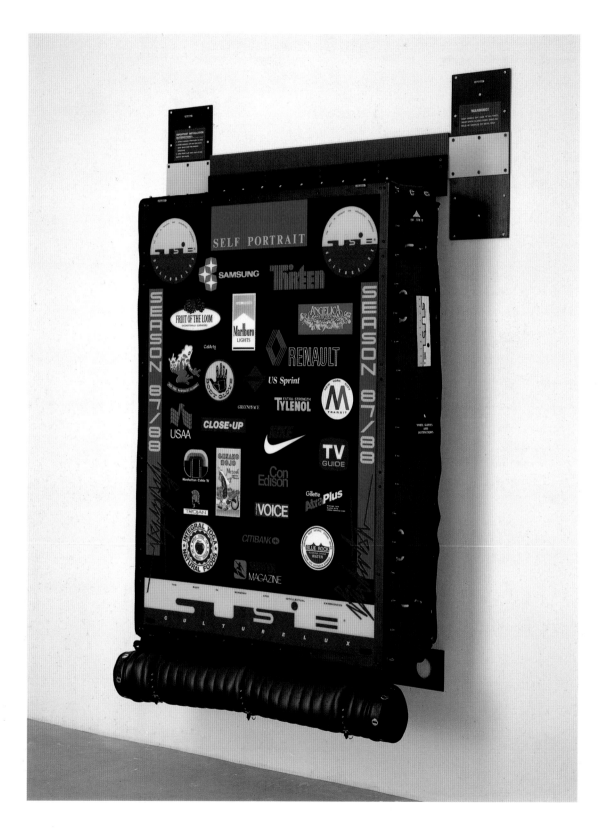

Plate 177. *New Hoover Deluxe Shampoo-Polishers, New Shelton Wet/Dry*
10-gallon Displaced Triple-decker, 1981–87
Four Hoover deluxe shampoo-polishers, one Shelton wet/dry
10-gallon vacuum cleaner, Plexiglas, and fluorescent tubes
91 x 54 x 28 in. (231 x 137 x 71 cm)
Cat. no. 72

Plate 178. *Three Ball Total Equilibrium Tank*, 1985
   Glass, iron, sodium chloride reagent, and basketballs
   60½ x 48 x 13¼ in. (154 x 124 x 34 cm)
   Cat. no. 73

Plate 179. *Louis XIV*, 1986
        Stainless steel
        46 x 27 x 15 in. (117 x 68 x 38 cm)
        Cat. no. 75

Plate 180. *Pink Panther*, 1988
Porcelain
41 x 20½ x 19 in. (104 x 52 x 48 cm)
Cat. no. 76

Plate 181. *untitled (football, clog)*, 1987
    Clog, straw, football, and laminated wooden shelf
    37½ x 74½ x 20 in. (95 x 189 x 51 cm)
    Cat. no. 167

Catalogue of the Collection

By Mary Murphy and Neal Benezra

Vito Acconci

Born 1940, Bronx, New York; lives and works in Brooklyn, New York

1. *Stretch*, 1969 (pl. 142)

Black-and-white photographs and text panels on foamcore
Nine parts, overall 54 x 54 in. (137 x 137 cm)

Provenance: Rhona Hoffman Gallery, Chicago.

Exhibitions: Rhona Hoffman Gallery, Chicago, 1988, "Vito Acconci, Photographic Works 1969–1970," ill. p. 6.

References: Vito Acconci, "Early Work: Moving My Body into Place," *Avalanche* 6 (Fall 1972), ill., n. pag.

2. *Making Shelter (House of Used Parts)*, 1985 (pl. 143)

Aluminum ladders, doors, windows, wood, canvas, and vinyl seat cushions
108 x 72 x 72 in. (274 x 183 x 183 cm)

Provenance: Rhona Hoffman Gallery, Chicago.

Exhibitions: La Jolla Museum of Contemporary Art, California, 1987, "Vito Acconci: Domestic Trappings," no. 29, ill. p. 20 (traveled 1987–88: Neuberger Museum of Art, State University of New York at Purchase; Aspen Art Museum, Colorado; Laumeier Sculpture Park, St. Louis).

Carl Andre

Born 1935, Quincy, Massachusetts; lives and works in New York

3. *Untitled*, 1963 (pl. 3)

Text on paper
11 x 8½ in. (28 x 22 cm)

Provenance: Paula Cooper Gallery, New York.

4. *Blue Wood Chain*, New York, 1964 (pl. 2)

Painted wood
26½ x 6 x 5½ in. (67 x 15 x 14 cm)

Provenance: Betty Parsons Gallery, New York; Jack Tilton Gallery, New York.

Exhibitions: The David and Alfred Smart Gallery, The University of Chicago, 1985, "Alumni Who Collect, II: Sculpture from 1600 to the Present," as *Blue Piece.*

References: Kunsthalle Bern, Switzerland, 1975, *Carl Andre, Sculpture 1958–1974*, p. 19, no. 1964–6; Haags Gemeentemuseum, The Hague, and Stedelijk Van Abbemuseum, Eindhoven, The Netherlands, 1987, *Carl Andre*, p. 16, no. 1964–6.

5. *Zinc-Lead Plain*, New York, 1969 (pl. 4)

Zinc and lead
Thirty-six units, overall ⅜ x 72 x 72 in. (1 x 183 x 183 cm); each ⅜ x 12 x 12 in. (1 x 31 x 31 cm)

Provenance: Dwan Gallery, New York; Carl Andre, New York; Paula Cooper Gallery, New York.

Exhibitions: The Solomon R. Guggenheim Museum, New York, 1970, "Carl Andre," no. 32, ill. p. 56, as *37 Pieces of Work*; Corcoran Gallery of Art, Washington, D.C., 1976–77, "Andre, Le Va, Long," ill. p. 9 and cover, as *17 Pieces of Work.*

References: Kunsthalle Bern, Switzerland, 1975, *Carl Andre, Sculpture 1958–1974*, p. 53, no. 1969-81; Museum of Contemporary Art, Los Angeles, 1986, *Individuals, A Selected History of Contemporary Art, 1945–1986*, ed. Julia Brown Turrell, ill. p. 166; Haags Gemeentemuseum, The Hague, and Stedelijk Van Abbemuseum, Eindhoven, The Netherlands, 1987, *Carl Andre*, p. 50, no. 1969–84.

N.B. *Zinc-Lead Plain* is one of the thirty-six floor pieces first shown together in the 1970 "Carl Andre" exhibition at the Guggenheim Museum under the title *37 Pieces of Work* (no. 32, ill. p. 56). Following the exhibition, the *Plains* were dispersed but the whole was refabricated in Cologne for the 1981 exhibition "Westkunst."

6. *Arcata Pollux*, Atlanta, 1983 (pl. 5)

Western red cedar
Seven parts, overall 48 x 36 x 36 in. (122 x 91 x 91 cm); each 12 x 12 x 36 in. (31 x 31 x 91 cm)

Provenance: Paula Cooper Gallery, New York.

Exhibitions: Heath Gallery, Atlanta, 1983, "Carl Andre: Sculpture 1983," no. 1, ill. p. 7; Paula Cooper Gallery, New York, 1988.

References: Haags Gemeentemuseum, The Hague, and Stedelijk Van Abbemuseum, Eindhoven, The Netherlands, 1987, *Carl Andre*, p. 152, no. 1983–69.

Georg Baselitz

Born 1938, Deutschbaselitz, Germany; lives and works in Derneburg, West Germany

7. *Das Malerbild*, 1987–88 (pl. 96)

Oil on canvas
110¼ x 177⅛ in. (280 x 450 cm)

Provenance: Galerie Michael Werner, Cologne.

Exhibitions: The Solomon R. Guggenheim Museum, New York, 1988–89, "Refigured Painting: The German Image 1960–1988," no. 23, ill. pp. 88–89 (traveled 1988–89: The Toledo Museum of Art, Ohio; Williams College Museum of Art, Williamstown, Massachusetts; Kunstmuseum, Düsseldorf; Schirn Kunsthalle, Frankfurt).

References: Andreas Franzke, *Georg Baselitz* (Munich, 1989), ills. pp. 246–49.

Lothar Baumgarten

Born 1944, Rheinsberg, Germany; lives and works in Düsseldorf

8. *Armadillo*, 1977–85 (pl. 144)

Black-and-white photographs
Three parts, overall dimensions variable;
each 26½ x 33 in. (67 x 84 cm)

Provenance: Marian Goodman Gallery,
New York.

Exhibitions: Marian Goodman Gallery,
New York, 1989, "A Group Show."

9. *Ana-Uaik (7 Venezuelan Rivers)*, 1985
(pl. 145)

Wall painting
39 x 47 in. (99 x 119 cm)

Provenance: Marian Goodman Gallery,
New York.

Exhibitions: Kunsthalle Bern, Switzerland,
1987, "El Dorado."

References: Max Wechsler, "Lothar
Baumgarten at Kunsthalle," *Artforum* 26, 3
(Nov. 1987), pp. 148–49; Christoph Schenker,
"Lothar Baumgarten at the Kunsthalle
Bern," *Flash Art* 137 (Nov.–Dec. 1987), p. 117.

Bernhard and Hilla Becher

Bernhard, born 1931, Siegen, Germany;
Hilla, born 1934, Potsdam, Germany; both
live and work in Düsseldorf

10. *Cooling Towers*, 1983 (pl. 146)

Black-and-white photographs
Twelve parts, each 20 x 16 in. (51 x 47 cm)

Provenance: Sonnabend Gallery, New York.

Ashley Bickerton

Born 1953, Barbados, West Indies; lives
and works in New York

11. *God*, 1986 (pl. 175)

Acrylic, aluminum paint, and resin on
wood with aluminum
48 x 96 x 11 in. (122 x 244 x 28 cm)

Provenance: Donald Young Gallery, Chicago.

Exhibitions: The Renaissance Society at
the University of Chicago, 1987, "Cal Arts:
Skeptical Belief(s)," ill. p. 22 (traveled:
Newport Harbor Art Museum, Newport
Beach, California).

References: Allan Jalon, "'Skeptical Belief(s)'
Exhibit Displays Varied Styles of Cal Arts
Graduates," *Los Angeles Times*, Jan. 24, 1988,
p. 49-c; John Welchman, "Cal-Aesthetics,"
Flash Art 141 (Summer 1988), p. 108; Rosetta
Brooks, "Altered States," *ZG*, 1988, ill. p. 76.

12. *Tormented Self-Portrait (Susie at
Arles) No. 2*, 1988 (pl. 176)

Mixed-media construction with leather
padding
90 x 69 x 18 in. (229 x 175 x 46 cm)

Provenance: Daniel Weinberg Gallery,
Los Angeles.

Exhibitions: Stedelijk Museum, Amsterdam,
1989, "Horn of Plenty," ill. p. 24; Whitney
Museum of American Art, New York, 1989,
"1989 Biennial Exhibition," ill. p. 27.

References: Shaun Caley, "Ashley Bickerton;
A Precise Enunciation of the Entire Art
Equation," *Flash Art* 141 (Summer 1988),
ill. p. 153; Shaun Caley, "Ashley Bickerton,"
Flash Art 143 (Nov.–Dec. 1988), p. 80; Uta M.
Reindl, "Horn of Plenty," *Kunstforum Inter-
national* 111 (Apr.–May 1989), ill. p. 408;
Christian Leigh, "Into the Blue," *Art &
Auction* 11, 10 (May 1989), ill. p. 263; Italo
Mussa, "Postmodernist Prophylaxis," *The
Journal of Art* 1, 6 (June–July 1989), ill. p. 9;
Holland Cotter, "Report from New York,"
Art in America 77, 9 (Sept. 1989), ill. p. 81.

Mel Bochner

Born 1940, Pittsburgh; lives and works in
New York

13. *Atoll*, 1983 (pl. 6)

Oil on canvas
108 x 83½ in. (274 x 212 cm)

Provenance: Sonnabend Gallery, New York.

Exhibitions: Carnegie-Mellon University
Art Gallery, Pittsburgh, 1985, "Mel Bochner:
1973–1985," no. 9, ill. p. 45 (traveled
1985–86: Kunstmuseum Luzern; Center
for the Fine Arts, Miami).

References: Jan van der Marck, "Mel
Bochner, Point to Point," *Artforum* 24, 8
(Apr. 1986), p. 105.

14. *Fjord*, 1984 (pl. 7)

Oil on canvas
93 x 94 in. (236 x 239 cm)

Provenance: Sonnabend Gallery, New York;
Gerald S. Elliott, Chicago; The Art Institute
of Chicago, gift of Gerald S. Elliott, 1985.1119.

Exhibitions: Sonnabend Gallery, New York,
1985, "Mel Bochner: Recent Paintings";
Carnegie-Mellon University Art Gallery,
Pittsburgh, 1985, "Mel Bochner: 1973–
1985," no. 15, ill. p. 51 (traveled 1985–86:
Kunstmuseum Luzern; Center for the Fine
Arts, Miami); The Detroit Institute of Arts,
1987, "Reconnecting," p. 17.

References: Stephen Westfall, "Bochner
Unbound," *Art in America* 73, 7 (July 1985),
p. 113; Donald Kuspit, "Mel Bochner at
Carnegie-Mellon University," *Artscribe* 56
(Feb.–Mar. 1986), ill. p. 72.

Marcel Broodthaers

Brussels 1924-1976 Cologne

15. *Corbeau et renard*, 1968 (pl. 147)

Paint on photographic linen
30¾ x 50¾ in. (78 x 129 cm)

Provenance: Marian Goodman Gallery,
New York.

16. *Chaise avec briques et pelle*,
1969–71–73 (pl. 148)

Chair, spade, wood, metal, bricks,
and paper
Chair, 34⅝ x 17 x 14¼ in. (88 x 43 x 36 cm);
spade, 45 x 7 in. (115 x 20 cm)

Provenance: Marian Goodman Gallery,
New York.

Exhibitions: Marian Goodman Gallery,
New York, 1984, "Marcel Broodthaers,"
no. 6, ill., n. pag.; Walker Art Center,
Minneapolis, 1989, "Marcel Broodthaers,"
ill. p. 143 (traveled 1989–90: The Museum
of Contemporary Art, Los Angeles; The
Carnegie Museum of Art, Pittsburgh;
Palais des Beaux-Arts, Brussels).

17. *La Soupe de Daguerre*, 1975 (pl. 149)

Color photographs on board
21 x 20½ in. (53 x 52 cm)

Provenance: Marian Goodman Gallery,
New York.

Sandro Chia

Born Florence, 1946; lives in Rome,
Ronciglione, Italy, and New York

18. *Malinconico Accampamento
(Melancholic Encampment)*, 1982 (pl. 100)

Oil on canvas
114⅛ x 159 in. (290 x 404 cm)

Provenance: Saatchi Collection, London;
Sperone Westwater Gallery, New York.

Exhibitions: West Berlin, 1982, "Zeitgeist,"
no. 39, ill. p. 107, as *Melancholic Camping*;
Fruitmarket Art Gallery, Edinburgh, 1983,
"Sandro Chia," no. 21, ill. cover, as
Melancholic Camping; The Museum of
Modern Art, New York, 1984, "An

International Survey of Recent Painting and Sculpture," ills. pp. 86, 359.

References: Achille Bonito Oliva, *Trans Avant-Garde International* (Milan, 1982), ill. p. 138, as *Ornamental Camping*; Andrea Hill, "Sandro Chia at the Fruitmarket, Edinburgh," *Artscribe* 43 (Oct. 1983), p. 50, as *Melancholic Camping*; Luciana Rogozinski, "La Position crépusculaire," *Parachute* 34 (Mar.–Apr.–May 1984), ill. p. 7; David Bourdon, "Uproar: Clutter and Clatter at The Modern," *Vogue* 178, 8 (Aug. 1984), ill. p. 72; Hilton Kramer, "MOMA Reopened," *The New Criterion*, Summer 1984, ill. p. 38; Klaus Otterman, Michael Kohn, and Kim Levin, "MOMA: An International Survey," *Flash Art* 118 (Summer 1984), ill. p. 62; Gerald Marzorati, "Your Show of Shows," *Artnews* 83, 7 (Sept. 1984), ill. p. 64.

Francesco Clemente

Born 1952, Naples; lives and works in Rome, Madras, India, and New York

19. *Untitled*, c. 1978 (pl. 101)

Gouache, oil, and pencil on paper on canvas
67 x 75 in. (170 x 190 cm)

Provenance: Marian Goodman Gallery, New York.

Exhibitions: John and Mable Ringling Museum of Art, Sarasota, Florida, 1985, "Francesco Clemente," pl. 37 (traveled 1986–87: Walker Art Center, Minneapolis; Dallas Museum of Art; University Art Museum, Berkeley, California; Albright-Knox Art Gallery, Buffalo; The Museum of Contemporary Art, Los Angeles); Winnipeg Art Gallery, 1988, "The Impossible Self," ill. p. 49.

N.B. Although the date of this work is uncertain, the painting closely resembles works such as *Bestiario* (1978), pl. 38 in the Ringling Museum catalogue listed above under Exhibitions.

20. *The Midnight Sun I*, 1982 (pl. 102)

Oil on canvas
79 x 98½ in. (170 x 250 cm)

Provenance: Anthony d'Offay Gallery, London.

Exhibitions: Anthony d'Offay Gallery, London, 1983, "The Midnight Sun."

References: Richard Shone, "Francesco Clemente: The Midnight Sun," *The Burlington Magazine* 125, 960 (Mar. 1983), p. 182.

21. *Analogy*, 1983 (pl. 103)

Fresco on radiator part
34 x 17 x 3¼ in. (86 x 43 x 8 cm)

Provenance: Sperone Westwater Gallery, New York.

Exhibitions: Walker Art Center, Minneapolis, 1984, "Images and Impressions: Painters Who Print," no. 47; John and Mable Ringling Museum of Art, Sarasota, Florida, 1985, "Francesco Clemente," ill. p. 66 (traveled 1986–87: Walker Art Center, Minneapolis; Dallas Museum of Art; University Art Museum, Berkeley, California; Albright-Knox Art Gallery, Buffalo; The Museum of Contemporary Art, Los Angeles); Fundación Caja de Pensiones, Madrid, 1987, "Francesco Clemente Affreschi," no. 79, ill. p. 140.

22. *Untitled*, 1983 (pl. 104)

Oil on canvas
78 x 93 in. (198 x 236 cm)

Provenance: Sperone Westwater Gallery, New York.

Exhibitions: Mary Boone Gallery, New York, 1983; Chicago Public Library Cultural Center, 1984, "Contemporary Italian Masters," p. 18, ill. p. 30; Walker Art Center, Minneapolis, 1984, "Images and Impressions: Painters Who Print," no. 45, ill. p. 24; John and Mable Ringling Museum of Art, Sarasota, Florida, 1985, "Francesco Clemente," pl. 61 (traveled 1986–87: Walker Art Center, Minneapolis; Dallas Museum of Art; University Art Museum, Berkeley, California; Albright-Knox Art Gallery, Buffalo; The Museum of Contemporary Art, Los Angeles); Milwaukee Art Museum, 1988, "Art Now: Selections from the Permanent Collection and Extended Loans."

References: John Russell, "The New European Painters," *New York Times Magazine*, Apr. 24, 1983, detail ill. cover; Richard Shone, "New York: Some Recent Exhibitions," *The Burlington Magazine* 125, 964 (July 1983), ill. p. 451; David Bourdon, "The Go-Betweens," *Vogue* 174, 9 (Sept. 1984), ill. p. 98; Judith Neisser, "A Magnificent Obsession," *Art & Auction* 10, 2 (Dec. 1987), p. 111; Charles Jencks, *Post-Modernism: The New Classicism in Art and Architecture* (New York, 1987), pl. 2.22.

23. *The Celtic Bestiary*, 1984 (pls. 120–27)

Pastel on paper
Eight works, each 26 x 19 in. (66 x 48 cm)

Provenance: Anthony d'Offay Gallery, London.

Exhibitions: Arts Council of Northern Ireland Gallery, Belfast, 1984, "Francesco Clemente in Belfast," no. 10, ills. of all works, n. pag., and cover; Power Gallery of Contemporary Art, University of Sydney, 1986, "Francesco Clemente, Pastels," ills. of all works, n. pag.

References: Richard Shone, "Francesco Clemente at Belfast Arts Council Gallery," *The Burlington Magazine* 127, 983 (Feb. 1985), p. 115; John Ashberry, "Under the Volcano," *Interview*, Mar. 1988, ills. pp. 64, 70 (*The Celtic Bestiary* no. 8 and no. 1).

24. *The Departure of the Argonaut*, 1985 (pl. 105)

Artist's book with text by Alberto Savinio
Forty-eight color lithographs, each 26 x 39 in. (66 x 99 cm)
Edition: 38/200, plus 32 artist's proofs
Published by Petersburg Press, New York and London

Provenance: Roger Ramsay Gallery, Chicago.

Exhibitions: L.A. Louver Gallery, Venice, California, 1986, "Four Books: The Union of Word and Image"; The Museum of Modern Art, New York, 1987, "The Departure of the Argonaut" (traveled 1987–89: Allen Memorial Art Museum, Oberlin College, Ohio; The Snite Museum of Art, University of Notre Dame, Indiana; The University of Oklahoma Museum of Art, Norman; Grunwald Center for Graphic Arts, University of California, Los Angeles; Tacoma Art Museum, Washington; Glenbow-Alberta Institute, Calgary; Dunlop Art Gallery, Regina Public Library, Canada; Winnipeg Art Gallery); Milwaukee Art Museum, 1988, "Francesco Clemente: The Graphic Work," no. 18 (Elliott version) (traveled 1988: St. Louis Art Museum; Museo Italoamericano, San Francisco).

References: Guy Burn, "Feature: Prints," *Arts Review* 38, 13 (Feb. 1986), p. 127; Gerrit Henry, "The Departure of the Argonaut: A Departure for Clemente," *Print Collector's Newsletter* 17, 3 (July–Aug. 1986), ill. pp. 88–89; Stephanie Bleecher, "The Departure of the Argonaut," *Arts Magazine* 60, 10 (Summer 1986), ill. p. 114; Buzz Spector, "The Departure of the Argonaut," *Artforum* 25, 6 (Feb. 1987), p. 114; Rainer Crone and Georgia Marsh, *Clemente* (New York, 1987), p. 53; Liliana Albertazzi, "Francesco Clemente," *Artefactum* 4, 21 (Nov. 1987–Jan. 1988), p. 6; Paul Vangelisti, "An Ambitious Argonaut," *Artweek* 19, 18 (May 7, 1988), ill. p. 6.

25. **Boat**, 1987 (pl. 106)

Oil on canvas
76 x 184 in. (193 x 467 cm)

Provenance: Galerie Bruno Bischofberger, Zurich.

Exhibitions: Museo d'Arte Contemporanea, Prato, Italy, 1988, "Europe Now," ill. p. 99.

26. **The Vocali (A E I O U) A = Eat**, 1989 (pl. 107)

Oil on linen
47 x 55 in. (119 x 140 cm)

Provenance: Sperone Westwater Gallery, New York.

Exhibitions: DIA Art Foundation, Bridgehampton, New York, 1989, "The Vocali (AEIOU)."

N.B. The *Vocali* series, composed of this and the following four works, was commissioned from the artist by Gerald S. Elliott.

27. **The Vocali (A E I O U) E = Love**, 1989 (pl. 108)

Oil on linen
47 x 55 in. (119 x 140 cm)

Provenance: Sperone Westwater Gallery, New York.

Exhibitions: See Exhibitions, cat. no. 26.

28. **The Vocali (A E I O U) I = Die**, 1989 (pl. 109)

Oil on linen
47 x 55 in. (119 x 140 cm)

Provenance: Sperone Westwater Gallery, New York.

Exhibitions: See Exhibitions, cat. no. 26.

29. **The Vocali (A E I O U) O = Sleep**, 1989 (pl. 110)

Oil on linen
47 x 55 in. (119 x 140 cm)

Provenance: Sperone Westwater Gallery, New York.

Exhibitions: See Exhibitions, cat. no. 26.

30. **The Vocali (A E I O U) U = Remember**, 1989 (pl. 111)

Oil on linen
47 x 55 in. (119 x 140 cm)

Provenance: Sperone Westwater Gallery, New York.

Exhibitions: See Exhibitions, cat. no. 26.

Tony Cragg

Born 1949, Liverpool; lives and works in Wuppertal, West Germany

31. **Red Bottle**, 1982 (pl. 128)

Plastic objects
84 x 24 in. (213 x 61 cm)

Provenance: Marian Goodman Gallery, New York.

32. **Drawn Objects: "Waiting,"** 1983 (pl. 129)

Mixed media and crayon
86½ x 26 x 28 in. (220 x 66 x 71 cm)

Provenance: Marian Goodman Gallery, New York.

References: Phyllis Freeman, Eric Himmel, Edith Pavese, Anne Yarowsky, eds., *New Art* (New York, 1984), ill. p. 61.

33. **Shed**, 1984 (pl. 130)

Stone, particle board, and wood
39 x 33 x 13½ in. (99 x 84 x 34 cm)

Provenance: Marian Goodman Gallery, New York.

34. **St. George and the Dragon**, 1985 (pl. 131)

Metal, plastic, and wood
71 x 102 x 40 in. (180 x 259 x 102 cm)

Provenance: Donald Young Gallery, Chicago.

References: Christoph Friedrich, "Alles und noch viel mehr: Kunstmuseum and Kunsthalle Bern," *Flash Art* 123 (Summer 1985), ill. p. 62.

35. **Membrane**, 1986 (pl. 132)

Wood, metal, and plaster
44½ x 46 x 32 in. (113 x 117 x 81 cm)

Provenance: Marian Goodman Gallery, New York.

References: Arts Council of Great Britain, Hayward Gallery, London, 1987, *Tony Cragg*, ill. p. 41, as *Stomach*.

36. **Spill**, 1987 (pl. 133)

Bronze
39 x 79 x 39 in. (100 x 200 x 100 cm)

Provenance: Galerie Bernd Klüser, Munich.

37. **Loco**, 1988 (pl. 134)

Wood
63 x 94½ x 86⅝ in. (160 x 240 x 220 cm)

Provenance: Marian Goodman Gallery, New York.

Exhibitions: Venice, 1988, "Tony Cragg: XLII Biennale di Venezia," ills. pp. 62–63 and frontispiece (unfinished).

References: Lynne Cooke, "Tony Cragg: Getrübtes Licht," *Parkette* 18 (1988), ill. p. 109; Stephan Schmidt-Wulffen, "Venice Biennial: Tony Cragg, British Pavilion," *Flash Art* 142 (Oct. 1988), p. 108; Tate Gallery, London, 1989, *Tony Cragg*, ill. p. 43.

Enzo Cucchi

Born 1950, Morro d'Alba, Italy; lives and works in Ancona, Italy

38. **Un quadro di fuochi preziosi (A Painting of Precious Fires)**, 1983 (pl. 112 and cover)

Oil on canvas with neon
117½ x 153½ in. (298 x 390 cm)

Provenance: Anthony d'Offay Gallery, London.

Exhibitions: Stedelijk Museum, Amsterdam, 1983–84, "Enzo Cucchi: Giulio Cesare Roma," no. 4 (traveled 1984: Kunsthalle Basel); Anthony d'Offay Gallery, London, 1984, "Enzo Cucchi: Italia," pl. IV; Chicago Public Library Cultural Center, 1984, "Contemporary Italian Masters," p. 19, ill. p. 35; Museum of Art, Carnegie Institute, Pittsburgh, 1985, "Carnegie International 1985," ill. p. 109; The Solomon R. Guggenheim Museum, New York, 1986, "Enzo Cucchi," pl. 34; Los Angeles County Museum of Art, 1987, "Avant-Garde in the Eighties," no. 126, ill., n. pag.; Milwaukee Art Museum, 1988, "Art Now: Selections from the Permanent Collection and Extended Loans," as *Precious Fires*.

References: Katharina Hegewisch, "Nachdenken ist so wichtig wie malen," *Art–Das Kunstmagazin* 11 (Nov. 1986), ills. pp. 30–31 and cover; Hugh Cumming, "Italian Art Today: A Survey," *Art & Design* 5, 1–2 (1989), ill. p. 31.

39. **Untitled**, 1986 (pl. 113)

Oil, sheet metal, and iron on canvas
119 x 153½ in. (302 x 390 cm)

Provenance: Sperone Westwater Gallery, New York.

Exhibitions: Städtische Galerie im Lenbachhaus, Munich, 1986, "Enzo Cucchi: Testa," vol. 1, ill. p. 131 (traveled: The

Fruitmarket Gallery, Edinburgh; Musée de la Ville de Nice).

References: Museo d'Arte Contemporanea, Prato, Italy, 1989, *Cucchi*, ill. p. 182.

Richard Deacon

Born 1949, Bangor, Wales; lives and works in London

40. *Falling on Deaf Ears No. 2*, 1984–85 (pl. 135)

Galvanized steel and canvas
48 x 48 x 48 in. (122 x 122 x 122 cm)

Provenance: Donald Young Gallery, Chicago.

References: The Douglas Hyde Gallery, Dublin, 1985, "The Poetic Object," ill. p. 18; Judith Russi Kirshner, "Tony Cragg, Richard Deacon at Donald Young Gallery," *Artforum* 23, 10 (Summer 1985), p. 113; Lewis Blackwell, "Making Sense," *Building Design*, Oct. 4, 1985, ill. p. 22; Jan Fonce, "Richard Deacon, for Those Who Have Eyes," *Artefactum* 5, 25 (Sept.–Oct. 1988), p. 25.

41. *Art for Other People No. 21*, 1986 (pl. 136)

Plastic and stainless steel
12 x 24 x 6 in. (30 x 60 x 15 cm)

Provenance: Marian Goodman Gallery, New York.

References: Brooks Adams, "Richard Deacon at Marian Goodman," *Art in America* 75, 1 (Jan. 1987), p. 131; Judith Neisser, "A Magnificent Obsession," *Art & Auction* 10, 2 (Dec. 1987), p. 109; Bonnefantenmuseum, Maastricht, The Netherlands, 1987, *Richard Deacon: Recent Sculpture 1985–87*, p. 25, pl. 13; Art Gallery of Windsor, Canada, 1987, *Richard Deacon*, ill., n. pag.; Marian Goodman Gallery, New York, 1988, *Richard Deacon*, fig. 4; Whitechapel Art Gallery, London, 1989, *Richard Deacon*, ill. p. 37.

42. *These Are the Facts*, 1987–88 (pl. 137)

Masonite, mild steel, carpet, and phosphor bronze
78 x 76 x 52 in. (198 x 193 x 132 cm)

Provenance: Marian Goodman Gallery, New York.

Exhibitions: Marian Goodman Gallery, New York, 1988, "Richard Deacon," ill., n. pag.; St. Louis Art Museum, 1988, "Cross Currents in Contemporary Sculpture"; Whitechapel Art Gallery, London, 1988–89, "Richard Deacon," ill. p. 59.

References: Frédéric Paul, "Richard Deacon," *Artstudio* 10 (Autumn 1988), ill. p. 89; Fundación Caja de Pensiones, Madrid, 1988, *Richard Deacon: Esculturas y Dibujos*, no. 45, ill. p. 67; Michael Archer, "Richard Deacon at the Whitechapel Art Gallery," *Artforum* 27, 7 (Mar. 1989), ill. p. 150; Michael Enrici, "Richard Deacon; Un Pan de Labeur Inestimable," *Galeries Magazine* 30 (Apr.–May 89), ill. p. 93.

Eric Fischl

Born 1948, New York; lives and works in New York

43. *Mother and Daughter*, 1984 (pl. 76)

Oil on canvas
84 x 204 in. (213 x 518 cm)

Provenance: Mary Boone Gallery, New York.

Exhibitions: Mary Boone Gallery, New York, 1984, "Eric Fischl"; Paris, 1985, "Nouvelle Biennale de Paris 1985," p. 325, ill. p. 233; Museum of Contemporary Art, Chicago, 1985–86, "Eric Fischl"; Art Gallery of New South Wales, Sydney, 1986, "Origins, Originality and Beyond; the Biennial of Sydney," p. 120; Milwaukee Art Museum, 1988, "Art Now: Selections from the Permanent Collection and Extended Loans."

References: John Yau, "Eric Fischl," *Artforum* 23, 5 (Feb. 1985), p. 86; Avis Berman, "Trouble in Paradise," *Architectural Digest* 42, 12 (Dec. 1985), ill. p. 76; *Museum of Contemporary Art Calendar* (Chicago), Jan.–Feb. 1986, ill., n. pag.; Charles Jencks, *Post-Modernism: The New Classicism in Art and Architecture* (New York, 1987), pl. 3.23.

44. *The Evacuation of Saigon*, 1987 (pl. 77)

Oil on linen
Three parts, overall 120 x 142 in. (305 x 361 cm)

Provenance: Mary Boone Gallery, New York.

Exhibitions: Mary Boone Gallery, New York, 1988, "Eric Fischl," ills., n. pag.

References: Lawrence Weschler, "The Art of Fischl," *Interview* 18, 5 (May 1988), ill. p. 70; Robert Hughes, "Discontents of the White Tribe," *Time* 131, 22 (May 30, 1988), ill. p. 71.

Dan Flavin

Born 1933, New York; lives and works in Garrison, New York

45. *the alternate diagonals of March 2, 1964 (to Don Judd)*, 1964 (pl. 8)

Red and yellow fluorescent light
145 x 12 x 4 in. (369 x 31 x 10 cm)

Provenance: Donald Judd; Young Hoffman Gallery, Chicago.

Exhibitions: Kaymar Gallery, New York, 1964, "some light."

References: Donald Judd, "In the Galleries," *Arts Magazine* 38 (Apr. 1964), p. 38, reprinted in Donald Judd, *Complete Writings 1959–1975* (Halifax and New York, 1975), p. 124 (Elliott version); Lucy Lippard, "New York Review; Dan Flavin at Kaymar Gallery," *Artforum* 11, 11 (May 1964), p. 54 (Elliott version); Grace Glueck, "ABC to Erotic," *Art in America* 54, 5 (Sept.–Oct. 1966), p. 107, as *Alternate Diagonals of March 3, 1964*; Joanna Eagle, "Artists as Collectors," *Art in America* 55, 6 (Nov.–Dec. 1967), ill. p. 60, as *8' + 4' – 2'* (Elliott version); The National Gallery of Canada, Ottawa, 1969, *fluorescent light, etc. from Dan Flavin*, p. 190; Phyllis Tuchman, "Minimalism and Critical Response," *Artforum* 15, 9 (1977), p. 26; Judith Neisser, "A Magnificent Obsession," *Art & Auction* 10, 2 (Dec. 1987), p. 110, as *Homage to Donald Judd* (Elliott version).

N.B. The title and form of this work were used in a number of subsequent pieces. This piece corresponds to the work exhibited at the Kaymar Gallery in 1964, with gold and red tubes.

46. *untitled (monument for V. Tatlin)*, 1970 (pl. 9)

Cool-white fluorescent light
96 x 31½ x 4 in. (244 x 80 x 10 cm)
Edition: 3/5

Provenance: Donald Young Gallery, Chicago.

Gunther Förg

Born 1952, Fussen, West Germany; lives and works in Areuse, Switzerland

47. *E.U.R. Palazzo della Civiltà*, 1983–88 (pl. 150)

Black-and-white photograph
71 x 47 in. (180 x 120 cm)

Provenance: Gallerie Vera Munro, Hamburg.

Exhibitions: Gallerie Vera Munro, Hamburg, 1987; Museum Haus Lange, Krefeld, West Germany, 1987, "Gunther Förg," no. 61/86, ill., n. pag., as *Palazzo Della Civilta, Rom* (traveled: Maison de la

Culture et de la Communication, Saint Etienne, France; Haags Gemeentemuseum, The Hague).

48. *Untitled*, 1987 (pl. 151)

Acrylic on lead on wood
100⅜ x 82⅝ in. (255 x 210 cm)

Provenance: Private collection, Connecticut; Luhring, Augustine & Hodes Gallery, New York.

Exhibitions: Galerie Christoph Durr, Munich, 1987, "Gunther Förg."

49. *Untitled*, 1988 (pl. 152)

Bronze
35½ x 23⅝ x 2 in. (90 x 60 x 5 cm)

Provenance: Luhring Augustine Gallery, New York.

References: Newport Harbor Art Museum, California, 1989, "Gunther Förg," ill. p. 75.

Dan Graham

Born 1942, Urbana, Illinois; lives and works in New York

50. *Bedroom Dining Room Model House*, 1967 (pl. 153)

Color photographs
29 x 39 x 2 in. (74 x 99 x 5 cm)

Provenance: Marian Goodman Gallery, New York.

Philip Guston

Montreal 1913–1980 Woodstock, New York

51. *Night Room*, 1976 (pl. 64)

Oil on canvas
80 x 69 in. (203 x 175 cm)

Provenance: David McKee Gallery, New York.

Exhibitions: XVI Bienal Internacional de São Paulo (organized by the San Francisco Museum of Modern Art for the International Communication Agency), 1981, "Philip Guston: Sus Ultimos Anos," fig. 9 (traveled 1982: Museo de Arte Moderno, Mexico City; Centro de Arte Moderno, Guadalajara, Mexico; Museo de Arte Moderno, Bogota).

References: Chicago Public Library Cultural Center, 1984, *Contemporary Italian Masters*, ill. p. 10.

52. *Untitled*, 1979 (pl. 1)

Mixed media on paper
11½ x 8½ in. (29 x 22 cm)

Provenance: The artist.

Jenny Holzer

Born 1950, Gallipolis, Ohio; lives and works in New York

53. *Untitled* from the *Living Series*, 1981 (pl. 154)

Bronze
7½ x 10 in. (19 x 25 cm)
Edition: 1/3

Provenance: Rhona Hoffman Gallery, Chicago.

54. *Essays*, 1982 (pl. 155)

Offset posters
Twenty-nine parts, each 17 x 17 in. (43 x 43 cm)

Provenance: Rhona Hoffman Gallery, Chicago.

55. *Selections from Under a Rock*, 1986 (pl. 156)

Electronic L.E.D. sign and red and green diodes
10 x 112½ x 4½ in. (25 x 286 x 11 cm)
Edition: 5/6

Provenance: Barbara Gladstone Gallery, New York.

56. *Untitled (Selections from Truisms)*, 1987 (pl. 157)

Danby royal marble
17 x 54 x 25 in. (43 x 137 x 64 cm)
Edition: 3/3

Provenance: Barbara Gladstone Gallery, New York.

Michael Hurson

Born 1941, Youngstown, Ohio; lives and works in New York

57. *Portrait of Gerald Elliott*, 1980 (pl. 65)

Pastel and gouache on paper
30 x 22 in. (76 x 56 cm)

Provenance: Dart Gallery, Chicago.

Exhibitions: The Clocktower, The Institute for Art and Urban Resources, New York, 1984, "Michael Hurson: Drawings,

1969–1983," no. 35 (traveled: The Art Institute of Chicago).

References: Alan G. Artner, "Black Folk Art: Charm, Little Insight," *Chicago Tribune*, May 4, 1984, sec. 5, p. 3.

N.B. This work was commissioned from the artist.

Neil Jenney

Born 1945, Torrington, Connecticut; lives and works in New York

58. *Man and Thing*, 1969 (pl. 66)

Acrylic on canvas
74 x 44½ in. (188 x 113 cm)

Provenance: Vivian Horan Gallery, New York.

59. *Vexation and Rapture*, 1969 (pl. 67)

Oil on canvas
62½ x 96½ in. (159 x 244 cm)

Provenance: Vivian Horan Gallery, New York.

60. *Implements Intrenchments*, 1970 (pl. 68)

Acrylic on canvas on wood
75½ x 63½ in. (192 x 161 cm)

Provenance: Vivian Horan Gallery, New York.

Donald Judd

Born 1928, Excelsior Springs, Missouri; lives and works in New York and Marfa, Texas

61. *Untitled*, 1962 (pl. 10)

Light cadmium red oil on Liquitex and sand on Masonite with yellow Plexiglas
48 x 96 x 2½ in. (122 x 244 x 6 cm)

Provenance: Gordon Locksley and George T. Shea, Minneapolis; Vivian Horan Gallery, New York.

Exhibitions: Locksley Shea Gallery, Minneapolis, 1973, "Donald Judd: Early Works–Recent Works"; Whitney Museum of American Art, New York, 1988, "Donald Judd," fig. 14 (traveled 1989: Dallas Museum of Art).

References: Dudley Del Balso, Roberta Smith, and Brydon Smith, "Catalogue Raisonné of Paintings, Objects, and Wood-Blocks 1960–1974," in The National Gallery of Canada, Ottawa, 1975, *Donald Judd*, no. 1962–30; Whitney Museum of American Art, 1984, *Blam! The Explosion of Pop, Minimalism, and Performance 1958–1964*, fig. 128; Kay Larson, "Industrial Light and Magic," *New York Magazine*, Nov. 7, 1988, p. 105; Donald B. Kuspit, "Red Desert and Arctic Dreams," *Art in America* 77, 3 (Mar. 1989), ill. p. 121; Francesco Poli, "Big Boxes for Smaller Ones," *Contemporanea* 2, 2 (Mar.–Apr. 1989), ill. p. 61.

62. *Untitled*, 1963 (pl. 11)

Black enamel on aluminum and raw sienna enamel and galvanized iron on wood
52 x 42⅛ x 5⅞ in. (132 x 107 x 15 cm)

Provenance: Julie Finch Judd, New York; Leo Castelli Gallery, New York; Donald Young Gallery, Chicago.

Exhibitions: Green Gallery, New York, 1963–64, "Don Judd"; Weatherspoon Art Gallery, Greensboro, North Carolina, 1967; The National Gallery of Canada, Ottawa, 1975, "Donald Judd," no. 16, ill. p. 58; Whitney Museum of American Art, New York, 1988, "Donald Judd," fig. 17 (traveled 1989: Dallas Museum of Art).

References: Sidney Tillim, "The New Avant-Garde," *Arts Magazine* 38, 5 (Feb. 1964), p. 20; John Coplans, "An Interview with Donald Judd," *Artforum* 9, 10 (June 1971), p. 42, fig. 7; Dudley Del Balso, Roberta Smith, and Brydon Smith, "Catalogue Raisonné of Paintings, Objects, and Wood-Blocks 1960–1974," in The National Gallery of Canada, Ottawa, 1975, *Donald Judd*, no. 1963–43.

63. *Untitled*, May 7, 1970 (pl. 12)

Anodized aluminum
6 x 110¾ x 6½ in. (15 x 280 x 17 cm)
Edition of three

Provenance: Galerie Bruno Bischofberger, Zurich; Private Collection; Waddington Gallery, London.

Exhibitions: The David and Alfred Smart Art Gallery, The University of Chicago, 1985, "Alumni Who Collect, II: Sculpture from 1600 to the Present."

References: Dudley Del Balso, Roberta Smith, and Brydon Smith, "Catalogue Raisonné of Paintings, Objects, and Wood-Blocks 1960–1974," in The National Gallery of Canada, Ottawa, 1975, *Donald Judd*, no. 1970–225.

64. *Untitled*, August 28, 1970 (pl. 13)

Stainless steel and green Plexiglas
Ten parts, each 6 x 27 x 24 in. (15 x 68 x 61 cm), with 6-inch intervals

Provenance: L. M. Asher Family Collection, Los Angeles; Larry Gagosian Gallery, Los Angeles.

References: Dudley Del Balso, Roberta Smith, and Brydon Smith, "Catalogue Raisonné of Paintings, Objects, and Wood-Blocks 1960–1974," in The National Gallery of Canada, Ottawa, 1975, *Donald Judd*, no. 1970–231; Judith Neisser, "A Magnificent Obsession," *Art & Auction* 10, 2 (Dec. 1987), p. 109.

65. *Untitled*, 1978 (pl. 14)

Red paint on plywood
19½ x 45 x 30½ in. (50 x 114 x 77 cm)

Provenance: Lone Star Foundation, New York; Dudley Del Balso, New York; Margo Leavin Gallery, Los Angeles; Vivian Horan Gallery, New York.

Exhibitions: Margo Leavin Gallery, Los Angeles, 1987, "Acquisitions: Painting and Sculpture."

66. *Untitled*, 1983 (pl. 15)

Plywood
Four parts, overall 39 x 216½ x 19⅝ in. (99 x 550 x 50 cm); each 39 x 39 x 19⅝ in. (99 x 99 x 50 cm)

Provenance: Leo Castelli Gallery, New York.

Exhibitions: Leo Castelli Gallery, New York, 1984, "Donald Judd."

References: Prudence Carlson, "Donald Judd's Equivocal Objects," *Art in America* 72, 1 (Jan. 1984), ill. p. 115.

67. *Untitled*, 1984 (pl. 16)

Painted aluminum
11⅞ x 70⅞ x 11⅞ in. (30 x 180 x 30 cm)

Provenance: The artist.

Anish Kapoor

Born 1954, Bombay; lives and works in London

68. *Hole and Vessel*, 1984 (pl. 138)

Polystyrene, cement, earth, acrylic medium, and pigment
37½ x 64 x 43 in. (95 x 162 x 109 cm)

Provenance: Barbara Gladstone Gallery, New York.

Exhibitions: Institute of Contemporary Art, Boston, 1985, "Anish Kapoor"; Albright-Knox Art Gallery, Buffalo, 1986, "Anish Kapoor," ill., n. pag.; University Gallery, University of Massachusetts, Amherst,

1986, "Anish Kapoor: Recent Sculptures and Drawings," fig. 3, n. pag.

Anselm Kiefer

Born 1945, Donaueschingen, West Germany; lives and works in Buchen/Hornbach, Odenwald, West Germany

69. *Die Donauquelle (The Source of the Danube)*, 1978–88 (pl. 95)

Mixed-media book construction with photographs
12 x 8 in. (30 x 20 cm)

Provenance: Marian Goodman Gallery, New York.

N.B. This book was published in 1978; the artist made additions in 1988.

70. *Untitled*, 1980–86 (pl. 98)

Emulsion, oil, acrylic, shellac, and charcoal on photograph mounted on cardboard, lead objects, and steel wire mounted on canvas
Three parts, overall 123 x 216 in. (312 x 548 cm); each 123 x 72 in. (312 x 183 cm)

Provenance: The artist.

Exhibitions: Stedelijk Museum, Amsterdam, 1986–87, "Anselm Kiefer: Bilder 1980–1986," p. 17, pl. 31; The Art Institute of Chicago and the Philadelphia Museum of Art, 1987–88, "Anselm Kiefer," pl. 78 (traveled: The Museum of Contemporary Art, Los Angeles; The Museum of Modern Art, New York); Musée National d'Art Moderne, Paris, 1989, "Magiciens de la Terre."

71. *The Studio of the Painter*, 1984 (pl. 97)

Oil, straw, emulsion, shellac, and woodcut on canvas
110 x 150 in. (279 x 381 cm)

Provenance: Anthony d'Offay Gallery, London.

Exhibitions: Musée d'Art Contemporain, Bordeaux, 1984, "Anselm Kiefer"; Milwaukee Art Museum, 1988, "1988: The World of Art Today," no. 32, ill. p. 80.

Jeff Koons

Born 1955, York, Pennsylvania; lives and works in New York

72. *New Hoover Deluxe Shampoo-Polishers, New Shelton Wet/Dry 10-gallon Displaced Triple-decker*, 1981–87 (pl. 177)

Four Hoover deluxe shampoo-polishers, one Shelton wet/dry 10-gallon vacuum cleaner, Plexiglas, and fluorescent tubes
91 x 54 x 28 in. (231 x 137 x 71 cm)

Provenance: Daniel Weinberg Gallery, Los Angeles.

Exhibitions: Museum of Contemporary Art, Chicago, 1988, "Jeff Koons," no. 7, ill. p. 14.

73. **Three Ball Total Equilibrium Tank**, 1985 (pl. 178)

Glass, iron, sodium chloride réagent, and three basketballs
60½ x 48¾ x 13¼ in. (154 x 124 x 34 cm)

Provenance: Sonnabend Gallery, New York.

Exhibitions: The Arts Club of Chicago, 1988, "The Objects of Sculpture," as *Three Ball 50-50 Tank*; Museum of Contemporary Art, Chicago, 1988, "Jeff Koons," no. 10, ill. p. 17.

References: Elizabeth Sussman, "The Problem of Primal Science," in Institute of Contemporary Art, Boston, 1988, *Utopia Post Utopia: Configurations of Nature and Culture in Recent Sculpture and Photography*, ill. p. 56.

74. **I Could Go for Something Gordon's**, 1986 (pl. 174)

Oil inks on canvas
45 x 86½ in. (114 x 220 cm)
Edition: 1/2

Provenance: Sonnabend Gallery, New York.

References: Alan Jones, "Jeff Koons 'Et qui libre?,'" *Galleries Magazine* 15 (Oct.– Nov. 1986), p. 96; Mary Ann Staniszewski, "Jeff Koons," *Flash Art* 142 (Nov.–Dec. 1988), ill. p. 114; Thomas Dreher, "Jeff Koons, Objekt-Bilder," *Artefactum* 6, 27 (Jan.–Feb. 1989), ill. p. 8.

75. **Louis XIV**, 1986 (pl. 179)

Stainless steel
46 x 27 x 15 in. (117 x 68 x 38 cm)
Edition: 2/3

Provenance: Sonnabend Gallery, New York.

Exhibitions: Milwaukee Art Museum, 1987-88, "Simulations: New American Conceptualism," no. 6, ill., n. pag. (Elliott version); Museum of Contemporary Art, Chicago, 1988, "Jeff Koons," no. 20, ill. p. 3 (Elliott version); University Art Galleries, Wright State University, Dayton, Ohio, 1988, "Redefining the Object" (Elliott version) (traveled: The Cleveland Center for Contemporary Art); Institute of Contemporary Art and Museum of Fine

Arts, Boston, 1988, "The BiNational: Art of the Late '80's," no. 41, ill. p. 127 (Elliott version) (traveled 1988–89: Städtische Kunsthalle, Düsseldorf).

References: Giancarlo Politi, "Luxury and Desire: An Interview with Jeff Koons," *Flash Art* 132 (Feb.–Mar. 1987), pp. 71-76, ill. p. 74; *Art in America* 76, 5 (May 1988), ills. p. 4 and cover (detail); Thomas Dreher, "Jeff Koons, Objekt-Bilder," *Artefactum* 6, 27 (Jan.–Feb. 1989), pp. 6–11; Sidney Tillim, "Ideology and Difference," *Arts Magazine* 63, 7 (Mar. 1989), p. 49; Klaus Kertess, "Bad," *Parkett* 19 (1989), ill. p. 41.

76. **Pink Panther**, 1988 (pl. 180)
Porcelain
41 x 20½ x 19 in. (104 x 52 x 48 cm)
Edition of three

Provenance: Sonnabend Gallery, New York.

References: Eleanor Heartney, "Jeff Koons at Sonnabend," *Artnews* 88, 2 (Feb. 1988), p. 138; Amei Wallach, "The Art and Power of Jeff Koons," *New York Newsday*, Dec. 1, 1988, part 2, cover ill.; Lawrence Chua, "Jeff Koons," *Flash Art* 144 (Jan.-Feb. 1989), p. 113; Adam Gopnik, "The Art World: Lost and Found," *The New Yorker*, Feb. 20, 1989, p. 107; Gregorio Magnani, "This Is Not Conceptual," *Flash Art* 145 (Mar.-Apr. 1989), ill. p. 85; Stuart Morgan, Jutta Koether, David Salle, Sherrie Levine, "Big Fun: Jeff Koons," *Artscribe* 74 (Mar.– Apr. 1989), ill. p. 49.

Jannis Kounellis

Born 1936, Piraeus, Greece; lives and works in Rome

77. **Untitled**, 1983 (pl. 114)

Wood and steel
66 x 95½ x 8 in. (167 x 243 x 20 cm)

Provenance: Barbara Gladstone Gallery, New York.

78. **Untitled**, 1988 (pl. 115)

Steel, wood, coal, and burlap
Two parts, overall 89 x 160 x 17 in. (226 x 406 x 43 cm)

Provenance: Donald Young Gallery, Chicago.

Exhibitions: Donald Young Gallery, Chicago, 1988.

References: Mary Sherman, "Sculptors Show at Young Gallery," *Chicago Sun-Times*, May 27, 1988, p. 73.

Louise Lawler

Born 1947, Bronxville, New York; lives and works in New York

79. **Between Reagan and Bush**, 1989 (pl. 158)

Cibachrome, painted wall, and text
24 x 20 in. (61 x 51 cm)
Edition of three (235A)

Provenance: Metro Pictures, New York.

Sherrie Levine

Born 1947, Hazelton, Pennsylvania; lives and works in New York

80. **Untitled (Chair Seat: No. 10)**, 1986 (pl. 159)

Casein on wood
18¼ x 18⅛ in. (47 x 46 cm)

Provenance: Rhona Hoffman Gallery, Chicago.

81. **Untitled (Copper Knots: No. 1)**, 1988 (pl. 160)

Metallic paint on wood
45¼ x 36 in. (115 x 92 cm)

Provenance: Mary Boone Gallery, New York.

Exhibitions: Whitney Museum of American Art, New York, 1989, "1989 Biennial," p. 247.

Sol LeWitt

Born 1928, Hartford, Connecticut; lives and works in Chester, Connecticut, and Spoleto, Italy

82. **Serial Project, Set D**, 1966 (pl. 17)

Painted steel
15½ x 55½ x 55½ in. (39 x 141 x 141 cm)

Provenance: Galerie Konrad Fischer, Düsseldorf; Hans Meyer, Düsseldorf; Salvatore Ala, Milan; Donald Young Gallery, Chicago.

Exhibitions: Kunsthalle Bern, 1972, "Sol LeWitt," ill., n. pag. (diagram).

References: Lucy Lippard, "Sol LeWitt: Non-Visual Structures," *Artforum* 5, 8 (Apr. 1967), p. 43; *Aspen Magazine* 1, 5–6 (Fall–Winter 1967), sec. 17, ills. (details), n. pag.; Michael Fried, "Art and Objecthood," *Artstudio* 5 (Summer 1987), ill. p. 23.

83. *Wall Drawing No. 311: Square, Circle, and Triangle on Red, Yellow, and Blue*, 1978 (pl. 18)

Wall drawing
Dimensions variable

Provenance: Young/Hoffman Gallery, Chicago.

References: Stedelijk Museum, Amsterdam, 1984, *Sol LeWitt Wall Drawings 1968–1984*, pp. 106, 188.

N.B. This work was commissioned from the artist by Gerald S. Elliott and was installed in the offices of Solomon, Rosenfeld, Elliott, Stiefel and Abrams, Chicago, from 1978 until 1988.

84. *1–2–3–4–5*, 1980 (pl. 19)

Painted aluminum
25¼ x 99¼ x 32¾ in. (64 x 252 x 83 cm)

Provenance: Rhona Hoffman Gallery, Chicago.

85. *Wall Drawing No. 358: A 12″ (30 cm) Grid Covering the Wall. Within Each 12″ (30 cm) Square, One Arc from the Corner. (The direction of the arcs and their placement are determined by the draftsman.)*, 1981 (pl. 20)

Wall drawing
Dimensions variable

Provenance: John Weber Gallery, New York.

Exhibitions: Addison Gallery of American Art, Phillips Academy, Andover, Massachusetts, 1981; John Weber Gallery, New York, 1986, "Wallworks," ill., n. pag.

References: Stedelijk Museum, Amsterdam, 1984, *Sol LeWitt Wall Drawings 1968–1984*, ill. p. 136.

86. *Untitled*, 1986 (pl. 21)

Painted wood
H. 78 in. (198 cm)

Provenance: Donald Young Gallery, Chicago.

Richard Long

Born 1945, Bristol, England; lives and works in Bristol

87. *Watermarks*, 1979 (pl. 139)

Photographs, pencil, and graphite on matboard
Two panels, each 34⅞ x 48½ in. (89 x 123 cm)

Provenance: Sperone Westwater Gallery, New York.

88. *Fire Rock Circle*, 1987 (pl. 140)

Sixty fire rock stones
Dia. 110 in. (280 cm)

Provenance: Donald Young Gallery, Chicago.

Robert Longo

Born 1953, Brooklyn, New York; lives and works in New York

89. *Untitled*, 1982 (pl. 78)

Charcoal, graphite, and ink on paper
96 x 48 in. (244 x 122 cm)

Provenance: Metro Pictures, New York.

Exhibitions: Metro Pictures, New York, 1982; Los Angeles County Museum of Art, 1989, "Robert Longo" (traveled 1989–90: Museum of Contemporary Art, Chicago; Wadsworth Atheneum, Hartford), ill., in press.

References: Stephen F. Eisenman, "Louise Lawler at Metro Pictures," *Arts Magazine* 57, 5 (Jan. 1983), ill. p. 41, as part of Louise Lawler's *Arrangements*, 1982; Carter Ratcliff, *Robert Longo* (New York, 1985), pl. 56; Richard Price, *Robert Longo: Men in the Cities 1979–1982* (New York, 1986), no. 33, ills. pp. 65, 106; Ronald Jones, "Hover Culture: The View from Alexandria," *Artscribe* 70 (Summer 1988), ill. p. 51, as part of Louise Lawler's *Arrangements*, 1982; Neal Benezra, "Overstated Means/Understated Meaning: Social Content in the Art of the 1980s," *Smithsonian Studies in American Art* 2, 1 (Winter 1988), ill. p. 21.

90. *Rock for Light*, 1983 (pl. 79)

Acrylic on paper, lacquer on wood, and acrylic on aluminum and copper
98 x 216 x 36 in. (249 x 549 x 91 cm)

Provenance: Metro Pictures, New York.

Exhibitions: Akron Art Museum, Ohio, 1984, "Robert Longo: Drawings and Reliefs," ill. p. 21; The Brooklyn Museum, New York, 1985, "Robert Longo: Temple of Love"; The Art Institute of Chicago, 1986, "75th American Exhibition," ill. pp. 48–49; Milwaukee Art Museum, 1988, "Art Now: Selections from the Permanent Collection and Extended Loans."

References: Grace Glueck, "The Very Timely Art of Robert Longo," *New York Times*, Mar. 10, 1985, p. 24; Charlotta Kotik, "Robert Longo's Temple of Love in the Grand Lobby," *The Brooklyn Museum*, Mar. 1985, ill. p. 3; Paul Gardner, "Longo: Making Art for Brave Eyes," *Artnews* 84, 5 (May 1985),

ill. p. 57; John Howell, "Robert Longo at The Brooklyn Museum," *Artforum* 14, 2 (Oct. 1985), pp. 120–21; Hal Foster, *Recodings: Art, Spectacle, Cultural Politics* (Port Townsend, WA, 1985), ill. p. 94; Carter Ratcliff, *Robert Longo* (New York, 1985), pl. 21; Judith Neisser, "A Magnificent Obsession," *Art & Auction* 10, 2 (Dec. 1987), pp. 112–13; Paul Bonaventura, "Robert Longo: A Report to the Future," *Artefactum* 6, 27 (Jan.–Feb. 1989), p. 14.

91. *Now Is the Creature (The Fly)*, 1986 (pl. 80)

Acrylic, graphite, and charcoal on linen and steel
82 x 140 x 26 in. (208 x 356 x 66 cm)

Provenance: Metro Pictures, New York.

Exhibitions: Spiral Garden, Wacola Art Center, Tokyo, 1986, "Robert Longo," ill., n. pag.; Los Angeles County Museum of Art, 1989, "Robert Longo" (traveled 1989–90: Museum of Contemporary Art, Chicago; Wadsworth Atheneum, Hartford), ill., in press.

References: Michael Brenson, "Art: Robert Longo and His 'Steel Angels,'" *New York Times*, May 16, 1986; Eleanor Heartney, "Robert Longo at Metro Pictures," *Artnews* 86, 1 (Jan. 1987), p. 155; Judith Neisser, "A Magnificent Obsession," *Art & Auction* 10, 2 (Dec. 1987), p. 110; Emily Prager, "Mondo Longo," *Interview* 18, 5 (May 1988), ill. p. 86.

Robert Mangold

Born 1937, North Tonawanda, New York; lives and works in Washingtonville, New York

92. *V Series: Central Section (Vertical)*, 1968 (pl. 22)

Acrylic on Masonite
48 x 48 in. (122 x 122 cm)

Provenance: John Weber Gallery, New York; The Oliver-Hoffmann Family Collection, Chicago; Donald Young Gallery, Chicago.

Exhibitions: Stedelijk Museum, Amsterdam, 1982, "Robert Mangold: Schilderijen/Paintings 1964–1982," no. 69, ill., n. pag.

93. *Circle Painting No. 5*, 1973 (pl. 23)

Acrylic and pencil on canvas
Dia. 72 in. (183 cm)

Provenance: Fay Jacoby, San Francisco; Daniel Weinberg Gallery, Los Angeles; Rhona Hoffman Gallery, Chicago.

Exhibitions: Stedelijk Museum, Amsterdam, 1982, "Robert Mangold: Schilderijen/Paintings 1964–1982," no. 173.

References: Joseph Masheck, "Robert Mangold: A Humanist Geometry," *Artforum* 12, 7 (Mar. 1974), p. 42 (diagram).

94. *Four Color Frame Painting No. 6*, 1984 (pl. 24)

Acrylic and pencil on canvas
99 x 72 in. (251 x 183 cm)

Provenance: Paula Cooper Gallery, New York.

Exhibitions: Stedelijk Museum, Amsterdam, 1984–85, "La Grande Parade," ill. p. 217; Museum of Art, Carnegie Institute, Pittsburgh, 1985, "Carnegie International 1985," ill. p. 183.

References: Judith Neisser, "A Magnificent Obsession," *Art & Auction* 10, 2 (Dec. 1987), p. 110.

Brice Marden

Born 1938, Bronxville, New York; lives and works in New York

95. *Tour IV*, 1972 (pl. 25)

Oil and wax on canvas
96 x 48 in. (244 x 122 cm)

Provenance: Galerie Alfred Schmela, Düsseldorf; Galerie Konrad Fischer, Düsseldorf; Inge Rodinstock, Munich; Jeffrey Hoffeld Gallery, New York.

Exhibitions: Stedelijk Museum, Amsterdam, 1975, "Fundamental Schilderkunst," no. 6.

References: Bruce Kurtz, "Documenta 5: A Critical Review," *Arts Magazine* 46, 8 (Summer 1972), p. 43.

96. *Grove Group V*, 1976 (pl. 26)

Oil and wax on canvas
72 x 108 in. (182 x 274 cm)

Provenance: Mr. and Mrs. Edward R. Hudson, Jr., Fort Worth; Larry Gagosian Gallery, New York.

Exhibitions: Royal Academy of Arts, London, 1981, "A New Spirit in Painting," no. 93, ill., n. pag.

97. *8*, 1987–88 (pl. 27)

Oil on linen
84 x 60 in. (213 x 152 cm)

Provenance: Mary Boone Gallery, New York.

Exhibitions: Mary Boone Gallery, New York, 1988, "Brice Marden."

References: Christian Leigh, "Into the Blue," *Art & Auction* 11, 10 (May 1989), ill., p. 264.

Mario Merz

Born 1925, Milan; lives and works in Turin, Italy

98. *Igloo*, 1984–85 (pl. 116)

Plate glass, steel, netting, neon, Plexiglas, and wax
39¼ x 98¼ x 118¼ in. (100 x 250 x 300 cm)

Provenance: Galerie Rudolf Zwirner, Cologne; Barbara Gladstone Gallery, New York.

Exhibitions: Galerie Rudolf Zwirner, Cologne, 1987; Kunsthaus Zurich, 1988, "Mario Merz"; Städtische Galerie im Prinz-Max-Palais, Karlsruhe, West Germany, 1988, "Zurück zur Natur, aber wie?," ill. p. 141; The Solomon R. Guggenheim Museum, New York, 1989, "Mario Merz," in press.

Robert Morris

Born 1931, Kansas City, Missouri; lives and works in New York

99. *Untitled*, 1984 (pl. 81)

Painted Hydrocal and oil on canvas
69½ x 86½ in. (177 x 200 cm)

Provenance: Sonnabend Gallery, New York.

Exhibitions: Newport Harbor Art Museum, California, and Museum of Contemporary Art, Chicago, 1986, "Robert Morris: Works of the Eighties," ill. p. 53; Milwaukee Art Museum, 1988, "Art Now: Selections from the Permanent Collection and Extended Loans."

Robert Moskowitz

Born 1935, New York; lives and works in New York

100. *Empire State*, 1984–86 (pl. 69)

Oil on canvas
96 x 32 in. (245 x 81 cm)

Provenance: Blum Helman Gallery, New York.

Exhibitions: Blum Helman Gallery, New York, "Robert Moskowitz," 1988;

Hirshhorn Museum and Sculpture Garden, Washington, D.C., 1989, "Robert Moskowitz," no. 62, ill., n. pag. (traveled 1989–90: La Jolla Museum of Contemporary Art, California; The Museum of Modern Art, New York).

References: Michael Kimmelman, "The Hypnotic Canvases of Robert Moskowitz," *New York Times*, Mar. 18, 1988, p. c-1.

101. *The Razor's Edge (for Bill Murray)*, 1985 (pl. 70)

Oil on canvas
30⅛ x 72 in. (76 x 183 cm)

Provenance: Blum Helman Gallery, New York.

Exhibitions: Blum Helman Gallery, New York, 1986, "Robert Moskowitz: Paintings and Drawings," ill. p. 9; Hirshhorn Museum and Sculpture Garden, Washington, D.C., 1989, "Robert Moskowitz," no. 61, ill., n. pag. (traveled 1989–90: La Jolla Museum of Contemporary Art, California; The Museum of Modern Art, New York).

References: Michael Brenson, "Art: Moskowitz's View of Sculptural and Architectural Icons," *New York Times*, Feb. 14, 1986, p. c-32.

Bruce Nauman

Born 1941, Fort Wayne, Indiana; lives and works in Pecos, New Mexico

102. *Untitled*, 1965 (pl. 31)

Fiberglass
83 x 8 x 83 in. (211 x 20 x 211 cm)

Provenance: Leo Castelli Gallery, New York; Mr. and Mrs. Eugene Schwartz, New York; The New Museum of Contemporary Art, New York; Donald Young Gallery, Chicago.

Exhibitions: Leo Castelli Gallery, New York, 1968, "Bruce Nauman," fig. 3; Kassel, West Germany, 1982, "Documenta 7," vol. 1, ill. p. 210.

References: Robert Mahoney, "New York in Review," *Arts Magazine* 63, 4 (Dec. 1988), p. 107; Coosje van Bruggen, *Bruce Nauman* (New York, 1988), ill. p. 30.

103. *Mold for a Modernized Slant Step*, 1966 (pl. 32)

Plaster
22 x 17 x 12 in. (56 x 43 x 31 cm)

Provenance: Nicholas Wilder Gallery, Los Angeles; Sperone Westwater Gallery, New York.

Exhibitions: Berkeley Gallery, San Francisco, 1966, "The Slant Step Show"; Nicholas Wilder Gallery, Los Angeles, 1966; Sperone Westwater Gallery, New York, 1988.

References: Leo Castelli Gallery, New York, 1968, *Bruce Nauman*, fig. 19; Philip Weidman, *Slant Step Book* (Sacramento, CA, 1969), p. 7; Cynthia Charters, "The Slant Step Saga," in Richard L. Nelson Gallery, University of California, Davis, 1983, *The Slant Step Revisited*, p. 9; Coosje van Bruggen, *Bruce Nauman* (New York, 1988), ill. p. 131.

104. *1/2 or 3/4" glass or plastic templates of my body separated by grease*, 1966 (pl. 33)

Watercolor and ink on paper
19 x 24 in. (48 x 61 cm)

Provenance: Blum Helman Gallery, New York; The Art Institute of Chicago, gift of Gerald S. Elliott, 1988.555.

References: Museum für Gegenwartskunst, Basel, 1986, "Bruce Nauman: Drawings 1965–1986," no. 39, fig. 23.

105. *Untitled*, 1966–67 (pl. 34)

Color photograph
20 x 23⅞ in. (51 x 61 cm)
Edition: 8/8

Provenance: Nicholas Wilder Gallery, Los Angeles; Leo Castelli Gallery, New York.

Exhibitions: Los Angeles County Museum of Art, 1972, "Bruce Nauman: Works 1965–1972," no. 21, ills. pp. 70–71, 101 (as part of *Untitled* set of eleven photographs) (traveled: Whitney Museum of American Art, New York; Kunsthalle Bern, Switzerland; Städtische Kunsthalle, Düsseldorf; Stedelijk Van Abbemuseum, Eindhoven, The Netherlands; Palazzo Reale, Milan; Contemporary Arts Museum, Houston; San Francisco Museum of Art); The Art Institute of Chicago, 1974, "Idea and Image in Recent Art," no. 40, ill. pp. 24–25 (as part of *Untitled* set of eleven photographs).

References: Robert Pincus-Witten, "Bruce Nauman at Leo Castelli," *Artforum* 6, 8 (Apr. 1968), pp. 57–58; Robert Pincus-Witten, "Bruce Nauman: Another Kind of Reasoning," *Artforum* 10,6 (Feb. 1972), p. 32; Coosje van Bruggen, "Entrance Entrapment Exit," *Artforum* 14, 10 (Summer 1986), p. 95; Coosje van Bruggen, *Bruce Nauman* (New York, 1988), ill. p. 46.

N.B. This and the ten subsequent works appear in the sources cited with often minor variations in title.

106. *Self-Portrait as a Fountain*, 1966–67 (pl. 35)

Color photograph
19¾ x 23¾ in. (50 x 60 cm)
Edition: 8/8

Provenance: Nicholas Wilder Gallery, Los Angeles; Leo Castelli Gallery, New York.

Exhibitions: See Exhibitions, cat. no. 105.

References: Fidel A. Danieli, "The Art of Bruce Nauman," *Artforum* 4, 4 (Dec. 1967), pp. 15–19; Robert Pincus-Witten, "Bruce Nauman at Leo Castelli," *Artforum* 6, 8 (Apr. 1968), pp. 57–58; Ursula Meyer, *Conceptual Art* (New York, 1972), ill. p. 186; Coosje van Bruggen, "Entrance Entrapment Exit," *Artforum* 14, 10 (Summer 1986), p. 95; Robert Storr, "Nowhere Man," *Parkett* 10 (July 1986), p. 71; Coosje van Bruggen, *Bruce Nauman* (New York, 1988), ill. p. 48; Nancy Goldring, "Identity: Representations of the Self," *Arts Magazine* 63, 7 (Mar. 1989), ill. p. 85.

107. *Drill Team*, 1966–67 (pl. 36)

Color photograph
19½ x 22½ in. (50 x 57 cm)
Edition: 8/8

Provenance: Nicholas Wilder Gallery, Los Angeles; Leo Castelli Gallery, New York.

Exhibitions: See Exhibitions, cat. no. 105.

References: See References, cat. no. 105.

108. *Feet of Clay*, 1966–67 (pl. 37)

Color photograph
22½ x 23½ in. (57 x 60 cm)
Edition: 8/8

Provenance: Nicholas Wilder Gallery, Los Angeles; Leo Castelli Gallery, New York.

Exhibitions: See Exhibitions, cat. no. 105.

References: See References, cat. no. 105.

109. *Waxing Hot*, 1966–67 (pl. 38)

Color photograph
19¾ x 20 in. (50 x 51 cm)
Edition: 8/8

Provenance: Nicholas Wilder Gallery, Los Angeles; Leo Castelli Gallery, New York.

Exhibitions: See Exhibitions, cat. no. 105.

References: Robert Pincus-Witten, "Bruce Nauman at Leo Castelli," *Artforum* 6, 8 (Apr. 1968), pp. 57–58; Robert Pincus-Witten, "Bruce Nauman: Another Kind of Reasoning," *Artforum* 10, 6 (Feb. 1972), ill. p. 34; Rijksmuseum Kröller-Müller, Otterlo, The Netherlands, 1981, *Bruce Nauman*,

1972–1981, ill. p. 29; Jeanne Silverthorne, "To Live and to Die," *Parkett* 10 (July 1986), ill. p. 27; Coosje van Bruggen, "Entrance Entrapment Exit," *Artforum* 14, 10 (Summer 1986), p. 95; Coosje van Bruggen, *Bruce Nauman* (New York, 1988), ill. p. 47.

110. *Finger Touch with Mirrors*, 1966–67 (pl. 39)

Color photograph
19¾ x 23¾ in. (50 x 60 cm)
Edition: 8/8

Provenance: Nicholas Wilder Gallery, Los Angeles; Leo Castelli Gallery, New York.

Exhibitions: See Exhibitions, cat. no. 105.

References: See References, cat. no. 105.

111. *Coffee Spilled Because the Cup Was Too Hot*, 1966–67 (pl. 40)

Color photograph
19¾ x 23¾ in. (50 x 60 cm)
Edition: 8/8

Provenance: Nicholas Wilder Gallery, Los Angeles; Leo Castelli Gallery, New York.

Exhibitions: See Exhibitions, cat. no. 105.

References: See References, cat. no. 105.

112. *Coffee Thrown Away Because It Was Too Cold*, 1966–67 (pl. 41)

Color photograph
19½ x 23 in. (50 x 58 cm)
Edition: 8/8

Provenance: Nicholas Wilder Gallery, Los Angeles; Leo Castelli Gallery, New York.

Exhibitions: See Exhibitions, cat. no. 105.

References: Fidel A. Danieli, "The Art of Bruce Nauman," *Artforum* 4, 4 (Dec. 1967), pp. 15–19; Robert Pincus-Witten, "Bruce Nauman at Leo Castelli," *Artforum* 6, 8 (Apr. 1968), pp. 57–58; Peter Plagens, "Roughly Ordered Thoughts on the Occasion of the Bruce Nauman Retrospective in Los Angeles," *Artforum* 11, 7 (Mar. 1973), p. 58; Coosje van Bruggen, "Entrance Entrapment Exit," *Artforum* 14, 10 (Summer 1986), p. 95; Coosje van Bruggen, *Bruce Nauman* (New York, 1988), ill. p. 46.

113. *Finger Touch Number 1*, 1966–67 (pl. 42)

Color photograph
19¾ x 23½ in. (50 x 60 cm)
Edition: 8/8

Provenance: Nicholas Wilder Gallery, Los Angeles; Leo Castelli Gallery, New York.

Exhibitions: See Exhibitions, cat. no. 105.

References: Robert Pincus-Witten, "Bruce Nauman at Leo Castelli," *Artforum* 6, 8 (Apr. 1968), pp. 57–58; Coosje van Bruggen, "Entrance Entrapment Exit," *Artforum* 14, 10 (Summer 1986), p. 95.

114. ***Eating My Words***, 1966–67 (pl. 43)

Color photograph
19¾ x 23¼ in. (50 x 59 cm)
Edition: 8/8

Provenance: Nicholas Wilder Gallery, Los Angeles; Leo Castelli Gallery, New York.

Exhibitions: See Exhibitions, cat. no. 105.

References: Robert Pincus-Witten, "Bruce Nauman at Leo Castelli," *Artforum* 6, 8 (Apr. 1968), pp. 57–58; Robert Pincus-Witten, "Bruce Nauman: Another Kind of Reasoning," *Artforum* 10, 6 (Feb. 1972), ill. p. 32; Coosje van Bruggen, "Entrance Entrapment Exit," *Artforum* 14, 10 (Summer 1986), p. 95.

115. ***Bound to Fail***, 1966–67 (pl. 44)

Color photograph
19¾ x 23¾ in. (50 x 60 cm)
Edition: 8/8

Provenance: Nicholas Wilder Gallery, Los Angeles; Leo Castelli Gallery, New York.

Exhibitions: See Exhibitions, cat. no. 105.

References: Robert Pincus-Witten, "Bruce Nauman at Leo Castelli," *Artforum* 6, 8 (Apr. 1968), pp. 57–58; Robert Pincus-Witten, "Bruce Nauman: Another Kind of Reasoning," *Artforum* 10, 6 (Feb. 1972), ill. p. 33; Ursula Meyer, *Conceptual Art* (New York, 1972), ill. p. 190; Edward Lucie-Smith, *Art Now, From Abstract Expressionism to Superrealism* (New York, 1977), pl. 357; Brenda Richardson, in The Baltimore Museum of Art, 1982–83, *Bruce Nauman: Neons*, ill. p. 22; Coosje van Bruggen, "Entrance Entrapment Exit," *Artforum* 14, 10 (Summer 1986), p. 95; Coosje van Bruggen, *Bruce Nauman* (New York, 1988), ill. p. 46.

116. ***Henry Moore Bound to Fail***, 1967 (pl. 45)

Cast iron
25½ x 23 x 3½ in. (65 x 58 x 9 cm)
Edition of nine

Provenance: Mr. and Mrs. Joseph Helman, Rome; Blum Helman Gallery, New York.

Exhibitions: Los Angeles County Museum of Art, 1972, "Bruce Nauman: Works 1965–1972," no. 30, ill. p. 77 (Elliott version) (traveled: Whitney Museum of American Art, New York; Kunsthalle Bern, Switzerland; Städtische Kunsthalle, Düsseldorf; Stedelijk Van Abbemuseum, Eindhoven, The Netherlands; Palazzo Reale, Milan; Contemporary Arts Museum, Houston; San Francisco Museum of Modern Art); Ace Gallery, Los Angeles, 1974; Stedelijk Museum, Amsterdam, 1982, "'60 '80: Attitudes/Concepts/Images," ill. p. 176 (Elliott version).

References: Robert Pincus-Witten, "Bruce Nauman: Another Kind of Reasoning," *Artforum* 10, 6 (Feb. 1972), p. 32; Brenda Richardson, in The Baltimore Museum of Art, 1982–83, *Bruce Nauman: Neons*, p. 22; Peter Plagens, "I Just Dropped in to See What Condition My Condition Was in...," *Artscribe* 56 (Feb.–Mar. 1986), p. 27; Joan Simon, "Breaking the Silence, An Interview with Bruce Nauman," *Art in America* 76, 9 (Sept. 1988), p. 144; Coosje van Bruggen, *Bruce Nauman* (New York, 1988), ill. p. 147.

117. ***Run from Fear, Fun from Rear***, 1972 (pl. 46)

Neon
Two parts, 7½ x 46 in.; 4¼ x 44½ in. (19 x 117 cm; 11 x 113 cm)
Edition of six

Provenance: Sperone Westwater Gallery, New York.

Exhibitions: The Baltimore Museum of Art, 1982–83, "Bruce Nauman: Neons," no. 16, ill. p. 73; Whitechapel Art Gallery, London, and Kunsthalle Basel, 1986–87, "Bruce Nauman," ill. p. 16 (traveled: ARC, Musée d'Art Moderne de la Ville de Paris).

References: Edward Lucie-Smith, *Art in the Seventies* (New York, 1980), ill. p. 27; Achille Bonito Oliva, *Quartetto: Beuys, Cucchi, Fabro, Nauman* (Milan, 1984), ill. pp. 92–93; Coosje van Bruggen, *Bruce Nauman* (New York, 1988), ill. p. 101.

118. ***3 Dead-End Adjacent Tunnels, Not Connected***, 1979 (pl. 47)

Plaster and wood
21 x 117 x 106 in. (54 x 297 x 268 cm)

Provenance: Leo Castelli Gallery, New York; Galerie Daniel Templon, Paris; Donald Young Gallery, Chicago.

Exhibitions: Whitechapel Art Gallery, London, and Kunsthalle Basel, 1986–87, "Bruce Nauman," ill., n. pag. (traveled: ARC, Musée d'Art Moderne de la Ville de Paris).

References: Coosje van Bruggen, *Bruce Nauman* (New York, 1988), ill. p. 68.

119. ***Life, Death, Love, Hate, Pleasure, Pain***, 1983 (pl. 48)

Neon
Dia. 70⅞ in. (180 cm)

Provenance: Barbara Gladstone Gallery, New York.

Exhibitions: Daniel Weinberg Gallery, Los Angeles, 1984; Museum of Contemporary Art, Chicago (333 East Wacker Drive Gallery), 1988, "Pop Art, Minimalism, and Earthart"; Fundaçao Calouste Gulbenkian, Lisbon, 1989, "Encontros: Signs of Life," pl. 16 (exhibition copy).

120. ***Chambre d'amis***, 1985 (pls. 49a–b)

Videotape installation: videotape (*Good Boy/Bad Boy*), audiotape (*Live and Die*), and neon (*Hanged Man*)
86⅝ x 55⅛ in. (220 x 140 cm)

Provenance: Galerie Konrad Fischer, Düsseldorf; Leo Castelli Gallery, New York.

Exhibitions: Museum Haus Lange and Museum Haus Esters, Krefeld, West Germany, 1985, "Dreissig Jahre durch die Kunst," vol. 1, no. 36, as *Untitled*, vol. 2, ills. pp. 42–43; Museum van Hedendaagse Kunst, Ghent, Belgium, 1986, "Chambre d'amis," ill. p. 161 (*Hanged Man*); Whitney Museum of American Art, New York, 1987, "Biennial 1987," ills. pp. 95–97, as *The Krefeld Piece* (*Good Boy/Bad Boy* and *Hanged Man*).

References: Chris Dercon, "Keep Taking It Apart: A Conversation with Bruce Nauman," *Parkett* 10 (July 1986), pp. 54–61 (*Good Boy/Bad Boy*), ill. p. 69 (installation); *Parkett* 10 (July 1986), p. 42 (*Hanged Man*); Peter Schjeldahl, "Bound and Disciplined," *7 Days* 1, 7 (May 11, 1988), p. 51 (*Hanged Man*); Joan Simon, "Breaking the Silence, an Interview with Bruce Nauman," *Art in America* 76, 9 (Sept. 1988), ill. p. 144 (*Hanged Man*); Coosje van Bruggen, *Bruce Nauman* (New York, 1988), ills. pp. 280–82; *ZG*, 1988, ill. cover (detail, *Hanged Man*).

121. ***Hanging Carousel (George Skins a Fox)***, 1988 (pl. 50)

Steel, polyurethane foam, and monitor
Dia. 204 in. (518 cm)

Provenance: Sperone Westwater Gallery, New York.

Exhibitions: Sperone Westwater Gallery, New York, 1988, "Bruce Nauman."

References: Joshua Decter, "Bruce Nauman at Sperone Westwater," *Flash Art* 143 (Nov.–Dec. 1988), ill. p. 118; Christopher Lyon, "Bruce Nauman at Sperone Westwater," *Art in America* 76, 12 (Dec. 1988), p. 145; Robert Mahoney, "New York in Review," *Arts Magazine* 63, 4 (Dec. 1988), p. 107; Patricia C. Phillips, "Bruce Nauman at Sperone Westwater," *Artforum* 27, 4 (Dec. 1988), p. 115; Amei Wallach, "Artist of the Showdown," *New York Newsday*, Jan. 8, 1989, part 2, ill. p. 5; Jerry Saltz, "Assault and Battery, Surveillance and Captivity," *Arts Magazine* 63, 8 (Apr. 1989), p. 13.

122. *Rats and Bats (Learned Helplessness in Rats) II*, 1988 (pl. 52)

Three ¾-inch U-matic videotapes, six television monitors, one projector, one live camera, and Plexiglas
Dimensions variable

Provenance: Leo Castelli Gallery, New York.

References: Robert C. Morgan, "Jasper Johns, David Salle, Bruce Nauman at Leo Castelli," *Flash Art* 144 (Jan.–Feb. 1989), ill. p. 123; Jerry Saltz, "Assault and Battery, Surveillance and Captivity," *Arts Magazine* 63, 8 (Apr. 1989), ill. p. 13.

123. *Above Yourself* (Study for "Elliott's Stones"), 1989 (pl. 53)

Graphite on paper
26¼ x 40 in. (67 x 102 cm)

Provenance: Sperone Westwater Gallery, New York.

N.B. This and the five subsequent works are preparatory studies for a series of carved granite sculptures commissioned from the artist by Gerald S. Elliott, which were unfinished at the time of publication.

124. *After Yourself* (Study for "Elliott's Stones"), 1989 (pl. 54)

Graphite on paper
26¼ x 40 in. (67 x 102 cm)

Provenance: Sperone Westwater Gallery, New York.

125. *Before Yourself* (Study for "Elliott's Stones"), 1989 (pl. 55)

Graphite on paper
26¼ x 40 in. (62 x 102 cm)

Provenance: Sperone Westwater Gallery, New York.

126. *Behind Yourself* (Study for "Elliott's Stones"), 1989 (pl. 56)

Graphite on paper
26¼ x 40 in. (67 x 102 cm)

Provenance: Sperone Westwater Gallery, New York.

127. *Beneath Yourself* (Study for "Elliott's Stones"), 1989 (pl. 57)

Graphite on paper
26¼ x 40 in. (67 x 102 cm)

Provenance: Sperone Westwater Gallery, New York.

128. *Beside Yourself* (Study for "Elliott's Stones"), 1989 (pl. 58)

Graphite on paper
26¼ x 40 in. (67 x 102 cm)

Provenance: Sperone Westwater Gallery, New York.

129. *Dog Biting Its Ass*, 1989 (pl. 51)

Foam
35 x 30 x 34 in. (89 x 76 x 86 cm)

Provenance: Texas Gallery, Houston.

Exhibitions: Texas Gallery, Houston, 1989, "Bruce Nauman: New Sculpture."

Tom Otterness

Born 1952, Wichita, Kansas; lives and works in New York

130. *The Doors*, 1985 (pl. 82)

Pressed wood and bronze
95½ x 60 x 5 in. (243 x 152 x 13 cm)
Edition: 4/9

Provenance: Brooke Alexander Gallery, New York.

References: Peter Frank and Michael McKenzie, *New, Used and Improved: Art for the 80's* (New York, 1987), ill. p. 32.

Mimmo Paladino

Born 1948, Paduli, near Benevento, Italy; lives and works in Milan

131. *Allegoria (Allegory)*, 1983 (pl. 117)

Bronze with gold mosaic
77 x 30 x 4½ in. (196 x 76 x 11 cm)
Edition: 1/4

Provenance: Sperone Westwater Gallery, New York.

Exhibitions: Sperone Westwater Gallery, New York, 1983, "Mimmo Paladino," ill., n.

pag., unfinished, as *Untitled*; Chicago Public Library Cultural Center, 1984, "Contemporary Italian Masters," p. 19, ill. p. 44, as *Untitled*; The David and Alfred Smart Gallery, The University of Chicago, 1985, "Alumni Who Collect, II: Sculpture from 1600 to the Present."

References: Alan G. Artner, "Young Italians: Europe's First Wave," *Chicago Tribune*, June 24, 1984, sec. 13, pp. 20–21, ill., as *Untitled*; Gillo Dorfles, *Mimmo Paladino, Veglia* (Milan, 1984), fig. 12; Städtische Galerie im Lenbachhaus, Munich, 1985, *Mimmo Paladino: Arbeiten von 1977 bis 1985*, ill. p. 109, unfinished plaster.

132. *Le Tane di Napoli (The Lairs of Naples)*, 1983 (pl. 118)

Oil on canvas and wood collage
107¼ x 83¼ in. (272 x 211 cm)

Provenance: Sperone Westwater Gallery, New York.

Exhibitions: Sperone Westwater Gallery, New York, 1983, "Mimmo Paladino," ill., n. pag.; Chicago Public Library Cultural Center, 1984, "Contemporary Italian Masters," p. 19, ill. p. 43; Krannert Art Museum, University of Illinois, Champaign, 1984, "New Painting"; Walker Art Center, Minneapolis, 1984, "Images and Impressions: Painters Who Print," no. 82, ill. p. 43; Städtische Galerie im Lenbachhaus, Munich, 1985, "Mimmo Paladino: Arbeiten von 1977 bis 1985," no. 30, ill. p. 63.

References: Donald B. Kuspit, "Mimmo Paladino at Sperone Westwater," *Art in America* 72, 2 (Feb. 1984), ill. p. 146; Nancy Princenthal, "Mimmo Paladino at Sperone Westwater," *Artnews* 83, 2 (Feb. 1984), pp. 164–66, ill., as *The Caves of Naples*.

133. *Untitled*, 1985 (pl. 119)

Oil and metal on limestone
47 x 20½ x 17¼ in. (119 x 52 x 44 cm)

Provenance: Sperone Westwater Gallery, New York.

Exhibitions: Institute of Contemporary Art, Boston, 1986, "Mimmo Paladino."

References: Judith Neisser, "A Magnificent Obsession," *Art & Auction* 10, 2 (Dec. 1987), p. 110.

Sigmar Polke

Born 1941, Oels, Germany [now Olesnica, Poland]; lives and works in Cologne and Hamburg

134. *Untitled*, 1982 (pl. 99)

Synthetic resin and mixed media on canvas
Three parts, overall 118 x 236 in. (300 x
600 cm); each 118 x 78¾ in. (300 x 200 cm)

Provenance: Anthony d'Offay Gallery,
London.

Exhibitions: Hayward Gallery, London,
1986, "Falls the Shadow: Recent British and
European Art," ill., n. pag.; The Art Institute
of Chicago, 1988–89.

Richard Prince

Born 1949, Panama Canal zone; lives and
works in New York

135. *Untitled (Sunset)*, 1981 (pl. 161)

Ektacolor print
30 x 45 in. (76 x 114 cm)
Edition: 4/5

Provenance: Barbara Gladstone Gallery,
New York.

Exhibitions: Magasin, Centre National d'Art
Contemporain de Grenoble, France, 1988,
"Richard Prince," ill., n. pag.

136. *Super-Heavy Santa*, 1986 (pl. 162)

Ektacolor print
86 x 48 in. (218 x 122 cm)
Artist's proof

Provenance: Barbara Gladstone Gallery,
New York.

Exhibitions: Kunsthalle Zürich, 1988,
"Richard Prince/Alan McCullom"; Magasin,
Centre National d'Art Contemporain de
Grenoble, France, 1988, "Richard Prince,"
n. pag.

References: Richard Prince and Barbara
Gladstone Gallery, *Richard Prince*
(New York, 1987), n. pag.

Gerhard Richter

Born 1932, Dresden; lives and works in
Cologne

137. *New York*, 1989 (pl. 163)

Oil on color photograph
4¼ x 5¾ in. (11 x 15 cm)

Provenance: Marian Goodman Gallery,
New York.

138. *Sils Maria*, 1989 (pl. 164)

Oil on color photograph
4¼ x 5¾ in. (11 x 15 cm)

Provenance: Marian Goodman Gallery,
New York.

139. *Sils Maria*, 1989 (pl. 165)

Oil on color photograph
4¼ x 5¾ in. (11 x 15 cm)

Provenance: Marian Goodman Gallery,
New York.

Susan Rothenberg

Born 1945, Buffalo; lives and works in
New York

140. *Kelpie*, 1978 (pl. 71)

Acrylic and flashe on canvas
76¾ x 109 in. (198 x 280 cm)

Provenance: Willard Gallery, New York;
Jeffrey Loria Gallery, New York.

Exhibitions: Larry Gagosian Gallery, New
York, 1987, "Susan Rothenberg: The Horse
Paintings 1974–1980," ill. p. 13.

References: Kunstmuseum Luzern, 1983,
*Back to the U.S.A.: American Art of the
70's and 80's*, ill. p. 177; Michael Brenson,
"Rothenberg Horses at the Gagosian
Gallery," *New York Times*, Jan. 23, 1987,
p. 23.

141. *Up, Down, Around*, 1985–87 (pl. 72)

Oil on canvas
89 x 93 in. (226 x 236 cm)

Provenance: Sperone Westwater Gallery,
New York.

Exhibitions: Sperone Westwater Gallery,
New York, 1987, "Susan Rothenberg:
Paintings," ill., n. pag.

Ulrich Ruckreim

Born 1938, Düsseldorf; lives and works
in Frankfurt

142. *Untitled*, 1988 (pl. 28)

Dolomite
86½ x 45½ x 12 in. (219 x 115 x 31 cm)

Provenance: Donald Young Gallery, Chicago.

Thomas Ruff

Born 1958, Zell am Harmersbach, West
Germany; lives and works in Düsseldorf

143. *Portrait*, 1988 (pl. 166)

Cibachrome print

83 x 65 in. (211 x 165 cm)
Edition: 2/4

Provenance: 303 Gallery, New York.

144. *Portrait*, 1988 (pl. 167)

Cibachrome print
83 x 65 in. (211 x 165 cm)
Edition: 3/4

Provenance: 303 Gallery, New York.

Robert Ryman

Born 1930, Nashville, Tennessee; lives and
works in New York

145. *Charter*, 1985 (pl. 59)

Oil on aluminum
82 x 31 in. (108 x 79 cm)

Provenance: Rhona Hoffman Gallery,
Chicago; promised gift to The Art Institute
of Chicago.

Exhibitions: Museum of Art, Carnegie
Institute, Pittsburgh, 1985, "Carnegie
International 1985," ill. p. 210; The Art
Institute of Chicago, 1987, "Robert Ryman,
The Charter Series: A Meditative Room for
the Collection of Gerald S. Elliott," ill., n.
pag. (traveled 1988: San Francisco Museum
of Modern Art); Museum of Art, Carnegie
Institute, Pittsburgh, 1988–89, "1988
Carnegie International," ill. p. 125.

References: Judith Neisser, "A Magnificent
Obsession," *Art & Auction* 10, 2 (Dec. 1987),
pp. 110, 113; Whitney Museum of American
Art, New York, 1987, *1987 Biennial
Exhibition*, ill. p. 117; Kenneth Baker,
"Ryman Art Opens 'New Work Series,'"
San Francisco Chronicle, Jan. 29, 1988;
Bill Berkson, "Robert Ryman at the San
Francisco Museum of Modern Art,"
Artforum 26, 9 (May 1988), p. 154; Gary
Garrels, "Interview with Robert Ryman at
the Artist's Studio," in Dia Art Foundation,
New York, 1988–89, *Robert Ryman*, p. 11.

N.B. As detailed in "Robert Ryman: *The
Charter Series…*," pp. 92–101, *Charter*
provided the basis for the four subsequent
paintings that Gerald S. Elliott commissioned from the artist.

146. *The Elliott Room: Charter II*, 1987
(pl. 60)

Acrylic on fiberglass with aluminum
93¾ x 93⅝ in. (238 x 238 cm)

Provenance: Rhona Hoffman Gallery and
Donald Young Gallery, Chicago; promised
gift to The Art Institute of Chicago.

Exhibitions: The Art Institute of Chicago, 1987, "Robert Ryman, *The Charter Series: A Meditative Room for the Collection of Gerald S. Elliott*," ill., n. pag. (traveled 1988: San Francisco Museum of Modern Art); Museum of Art, Carnegie Institute, Pittsburgh, 1988–89, "1988 Carnegie International," ill. p. 126.

References: See References, cat. no. 145.

147. *The Elliott Room: Charter III*, 1987 (pl. 61)

Acrylic on fiberglass with aluminum
84¼ x 84 in. (214 x 213 cm)

Provenance: Rhona Hoffman Gallery and Donald Young Gallery, Chicago; promised gift to The Art Institute of Chicago.

Exhibitions: See Exhibitions, cat. no. 146.

References: See References, cat. no. 145.

148. *The Elliott Room: Charter IV*, 1987 (pl. 62)

Acrylic on fiberglass with aluminum
72⅜ x 72 in. (184 x 183 cm)

Provenance: Rhona Hoffman Gallery and Donald Young Gallery, Chicago; promised gift to The Art Institute of Chicago.

Exhibitions: See Exhibitions, cat. no. 146.

References: See References, cat. no. 145.

149. *The Elliott Room: Charter V*, 1987 (pl. 63)

Acrylic on fiberglass with aluminum
95½ x 95½ in. (243 x 243 cm)

Provenance: Rhona Hoffman Gallery and Donald Young Gallery, Chicago; promised gift to The Art Institute of Chicago.

Exhibitions: See Exhibitions, cat. no. 146.

References: See References, cat. no. 145.

David Salle

Born 1952, Norman, Oklahoma; lives and works in New York

150. *His Brain*, 1984 (pl. 83)

Oil and acrylic on canvas and fabric
117 x 108 in. (279 x 274 cm)

Provenance: Mary Boone Gallery and Leo Castelli Gallery, New York.

Exhibitions: Paris, 1985, "Nouvelle Biennale de Paris 1985," p. 328; The Art Institute of Chicago, 1986, "75th American Exhibition," p. 56; Institute of Contemporary Art,

University of Pennsylvania, Philadelphia, 1986, "David Salle," ill. p. 56 (traveled 1986–88: Whitney Museum of American Art, New York; The Museum of Contemporary Art, Los Angeles; Art Gallery of Ontario, Toronto; Museum of Contemporary Art, Chicago); Milwaukee Art Museum, 1988, "Art Now: Selections from the Permanent Collection and Extended Loans."

References: Michael Brenson, "Art: Variety of Forms for David Salle Imagery," *New York Times*, Mar. 23, 1984, p. C–20; Roberta Smith, "Quality Is the Best Revenge," *Village Voice*, Apr. 3, 1984, p. 79, ill.; Michael Kohn, "David Salle at Leo Castelli," *Flash Art* 83, 6 (Summer 1984), p. 68; Gerald Marzorati, "The Artful Dodger," *Artnews* 83, 6 (Summer 1984), ill. p. 49; Peter Schjeldahl, "The Real Salle," *Art in America* 72, 8 (Sept. 1984), ill. p. 183; "Letters: On Schjeldahl on Salle," *Art in America* 73, 2 (Feb. 1985), p. 5; Kristin Olive, "David Salle's Deconstructive Strategy," *Arts Magazine* 60, 3 (Nov. 1985), p. 85; Editions Gallery, Bruno Bischofsberger, Zurich, 1986, *David Salle*, p. 23; Tony Godfrey, *The New Image: Painting in the 1980's* (New York, 1986), p. 141, ill. p. 133; Barbara Rose, *American Painting: The Twentieth Century* (New York, 1986), ill. p. 158; Lisa Liebmann, "Harlequin for an Empty Room: On David Salle," *Artforum* 25, 6 (Feb. 1987), p. 98; Catherine Millet, "David Salle," *Flash Art* 123 (Summer 1987), pp. 30–34; Peter Schjeldahl, *Salle* (New York, 1987), p. 41.

151. *Dusting Powders*, 1986 (pl. 84)

Acrylic and oil with wooden chair parts on canvas
108 x 156 in. (274 x 396 cm)

Provenance: Leo Castelli Gallery, New York.

Exhibitions: Leo Castelli Gallery, New York, 1986, "David Salle"; Institute of Contemporary Art, University of Pennsylvania, Philadelphia, 1986, "David Salle," ill. p. 80 (traveled 1986–88: Whitney Museum of American Art, New York; The Museum of Contemporary Art, Los Angeles; Art Gallery of Ontario, Toronto; Museum of Contemporary Art, Chicago); The Menil Collection, Houston, 1988, "David Salle."

References: Phyllis Tuchman, "David Salle, Emerging as a Young Master," *New York Newsday*, Apr. 20, 1986, ill., part 2, p. 11; François Duret-Robert, "Les Peintres d'aujourd'hui dont on parlera demain," *Connaissance des arts* 413/414 (July–Aug. 1986), ill. p. 47, as unfinished; Stellan Holm, "David Salle: ett mysterium utan kom-

mentarer," *Clic*, Sept. 1986, ill. p. 121; Lisa Liebmann, "Harlequin for an Empty Room: On David Salle," *Artforum* 25, 6 (Feb. 1987), pp. 94–99; Judith Neisser, "A Magnificent Obsession," *Art & Auction* 10, 2 (Dec. 1987), p. 108; Dodie Kazanjian, "Lining Up for Art," *House and Garden* 160, 3 (Mar. 1988), ill. p. 33, detail; Eleanor Heartney, "David Salle: Impersonal Effects," *Art in America* 76, 6 (June 1988), p. 127.

Julian Schnabel

Born 1951, New York; lives and works in New York

152. *Conversion of St. Paul*, 1980 (pl. 85)

Oil on canvas
96 x 84 in. (244 x 213 cm)

Provenance: Mary Boone Gallery, New York; Perry Rubenstein Gallery, New York; Larry Gagosian Gallery, Los Angeles.

Exhibitions: Venice Biennale, 1980, "La Biennale di Venezia," p. 63, no. 5.

References: Donald Kuspit, "Julian Schnabel's 'Profundity': Not an Apologia Vita Sua," *C*, Fall 1984, p. 18.

153. *Aorta*, 1981 (pl. 86)

Oil on sisal rug with wooden frame
118 x 165¼ in. (300 x 420 cm)

Provenance: Mary Boone Gallery, New York; Saatchi Collection, London; Larry Gagosian Gallery, New York.

Exhibitions: Tate Gallery, London, 1982, "Julian Schnabel," no. 11, ill. p. 9; Akron Art Museum, Ohio, 1983, "Julian Schnabel," ill., n. pag.; Leo Castelli Gallery, New York, 1983, "Julian Schnabel"; West Berlin, 1983, "Zeitgeist," ill. p. 229.

References: Caroline Collier, "Julian Schnabel at the Tate Gallery," *Flash Art* 109 (Nov. 1982), p. 66; Robert Pincus-Witten, "Entries: Vaulting Ambition," *Arts Magazine* 57, 6 (Feb. 1983), ill. p. 75; Rudi Fuchs, Hilton Kramer, and Peter Schjeldahl, *Art of Our Time: The Saatchi Collection* (London, 1984), vol. 3, pl. 95; Whitechapel Art Gallery, London, 1986, *Julian Schnabel, Paintings 1975–1986*, ill. p. 110.

154. *Private School in California*, 1984 (pl. 87)

Oil and modeling paste on velvet
120 x 84 in. (305 x 213 cm)

Provenance: Edwin L. Stringer, Toronto; Pace Gallery, New York.

Exhibitions: Pace Gallery, New York, 1984, "Julian Schnabel," pl. 10; Fort Lauderdale Museum of Art, Florida, 1986, "An American Renaissance: Painting and Sculpture Since 1940," p. 232, ill. p. 124; Milwaukee Art Museum, 1987, "Julian Schnabel," no. 11, pl. 11; Milwaukee Art Museum, 1988.

References: Roberta Smith, "Weighing In," *Village Voice*, Nov. 27, 1984, p. 113.

155. *Vita*, 1984 (pl. 88)

Oil and bondo with plates on wood
120 x 120 in. (305 x 305 cm)

Provenance: Pace Gallery, New York.

Exhibitions: Musée d'Art Contemporain, Bordeaux, 1984, "Légendes," ill. p. 71; Pace Gallery, New York, 1984, "Julian Schnabel," pl. 1; Whitechapel Art Gallery, London, 1986, "Julian Schnabel, Paintings 1975–1986" (traveled 1986–87: Musée National d'Art Moderne, Paris; Städtische Kunsthalle, Düsseldorf).

References: Roberta Smith, "Weighing In," *Village Voice*, Nov. 27, 1984, p. 113; Arthur C. Danto, *The State of the Art* (New York, 1987), ill. p. 101; Julian Schnabel, *CVJ: The Nicknames of Maitre d's and Other Excerpts from Life* (New York, 1987), ill. p. 148.

156. *Untitled*, 1988 (pl. 89)

Oil on tarpaulin
126 x 96½ in. (320 x 244 cm)

Provenance: Pace Gallery, New York.

Richard Serra

Born 1939, San Francisco; lives and works in New York and Nova Scotia, Canada

157. *Another Look at a Corner*, 1985 (pl. 29)

Steel
55½ x 54 x 106½ in. (141 x 137 x 271 cm)

Provenance: Marian Goodman Gallery, New York.

Exhibitions: List Visual Arts Center, Massachusetts Institute of Technology, Cambridge, 1986, "Natural Forms and Forces: Abstract Images in American Sculpture," ill., n. pag.

158. *Five Plate Pentagon*, 1988 (pl. 30)

Corten steel
Five parts, each 60 x 1½ x 60 in. (152 x 4 x 152 cm)

Provenance: Marian Goodman Gallery, New York.

Joel Shapiro

Born 1941, New York; lives and works in New York

159. *Untitled*, 1981–84 (pl. 73)

Bronze
47¼ x 46⅞ x 46½ in. (120 x 119 x 118 cm)
Edition: 1/3

Provenance: Paula Cooper Gallery, New York.

160. *Untitled (Arching Figure)*, 1985 (pl. 74)

Bronze
38½ x 28½ x 14 in. (98 x 72 x 36 cm)
Edition: 1/3

Provenance: Paula Cooper Gallery, New York.

Exhibitions: Stedelijk Museum, Amsterdam, 1985, "Joel Shapiro," no. 37, ill. pp. 45, 55 (traveled 1985–86: Kunstmuseum Düsseldorf; Staatliche Kunsthalle Baden-Baden, West Germany).

161. *Untitled (for G.S.E.)*, 1986–87 (pl. 75)

Bronze
64½ x 69½ x 49 in. (164 x 176 x 124 cm); base 26½ x 34¼ x 48⅜ in. (67 x 87 x 123 cm)

Provenance: Paula Cooper Gallery, New York.

References: Judith Neisser, "A Magnificent Obsession," *Art & Auction* 10, 2 (Dec. 1987), p. 113.

N.B. This work was commissioned from the artist by Gerald S. Elliott.

Cindy Sherman

Born 1954, Glen Ridge, New Jersey; lives and works in New York

162. *Untitled #88*, 1981 (pl. 90)

Color photograph
24 x 48 in. (61 x 122 cm)
Artist's proof

Provenance: Metro Pictures, New York; Gerald S. Elliott, Chicago; The Art Institute of Chicago, gift of Gerald S. Elliott in memory of Ann Elliott, 1988.118.

Exhibitions: Whitney Museum of American Art, New York, 1987, "Cindy Sherman," no. 54, ill., n. pag.

References: Mark Holborn, "Color Codes," *Aperture* 69 (Fall 1984), ill. p. 15; Peter Schjeldahl and I. Michael Danoff, *Cindy Sherman* (New York, 1984), pl. 54, n. pag.

163. *Untitled #137*, 1984 (pl. 91)

Color photograph
70½ x 47¾ in. (179 x 119 cm)
Edition: 2/5

Provenance: Metro Pictures, New York.

Exhibitions: Whitney Museum of American Art, New York, 1987, "Cindy Sherman," no. 92, ill., n. pag.; Milwaukee Art Museum, 1988, "Art Now: Selections from the Permanent Collection and Extended Loans."

References: Ken Johnson, "Cindy Sherman and the Anti-Self: An Interpretation of Her Imagery," *Arts Magazine* 63, 2 (Nov. 1987), ill. p. 50.

164. *Untitled #147*, 1985 (pl. 92)

Color photograph
49½ x 72½ in. (153 x 184 cm)
Edition: 1/6

Provenance: Metro Pictures, New York.

Exhibitions: Westfälischer Kunstverein, Münster, 1985–86, "Cindy Sherman-Photographien," ill. p. 13; The Contemporary Arts Center, Cincinnati, 1986, "Jenny Holzer/Cindy Sherman"; Los Angeles County Museum of Art, 1987, "Avant Garde in the Eighties," no. 103; Whitney Museum of American Art, New York, 1987, "Cindy Sherman," no. 100, ill., n. pag.

165. *Untitled #152*, 1985 (pl. 93)

Color photograph
72½ x 49⅜ in. (184 x 151 cm)
Edition: 5/6

Provenance: Metro Pictures, New York.

Exhibitions: Westfälischer Kunstverein, Münster, 1985–86, "Cindy Sherman Photographien," ill. p. 26; Whitney Museum of American Art, New York, 1987, "Cindy Sherman," no. 99, ill., n. pag.

References: Paul Taylor, "Cindy Sherman," *Flash Art* 124 (Oct.–Nov. 1985), ill. p. 79; Larry Frascella, "Cindy Sherman's Tales of Terror," *Aperture* 103 (Summer 1986), ill. p. 48.

166. *Untitled #188*, 1989 (pl. 94)

Color photograph
45¼ x 67 in. (115 x 170 cm)
Edition: 3/6

Provenance: Metro Pictures, New York.

Exhibitions: Metro Pictures, New York, 1989, "Cindy Sherman."

References: Peter Schjeldahl, "Little Show of Horrors," *7 Days*, Apr. 12, 1989, p. 62; Laura Cottingham, "The Feminine De-Mystique," *Flash Art* 147 (Summer 1989), ill. p. 91; David Rimanelli, "Cindy Sherman at Metro Pictures," *Artforum* 28, 10 (Summer 1989), ill. p. 137.

Haim Steinbach

Born 1944, Israel; lives and works in Brooklyn, New York

167. ***untitled (football, clog)***, 1987 (pl. 181)

Clog, straw, football, and laminated wooden shelf
37½ x 74½ x 20 in. (95 x 189 x 51 cm)

Provenance: Rhona Hoffman Gallery, Chicago.

Exhibitions: Rhona Hoffman Gallery, Chicago, 1987, "Haim Steinbach."

Thomas Struth

Born 1954, Geldern, West Germany; lives and works in Düsseldorf

168. ***The Shimada Family, Yamaguchi 1986***, 1988 (pl. 168)

Color photograph
26½ x 33½ in. (67 x 85 cm)
Edition of ten

Provenance: Marian Goodman Gallery, New York.

169. ***Via Giovanni a Mare, Rome***, 1988 (pl. 169)

Black-and-white photograph
With frame 26½ x 33¾ in. (67 x 86 cm)
Edition of ten

Provenance: Luhring Augustine Gallery, New York.

Exhibitions: Luhring Augustine Gallery, New York, 1989, "Jon Kessler, Stephen Prina, Thomas Struth."

170. ***Via Medina, Naples***, 1988 (pl. 170)

Black-and-white photograph
With frame 26½ x 33¾ in. (67 x 86 cm)
Edition of ten

Provenance: Luhring Augustine Gallery, New York.

Exhibitions: Luhring Augustine Gallery, New York, 1989, "Jon Kessler, Stephen Prina, Thomas Struth."

171. ***Via Sanità, Naples***, 1988 (pl. 171)

Black-and-white photograph
With frame 26½ x 33¾ in. (67 x 86 cm)
Edition of ten

Provenance: Luhring Augustine Gallery, New York.

Exhibitions: Luhring Augustine Gallery, New York, 1989, "Jon Kessler, Stephen Prina, Thomas Struth."

Jeff Wall

Born 1946, Vancouver; lives and works in Vancouver

172. ***Pleading***, 1989 (pl. 172)

Steel, Plexiglas, and Cibachrome print
54 x 73½ x 9¼ in. (137 x 187 x 24 cm)

Provenance: Marian Goodman Gallery, New York.

Lawrence Weiner

Born 1942, New York; lives and works in New York and Amsterdam

173. ***From Major to Minor, From Small to Large***, 1974–86 (pl. 173)

Wall painting
Dimensions variable

Provenance: Leo Castelli Gallery, New York.

Installations: Piwna, Warsaw, 1981; Leo Castelli Gallery, New York, 1986, "Water under the Bridge."

Bill Woodrow

Born 1948, Henley, England; lives and works in London

174. ***On the Other Hand***, 1987 (pl. 141)

Roto-dryer with acrylic and spray enamel
39 x 72 x 12 in. (99 x 183 x 30 cm)

Provenance: Donald Young Gallery, Chicago.

Exhibitions: The Arts Club of Chicago, 1988, "The Objects of Sculpture," ill. p. 4.

Index

cat. no. 120, pls. 49a–b, pp. 84–85; *Coffee Spilled Because the Cup Was Too Hot* (1966–67), cat. no. 111, pl. 40, p. 77; *Coffee Thrown Away Because It Was Too Cold* (1966–67), cat. no. 112, pl. 41, p. 77; *Dog Biting Its Ass* (1989), cat. no. 129, pl. 51, p. 87; *Drill Team* (1966–67), cat. no. 107, pl. 36, p. 74; *Eating My Words* (1966–67), cat. no. 114, pl. 43, p. 78; *Feet of Clay* (1966–67), cat. no. 108, pl. 37, p. 75; *Finger Touch Number 1* (1966–67), cat. no. 113, pl. 42, p. 78; *Finger Touch with Mirrors* (1966–67), cat. no. 110, pl. 39, p. 76; *Hanging Carousel (George Skins a Fox)* (1988), cat. no. 121, pl. 50, p. 86; *Henry Moore Bound to Fail* (1967), cat. no. 116, pl. 45, p. 80; *Life, Death, Love, Hate, Pleasure, Pain* (1983), cat. no. 119, pl. 48, p. 83; *Mold for a Modernized Slant Step* (1966), cat. no. 103, pl. 32, p. 71; *½ or ¾″ glass or plastic templates of my body separated by grease* (1966), cat. no. 104, pl. 33, p. 72; *Rats and Bats (Learned Helplessness in Rats) II* (1988), cat. no. 122, pl. 52, p. 88; *Run from Fear, Fun from Rear* (1972), cat. no. 117, pl. 46, p. 81; *Self-Portrait as a Fountain* (1966–67), cat. no. 106, pl. 35, p. 73; *3 Dead-End Adjacent Tunnels, Not Connected* (1979), cat. no. 118, pl. 47, p. 82; *Untitled* (1965), cat. no. 102, pl. 31, p. 70; *Untitled* (1966–67), cat. no. 105, pl. 34, p. 73; *Waxing Hot* (1966–67), cat. no. 109, pl. 38, p. 76

Otterness, Tom: *The Doors* (1985), cat. no. 130, pl. 82, p. 134

Paladino, Mimmo: *Allegoria (Allegory)* (1983), cat. no. 131, pl. 117, p. 194; *Le Tane di Napoli (The Lairs of Naples)* (1983), cat. no. 132, pl. 118, p. 195; *Untitled* (1985), cat. no. 133, pl. 119, p. 196

Polke, Sigmar: *Untitled* (1982), cat. no. 134, pl. 99, pp. 158–59

Prince, Richard: *Super-Heavy Santa* (1986), cat. no. 136, pl. 162, p. 267; *Untitled (Sunset)* (1981), cat. no. 135, pl. 161, p. 266

Richter, Gerhard: *New York* (1989), cat. no. 137, pl. 163, p. 268; *Sils Maria* (1989), cat. no. 138, pl. 164, p. 269; *Sils Maria* (1989), cat. no. 139, pl. 165, p. 269

Rothenberg, Susan: *Kelpie* (1978), cat. no. 140, pl. 71, p. 115; *Up, Down, Around* (1985–87), cat. no. 144, pl. 72, p. 116

Ruckreim, Ulrich: *Untitled* (1988), cat. no. 142, pl. 28, p. 55

Ruff, Thomas: *Portrait* (1988), cat. no. 143, pl. 166, p. 270; *Portrait* (1988), cat. no. 144, pl. 167, p. 271

Ryman, Robert: *Charter* (1985), cat. no. 145, pl. 59, p. 97; *The Elliott Room: Charter II* (1987), cat. no. 146, pl. 60, p. 98; *The Elliott Room: Charter III* (1987), cat. no. 147, pl. 61,

p. 99; *The Elliott Room: Charter IV* (1987), cat. no. 148, pl. 62, p. 100; *The Elliott Room: Charter V* (1987), cat. no. 149, pl. 63, p. 101

Salle, David: *Dusting Powders* (1986), cat. no. 151, pl. 84, p. 136; *His Brain* (1984), cat. no. 150, pl. 83, p. 135

Schnabel, Julian: *Aorta* (1981), cat. no. 153, pl. 86, p. 138; *Conversion of St. Paul* (1980), cat. no. 152, pl. 85, p. 137; *Private School in California* (1984), cat. no. 154, pl. 87, p. 139; *Untitled* (1988), cat. no. 156, pl. 89, p. 141; *Vita* (1984), cat. no. 155, pl. 88, p. 140

Serra, Richard: *Another Look at a Corner* (1985), cat. no. 157, pl. 29, p. 56; *Five Plate Pentagon* (1988), cat. no. 158, pl. 30, p. 57

Shapiro, Joel: *Untitled* (1981–84), cat. no. 159, pl. 73, p. 117; *Untitled (Arching Figure)* (1985), cat. no. 160, pl. 74, p. 118; *Untitled (for G.S.E.)* (1986–87), cat. no. 161, pl. 75, p. 119

Sherman, Cindy: *Untitled #88* (1981), cat. no. 162, pl. 90, p. 142; *Untitled #137* (1984), cat. no. 163, pl. 91, p. 143; *Untitled #147* (1985), cat. no. 164, pl. 92, p. 144; *Untitled #152* (1985), cat. no. 165, pl. 93, p. 144; *Untitled #188* (1989), cat. no. 166, pl. 94, p. 145

Steinbach, Haim: *untitled (football, clog)* (1987), cat. no. 167, pl. 181, p. 293

Struth, Thomas: *The Shimada Family, Yamaguchi 1986* (1988), cat. no. 168, pl. 168, p. 272; *Via Giovanni a Mare, Rome* (1988), cat. no. 169, pl. 169, p. 272; *Via Medina, Naples* (1988), cat. no. 170, pl. 170, p. 273; *Via Sanità, Naples* (1988), cat. no. 171, pl. 171, p. 273

Wall, Jeff: *Pleading* (1989), cat. no. 172, pl. 172, p. 274

Weiner, Lawrence: *From Major to Minor, From Small to Large* (1974–86), cat. no. 173, pl. 173, p. 275

Woodrow, Bill: *On the Other Hand* (1987), cat. no. 174, pl. 141, p. 236

Photography Credits